*Philosophy
and the Self:
East and West*

Other Works by Troy Wilson Organ:

An Index to Aristotle (1949)
The Examined Life (1956)
The Self in Indian Philosophy (1965)
The Art of Critical Thinking (1965)
The Hindu Quest for the Perfection of Man (1970)
Hinduism, Its Historical Development (1974)
Western Approaches to Eastern Philosophy (1975)
Third Eye Philosophy (1987)

Philosophy and the Self: East and West

Troy Wilson Organ

Selinsgrove: Susquehanna University Press
London and Toronto: Associated University Presses

© 1987 by Associated University Presses, Inc.

Associated University Presses
440 Forsgate Drive
Cranbury, NJ 08512

Associated University Presses
25 Sicilian Avenue
London WC1A 2QH, England

Associated University Presses
2133 Royal Windsor Drive
Unit 1
Mississauga, Ontario
Canada L5J 1K5

The paper used in this publication meets the requirements
of the American National Standard for Permanence of Paper
for Printed Library Materials Z39.48-1984.

Library of Congress Cataloging-in-Publication Data

Organ, Troy Wilson.
  Philosophy and the self.

  Bibliography: p.
  Includes index.
  1. Self (Philosophy) I. Title.
BD450.072 1987   126   86-62506
ISBN 0-941664-80-5 (alk. paper)

Printed in the United States of America

Contents

Preface	7
1 The Human Being as Philosopher	11
2 The Human Being as Speaker	43
3 The Human Being as Knower	66
4 The Human Being as Self-Knower	106
5 The Theories of the Self	128
6 The Self-Realization of Human Beings	173
Notes	201
Recommended Readings	223
Index	236

Preface

Plato's *Apology* is a record of Socrates' defense of his intellectual life when he was placed on trial at age seventy. Socrates reported that two injunctions had shaped his adult life: "Seek to know yourself" and "Examine your life." This volume is my apology for many years of study of philosophical problems—and especially the problem of the self—in East-West contexts.

I wish to state at once that I do not anticipate nor favor the creation of "East-West Philosophy," "World Philosophy," "Global Philosophy," "Whole Earth Philosophy," "Philosophy of Our Space Ship," or the "Planétisation of Culture." Such would be an intellectual smörgåsbord or a "pathological eclecticism."[1] Hippie Hinduism, European Zen, and Occidental versions of Sikhism and Taoism are pathetic imitations of the genuine articles. Nirad C. Chaudhuri condemns the "Western idiot who seeks salvation *à la hindoue*."[2] According to Louis Renou "the movements created in Europe, though claiming that their authority comes from her [India], are rarely a faithful reflection. No real yogin and no traditionally inclined Indian would find his proper nourishment among them. . . . Indian spirituality . . . is not designed for export. It is the result of intimate experience, and of experiment even more than of speculative thought; it is a whole, and can be understood only if considered as a whole."[3] There is a vast difference between a patchwork philosophy made up of snippets from East and West and the philosophy of a Western or an Eastern person alert and receptive to ideas from the other hemisphere.

One must maintain a base from which one accepts, rejects, or modifies another culture's insights and methodologies. Arthur O. Lovejoy stated the problem in memorable words: "To say 'Yes' to everything and everybody is manifestly to have no character at all. The delicate and difficult art of life is to find, in each turn of experience the *via media* between two extremes: to be catholic without being characterless; to have and apply standards, and yet to be on guard against their desensitizing and stupefying influence, their tendency to blind us to the diversities of concrete situations and to previously unrecognized values; to know when to tolerate, when to embrace, and when to fight."[4] Mahatma Gandhi expressed this a bit differently: "I do not want my house to be walled in on all sides and my windows to be stuffed. I want the cultures of all lands to be blown about my house as freely as possible. But I refuse to be blown off my feet."[5]

The focus on the self I have found to be salutary both in my teaching and in my efforts to form a personal philosophy of life adequate for meaningful existence in this tumultuous century. The philosophy we need is one that assists us solve the problems of overpopulation, unemployment, human exploitation, pollution of the environment, energy shortage, and, above all, depopulation of the planet through the use of nuclear weapons. Yet I am haunted with this thought: What is the profit if we solve social, political, economic, and environmental problems but do not know who we are?

*Philosophy
and the Self:
East and West*

1
The Human Being as Philosopher

A book on philosophy Eastern and Western written by a Western man in a Western language can deteriorate into presentation of Western thought with some references to similar but inferior thought from Eastern sources or into sentimental charity that compares Eastern profundities with Western superficialities. I hope to avoid both errors. Neither East nor West has sole possession of truth or value. The word *philosophy* is Western. There is no term in Sanskrit or Chinese synonymous with it. The word was coined in the sixth century B.C. by Pythagoras. In ancient Greece seven men were distinguished for their sagacity: Solon of Athens, Chilon of Lacedaemon, Pittacus of Mitylene, Bias of Priene, Periander of Corinth, Cleonbulus of Lindus, and Thales of Miletus. Pythagoras, when asked if he also was a sage, replied, "I am not a *sophós* (wise person). I am only a *philósophos* (person in love with wisdom)." Western historians of philosophy sometimes state that "the first philosopher" was indeed one of the seven sages of the Greek world, namely, Thales. He is given that appellation because he was the first Western person who rejected the accepted mythology, holding that each has the right to offer an alternative to the reigning Olympianism. Thales may also be called "the first scientist," since he claimed water was the basic stuff of all things. The distinction between philosophy and science is that, whereas philosophy considers reality from the standpoints of both knowing and valuing, the sciences seek knowledge that is free from all value considerations. Thales' credentials as a sage were established on 28 May 585 B.C. at 6:13 P.M. This remarkable statement is based on modern astronomical calculations that an eclipse of the sun took place in Asia Minor at that time. Thales' prediction grew out of his studies of Babylonian records of eclipses. The Babylonians had recorded for centuries the appearance of eclipses, but none before Thales had, noting the regularity, predicted the next eclipse.

Thales may have been the first philosopher in the Western world, but it is presumptuous to call him the first philosopher. The remains of Cro-Magnon man in Dordogne (France) indicate that man 30,000 years ago had a feeling for beauty and a desire to separate reality from appearance. Was the first *homo sapiens* a philosophical thinker? Perhaps, in a sense. But to call the first man a philosopher would be misleading, although his arrival brought a new kind of being into the world—a being who is a problem to himself.

1. *Professional Philosophy and Everyone Philosophy*

A distinction must be made between a general activity that might be called "being philosophical" and a special activity known as "philosophizing." The former connotes mental attitudes such as doubting, opining, speculating, and expressing prejudices; the latter is a specific activity conducted with certain rules and guiding principles. The former is unplanned; the latter is a conscious and responsible activity. Every person at some time or other expresses what Wittgenstein called the basic philosophical problem: "I don't know my way about." The former is the philosophy of everyone; the latter is the philosophy of the philosopher. Some of the chief differences are that whereas the philosophy of everyone is unplanned, unsystematic, and unsustained, the philosophy of the philosopher is planned, systematic, and sustained. But the chief difference is that the philosopher examines assumptions. An assumption is an idea, belief, or evaluation that is taken for granted as a basis of argument and/or action. The philosopher questions, analyzes, and evaluates the starting points. A student of ethics has written of Nietzsche that his "main concern was to examine all presuppositions which lay behind philosophical systems and customary moralities."[1] This is an exaggeration. No philosopher examines *all* assumptions. Moreover, each philosopher has to decide when to stop examining assumptions and when to start acting upon the basis of assumptions. When Plato cautioned, "Too much philosophy is the ruin of human life,"[2] perhaps he had in mind the philosopher who did not know when to stop philosophizing.

The distinction between the philosophy of everyone and the philosophy of the philosopher is similar to a distinction Nietzsche made between "philosophical laborers" and "philosophers proper." The former systematize and defend the beliefs of their times; the latter analyze, and often reject, the prevailing beliefs and values. An Indologist had this distinction in mind when he warned readers of professional Indian philosophers "not to jump to conclusions about Indian philosophy and religion from a perusal of their works." One must balance a study of "the greatest thinkers and literary artists which India has produced" with a study of "the great mass of believers, or, perhaps one might better say, acquiescers."[3] Philosophers are not necessarily heretical to received opinions and values, although they often criticize traditional wisdom. A philosopher, according to Socrates, is a gadfly that stings sluggish minds.

The earlier *Upaniṣads* in India and the *Liu Yi* (Six Classics) of China predate Thales. That marvelously creative century—the sixth century B.C., which is often called "The Pivotal Age"—was the century not only of the Seven Sages of Greece but also of Jeremiah, Zoroaster, Gautama, Confucius, and Lao Tzu. Historians puzzle over this concurrent emergence of new thoughts and values in Europe and Asia. Why should creative thinkers in each of these cultures have decided almost simultaneously that the unexamined life is not a fit life for human beings? A study of this century is an excellent cure for what Mircea Eliade called the "provincializing" of Western philosophy. Frederick Copleston, after writing a series that has been proclaimed as "the best text of the history of philosophy now available in English," realized that "it is highly desirable that we should widen our horizons and acquire some knowledge of the ways of thought of other peoples, of cultures other than our own. Philosophy in a given country can become extremely parochial or provincial. Perhaps this is only to be expected, when philosophy has become a highly specialized discipline. Students are naturally not encouraged to dissipate their energies. We cannot, however, leave the task of increasing mutual understanding among peoples simply to politicians and traders."[4]

2. Science, Philosophy, and Religion

The distinction between sophists and philosophers continues to this day. It is found in the distinction between scientists and philosophers. The word *science* comes from the Latin verb *scire* (to know). Scientists know but philosophers love wisdom. The difference is made more obvious by noting that the opposite of knowledge is ignorance and the opposite of wisdom is foolishness. Scientists classify human beings into knowers and ignoramuses. Philosophers refer to the wise and the foolish. The two classifications are not unrelated; a person may know without being wise, but a person cannot be wise in the absence of knowledge.

Scientists seek factual knowledge. Factual knowledge, they insist, is knowledge free from values. Knowers must carefully eliminate from their knowledge all that they *want* to believe. Philosophers do not deny the importance of facts, but they insist that human beings live in a world of values as well as a world of facts. "What can I hope?" is as important as "What can I know?" An American philosopher once facetiously said that a philosopher has "too little knowledge to be a scientist . . . too little faith to be a saint."[5] But philosophers differ widely as to how much weight should be given to hope.

Montaigne said there were three classes of philosophers: (1) the Dogmatic, who claim "I have found the truth"; (2) the Skeptical, who warn, "Truth cannot be found"; (3) the Persistent, who affirm, "I am still in quest of truth." William James thought that there are two kinds of philosophers: (1) the Tender-minded, who appeal to principles; (2) the Tough-minded, who appeal to facts.[6]

3. Attempts to Define Philosophy

One of the puzzling facts about philosophy is that philosophers do not agree what philosophy is. Friedrich Waismann, a professor of philosophy at Oxford University, begins his book *How I See Philosophy* with this confession: "What philosophy is? I don't know, nor have I a set formula to offer." He adds "It is perhaps easier to say what philosophy is not than what it is. The first thing, then, I should like to say is that philosophy, as it is practised today, is very unlike science; and this in three aspects: in philosophy there are no proofs; there are no theorems; and there are no questions which can be decided, Yes or No. . . . a philosopher is a man who senses as it were hidden crevices in the build of our concepts where others only see the smooth part of commonplaceness before them."[7] In the closing months of World War II the American Philosophical Association, deciding it was time to examine philosophy before American educators plunged into the serious problems of educating the returning war veterans, appointed a committee to study the function of philosophy in liberal education. The committee found "the skeleton in the American philosophical closet" was that philosophers held two divergent views as to the goals of philosophy: "On the one side are those for whom philosophy is contemplation; on the other, those for whom it is a preface to action. One party believes that the prime business of intelligence, and therefore of philosophy, is to lay bare the nature of things, to lay hold of the constitutive principles of goodness, truth, and beauty, and to understand as completely as may be the permanent structure of the world. The other party believes that the business of intelligence is instrumental, that it is an agency of adjustment, a means for molding nature and human nature into the service of human desire. One party believes that intellect has an end of its own, which is theoretical understanding, and that this understanding can be achieved only by following the lines of an independent order of nature. The other believes that intellect has no end, and truth no meaning, apart from the process of human growth and adjustment."[8]

One of the favorite games philosophers play is trying to outdo one another in fashioning definitions of philosophy. A definition regarded as classic for centuries in the West is that of Cicero: *"Nec quicquan aliud est philosophia, si interpretari velis, praeter studium sapientiae; sapientia autem est rerum di-*

vinarum et humanarum causarumque quibus eae res continentur scientia." (Nor, should one want to translate the word, is philosophy anything other than the pursuit of wisdom; now wisdom is the knowledge of things human and divine and of the causes by which these things are controlled.)[9] Sometimes philosophers attempt clever definitions of philosophy, for example, "the techniques of illusionectomy," "the disambiguation of ideas," "the disease of which it should be the cure," "the systematic effort to avoid the systematic deadening of the systematizing imagination," and "the study of those subjects which no one but a philosopher would think of studying." But usually philosophers make a serious and honest effort to define the philosophical discipline.

The following definitions and descriptions culled from philosophical books, articles, and essays reveal diverse interpretations. A reading of these will evidence the truth expressed in a brief guide for undergraduates prepared by a committee of the American Philosophical Association: "Philosophy is quite unlike any other field. It is unique both in its methods and in the nature and breadth of its subject matter. Philosophy pursues questions in every dimension of human life, and its techniques apply to problems in any field of study or endeavor. No brief definition expresses the richness and variety of philosophy."[10]

1. The art of thinking things through.
2. Critical analysis of concepts and discovery of relations among them.
3. The integration, unification, and interpretation of knowledge.
4. Reflective thinking, i.e., thinking on thinking.
5. An unusually persistent effort to think clearly.
6. The cultural study of meanings and values.
7. An interpretation of life.
8. An attempt to see life steadily and see it whole.
9. An attempt by use of scientific methods to understand the world in which we live.
10. An attempt to make the implicit explicit.
11. An effort to form a consistent world view.
12. The search for unity and truth.
13. A comprehensive view of reality.
14. The effort to place values in the world of facts.
15. Thought of the second degree, i.e., thought about thought.
16. A critique of language, of communicated meanings.
17. A quest to understand the nature of conceptual systems.
18. An examination of the grounds of belief.
19. A descriptive examination of the ways words and expressions are used in their natural employment in a natural language.
20. A therapy for correcting the misuses of language.

21. An interpretation of existence from the standpoint of value.
22. An effort to teach how to live without certainty.
23. The reaction of the whole of man to the whole of reality.
24. A spiritual endeavor of the whole of man's being.
25. An effort of human thought to face the mystery and complexity of life without passion or attachment to any particular creed.
26. A criticism of what is done by man, i.e., of human action and human production.
27. The most general science, the science of sciences, the parent science.
28. The criticism and systematization or organization of all knowledge, drawn from empirical science, rational learning, common experience, or whatever.
29. The attempt to think clearly and methodologically about certain notions that are always turning up in our thinking and that seem necessary to our thinking but that the special sciences do not tell us about.
30. An effort to combine the common experiences of life on the one hand and the results of the special sciences on the other into a consistent and harmonious world-theory.
31. Talk about the uses of talk.
32. An attempt to express the infinity of the universe in terms of the limitations of language.
33. The attempt to make manifest the fundamental evidence as to the nature of things.
34. The criticism of abstractions that govern special modes of thought.
35. The endeavor to find a conventional phraseology for the vivid suggestiveness of the poet.
36. The understanding of the interfusion of modes of existence.
37. An attitude of mind toward doctrines ignorantly entertained.
38. An attempt to enlarge the understanding of the scope of application of every notion that enters into our current thought.
39. An attempt to rationalize mysticism.
40. The development of the logic and methodology of science.
41. A survey of possibilities and their comparison with actualities.
42. The clarification of propositions.
43. Linguistic therapy designed to clear up logical confusion.
44. The criticism and clarification of notions that are apt to be regarded as ultimate and to be accepted in an uncritical manner.
45. The search for a comprehensive view of nature.
46. An attempt at a universal explanation of things.
47. The summary of the sciences and their completion.
48. The theory of a subject matter taken as a whole or organized unity,

containing principles that bind together a variety of particular truths and facts, and requiring a harmony of theory and practice.
49. The pursuit of wisdom and its formulation in words.
50. The critical inquiry into what one is actually doing in the world.
51. The attempt to ask and answer in a formal and disciplined way the great questions of life that ordinary men put to themselves in reflective moments.
52. An effort to become sensitively aware of the essential humanness in every position that human beings take.
53. The peculiar mode of thinking that gives humanity its distinctive character.
54. An effort to reconcile self-conscious reason with actuality.
55. An attempt to achieve an overall, integrated understanding of whatever constitutes the world for an individual in such a way that the individual's place in the world is understandable and meaningful.
56. A search for the ultimate meaning by which we live.
57. The endeavor to frame a coherent, logical, necessary system of general ideas in which every element of our experience can be interpreted.
58. The study of symbol and meaning.
59. Questions to which at present no definite answers can be given.
60. An attempt to examine the world under the aspect of eternity.
61. An effort to make sense of things.
62. The elucidation of statements made by scientists.
63. The rational explanation of anything.
64. The science of the first principles of being.
65. The unique and irreplaceable human discipline of man's spiritual quest.
66. The study that takes the concepts we use in common life and science, analyzes them, and determines their precise meaning and their mutual relations.
67. An attempt to help human beings understand themselves.
68. A quest for Ultimate Truth about the Absolute.
69. An effort to guide human beings toward the realization of the right moral goals.
70. The breaking up of those fetters which bind us to inherited preconceptions, so as to attain a new and broader way of looking at things.
71. An attempt to make comprehensive sense of the full range of facts.
72. The knowledge of things in general by their ultimate causes, as far as natural reason can attain to such knowledge.
73. The principle of concentration through which man becomes himself by partaking of reality.

74. A living expression of the basic universality of man, of the bond between all men.
75. The dialogue between Being and being, between groundless ground and man.
76. The study of man and his place in the universe, and the study of the values that ought to be recognized in the aesthetic, ethical and religious realms.
77. The attempt to penetrate the nature of reality and to do so by means of an adequate mode of knowledge-discovery.
78. The study of those subjects which can be understood only by considering the ways in which they are talked about.
79. The thinking we do when we ask ourselves whether something we believe is reasonable to believe.
80. A kind of concept analysis, exposing the implications encased in the meanings of ordinary words, ideas, and beliefs.
81. The science of things in their first causes.
82. An attempt to discover and articulate the ultimate principles in terms of which everything can be understood.
83. An effort to attain a conception of the frame of things that will on the whole be more rational than the somewhat chaotic view that everyone by nature carries about with him under his hat.
84. An analytic study of concepts.
85. The thinking study of things.
86. The study of man as a reasonable rather than an active being, i.e., an endeavor to form his understanding more than to cultivate his manners.
87. The synthetic interpretation of all experience.
88. An attempt to answer the question "What is it all about?"
89. A survey of possibilities and their comparison with actualities.
90. An attempt to enlarge the understanding of the scope of application of every notion that enters into current thought.
91. An attempt to take every word and every phrase in the verbal expression of thought and ask "What does it mean?"
92. An effort to harmonize, refashion, and adjust divergent intuitions as to the nature of things.
93. The survey of the ultimate ideas and the retention of the whole of the evidence in shaping a cosmological scheme.
94. An effort to render explicit, and—as far as may be—efficient, a process that otherwise is unconsciously performed without rational tests.
95. The welding of imagination and common sense into a restraint upon specialists, and also into an enlargement of their imaginations.
96. An effort to provide the generic notions that should make it easier to

conceive the infinite variety of specific instances that rest unrealized in the womb of nature.
97. An attempt to understand the stable features of the world and to solve the problems that arise from man's ability to reflect on his experience.
98. The experiential or empirical study of the nonempirical or *a priori*, and of such questions as arise out of the relation of the empirical to the *a priori*.
99. The study that, having learned from the sciences what life or matter or mental action is, asks how these orders of facts are related to one another and to the fundamental nature of things.
100. The persistent questioning of receiving opinions.
101. The return of thought upon itself.
102. The investigation of all things.
103. The study of being qua being.
104. The pursuit of goodness, beauty, and truth.
105. An attempt to know the meaning, nature, and causes of all things human and divine, and to understand and realize in practice the whole theory of morality.
106. A reasoned pursuit of fundamental truths.
107. The pursuit of knowledge of things and their causes, whether theoretical or practical.
108. The study that deals with ultimate reality, or with the most general causes and principles of things.
109. The intellectual answer of man to the problem of existence.
110. An effort to weaken the hold of blind custom on the imagination and on the energies of men and to keep alive the sense of human life as a creative adventure.
111. The exposition of one's mode of being in the world.
112. The analysis, interpretation, and evaluation of those symbol-bound activities or experiences of man which constitute or affect his qualitative growth and progress.
113. The instrument that enables man to make his pursuit of values a consciously directed activity.
114. The search for that which if discovered and attained would enable man to enjoy continuous, supreme, and unending happiness.
115. An inquiry into the means of terminating human misery.
116. The science of the general laws of being (i.e., nature and society), human thinking, and the process of knowledge.
117. The science of the relation of thinking to being.
118. The study of the relationship of consciousness to being, examined from two aspects: first, what is primary—spirit or matter? and second, how is knowledge of the world related to the world itself?

119. The conclusions of one who is not interested in each thing in its private existence but in the aggregate of all there is.
120. *Hē epistēmē tòn eleuthéron.* (The sportive science.)

An effort to classify the above definitions may not be so hopeless as first appears. Some philosophers think of philosophy as analysis. Some philosophers think of philosophy as synthesis. The approach of the former is prescientific in the sense that they critically examine the assumptions, methodologies, and terminologies of the process that arrives at human knowledge. The approach of the latter is transscientific in the sense that they, while not rejecting the analytic approach, hold that philosophers should also construct integrative and comprehensive systems that give meaning and focus to human existence.

4. *The Role of Philosophy in the West*

The wide variety of views about philosophy is reflected in the history of Western philosophy. There have been at least ten views of the role of philosophy in the 2,500 years of its existence in the West:

1. Rejection of mythology as explanation of the nature of the world. Search for a natural source of motion and for a physical stuff from which all things came. E.g., the Presocratics.
2. Search for knowledge of the self and for ethical standards. E.g., Socrates.
3. Attempt to discover how man can know the world. E.g., Plato, Aristotle.
4. Search for a way of life in a time of political turmoil that has been described as "a failure of nerve." E.g., the Stoics and the Epicureans.
5. Attempt to find ways of giving rational defense of religious beliefs. E.g., the Christian philosophers up to the Renaissance.
6. Quest for ways of knowing the world to replace the religious authorities that no longer held control over the minds of men. E.g., the seventeenth-century rationalists and the eighteenth-century empiricists.
7. Attempts to find methods of integrating the new scientific studies into the thought of the times. E.g., Francis Bacon, Herbert Spencer, John Dewey.
8. Search for language procedures to handle knowledge. Logical clarification of thought. E.g., the logical positivists and the language analysts.

9. Quest for a world philosophy that will overcome the tensions of our times. E.g., William Ernest Hocking, F. S. C. Northrop, Charles A. Moore.
10. Revolt against the intellectualizing of life in an effort to return to the ultimate problems. E.g., the existentialists.

These ten views of the role of philosophy must not hide the fact that philosophy in the West is a shifting balance among three traditions: the classical Greek, the Judaeo-Christian, and the modern scientific. Chronologically they are the ancient, the medieval, and the modern. The ideal figures in each are Plato, Aquinas, and Francis Bacon. The goal of the classical Greek tradition is to live wisely and harmoniously in the natural and social worlds; the goal of the Judaeo-Christian tradition is to glorify God and enjoy him forever; the goal of the modern scientific tradition is to acquire knowledge of and power over the natural world. Today in the West there are philosophers committed to each of the three traditions. Whereas the long-range view may be that the philosophical community is trying to find a *modus operandi* that does justice to all three traditions, the short-range view is that philosophers are engaged in a dogfight for survival and supremacy. In the current conflict some fear that the dominance of the scientific tradition may result in scientism, that is, ". . . a form of reductionism . . . which insists that all facts of human experience can ultimately be interpreted in terms of quantitative categories and/or external causal conditions, and which insists also that the methods of science are the only methods we have for discovering truth."[11] Others fear that people living under the threat of extermination in nuclear warfare may be willing to support any irrational faith that promises security.

5. *The Divisions of Philosophy*

Philosophy raises three questions about any subject matter: "What is its reality?", "How is it known?", and "What is its value?"

Metaphysics is the general term for the study of reality. Its Greek derivation means that it is a higher study of the physical or natural. The term *ontology*, which means study of being, is a synonym. Such questions as the following are raised: "What does it mean to be?", "What is the real nature of things?", "What is the difference between appearance and reality?"

Epistemology is the general term for the study of knowledge. Its questions include: "What are the sources of knowledge?", "What is the meaning of truth?", "What are the tests of true statements?", "What rules govern how one may argue validly from known truth to new truths?"

Axiology is the general term for the study of value. In this branch of philosophy questions such as the following are raised: "Does man create or discover values?", "Are values the same for all?", "What makes an act right?", "What makes a human goal good?", "What is meant when an art object is said to be beautiful?"

The systems of philosophy may be distinguished according to whether reality, knowledge, or value is given prior consideration.

The proponents of one system ask, "Reality being what it is, what can be known and what ought to be valued?" According to systems of this type, methodologies and values are chosen on the basis of their consistency with prior metaphysical conclusions. For example, a supernaturalist, having postulated the existence of God, concludes that morality consists in obedience to the will of God, and that the ultimate truth is revealed by God in sacred Scriptures and in mystical experiences. The supernaturalist will not tolerate a way of knowing that excludes the possibility of God. These systems can be subdivided into those which begin with an analysis of nature with man removed and make man like nature, and those which begin with man removed from nature and make nature like man. The former, by abstracting man from nature, reduces nature to a machine. When they turn to man, they also make man machinelike. Thus arise the materialistic ontologies. The latter by considering man apart from nature concludes that man's essential characteristic, and hence the essential characteristic of nature, is mind, or will, or feeling. Thus arise the idealistic ontologies.

The proponents of another system ask, "Knowledge being what it is, what is valuable and real?" A classic example of this type is the philosophy of Kant. Kant instituted what he called a "Copernican Revolution" in philosophy by pointing out that the mind in its psychological process of knowing determines the nature of the known world. Some of the systems in this class originate in a commitment to a method of acquiring knowledge, for example, authoritarianism, rationalism, intuitionism, and empiricism; others are epistemologically oriented, for example, Berkeley's mentalism, which starts with the view that things in the object world exist only when they are in a knowing relationship, and still others begin with an analysis of the constitution of the meaningful use of language, for example, logical positivism, which according to some of its early supporters held that sentences are meaningful only when they refer to entities that can be tested scientifically.

The proponents of a third system ask, "Evaluation being what it is, what is real and true?" Pragmatism is an example of such a system. It holds that reality is molded by human expectations, volitions, and desires, and also that logic itself is a form of evaluation. The pragmatists claim that all of us, far more than we may like to admit, allow our views of the universe, of ourselves, and of our place in the universe to be shaped by our wishes and hopes. Reality is what we want reality to be.

6. Philosophy West and East

What we have been considering thus far in this chapter is philosophy as it is conceived and practiced in the West. The love of wisdom, which sought the enrichment of human life in the ancient Greek world, became the handmaiden of the Christian Church in the Middle Ages. Today, for many professional philosophers in the West, philosophy is still a handmaiden, but she serves the sciences rather than the Church. Rather than having a life of her own, she examines, clarifies, and modifies the language of sciences, arts, theology, law, history, sociology, and psychology. Her subject matter is knowledge wherever it is found. This view of the role of philosophy is well stated by Bertrand Russell, as follows: "The philosophy . . . which is to be genuinely inspired by the scientific spirit, must deal with somewhat dry and abstract matters, and must not hope to find an answer to the practical problems of life. . . . Many hopes which inspired philosophers in the past it cannot claim to fulfil; but other hopes, more purely intellectual, it can satisfy more fully than former ages could have deemed possible for human minds."[12]

I cannot fully support this narrowing of the function of philosophy, believing as I do in the need for philosophers to return to the Pythagorean love of wisdom as a guide to both thought and life.[13] Eastern philosophy has remained closer to the Pythagorean ideal than has Western philosophy. But is Eastern philosophy "philosophy" in the Western sense? William S. Haas has raised some doubts about this: "Upon a first open-minded approach to Eastern philosophy immediately the notion arises that there is a basic distinction between it and Western philosophy. On deeper investigation this notion is intensified. And then comes the realization that the term philosophy is actually inapplicable—that it serves to obscure and to falsify the spirit of Eastern thought. Neither the origin, the purpose, nor the intellectual means and methods are the same in the East as in the West. No universal term exists that is sufficiently suggestive to embrace the approach of both West and East."[14] Agehananda Bharati offers the same caveat in the opening sentence of his *The Tantric Tradition:* "Throughout this book I shall keep cautioning readers about the use of 'philosophy' and 'philosophical' in our context."[15] He adds that "it might have been wise to substitute 'philosophy' by some such word as 'ideology' or 'speculative patterns,' [or] . . . 'psycho-experimental-speculations.' "[16] Haas creates the term *philousia* (love of isness). Western philosophy seeks intellectual illumination; Eastern philosophy seeks psychological liberation. Western philosophy has traditionally been essentialistic; Eastern philosophy has been existentialistic. *Essentialism* is the view that the nature of things can be expressed in concepts, and that the worth of knowledge is measured in relation to truth. *Existentialism* denies both. Existentialism repudiates the building of philosophical systems. It would bring philosophy down to earth, contending that the worth of a philosophy is in its application to life. Essentialism holds that essence is prior in reality to existence. Existentialism holds that existence is prior to essence. Platonism is the archetypal form of essentialism. Existentialism broke into Western philosophy in the works of Dostoevski, Kierkegaard, Nietzsche, Kafka, Jaspers, Heidegger, Sartre, and Camus. In Eastern philosophical thinking an existential protest and revolt against essentialism has not occurred because Eastern thinking has always been existential. One student of Eastern philosophy has written as follows about the Indian intellectuals: "Essence . . . cannot be conceived of apart from existence; nor can anything 'exist' except 'essence' . . . perhaps the concept 'essence' is unknown to Indians."[17] The East attempts to establish immediate contact with the real. However, this desire is linked with restraining traditions rather than intellectual curiosity so that in the East, despite its existentialism, discoveries are not fully implemented in society; for example, Indians developed the number system, but it was the West that developed analytic geometry and the calculus; the Chinese invented printing but published few books, discovered gunpowder but limited its use to firecrackers, and constructed a compass but did not become a seafaring people.

Modern Western people are often puzzled by the willingness of Eastern people to live comfortably within their traditions. Thomas Whittaker, writing in 1918, made this statement: "Nowhere in Asia of course has there been that self-conscious break with traditional authority which we find in ancient Greece and in modern Europe."[18] He was thinking of such breaks as the rise of Greek philosophy, the fall of the Roman Empire, the Protestant Reformation, the Italian Renaissance, and the industrial revolution. Much has happened in the East since 1918. It may be too early to draw reliable conclusions, but the changes that have taken place in India, China, Japan, Korea, and Southeast Asia in the twentieth century have deeply affected the traditional cultures of Asia. Future historians may refer to this century as "The Century of the Asian Renaissance."

Eastern knowledge is a form of being. It is lucid and self-sufficient. It is oriented to pure consciousness—a consciousness that is not the consciousness of anything, a consciousness without objects. Western knowledge is a form of having. It needs an instrument—an object—to seize and possess. This is the concept. The concept links subject and object together—and also keeps them apart.

The ideal goal of knowing in the West is to capture the "object" as it is, without an adulteration of categories introduced by the knower. The ideal goal of knowing in the East is to discover the "subject," without any relationship to the object. Psychologically it can be described as a state of objectless awareness. Tu Wei-ming has written that "to follow the path of knowledge backward, as it were, to the starting point of the true self is the aim of East Asian thought."[19] Yet, to identify the goal of Western thought as pure object and the goal of Eastern thought as pure subject is not apropos, since the goal of the former is to transcend the object of the knowing relationship and the goal of the latter is to transcend the subject of the knowing relationship. Perhaps *thing-in-itself* and *self-in-itself* are the least confusing terms. With their use the ideal goals of Western and Eastern thought can be illustrated as follows:

The epistemic goal of Western thought:

- The thing-in-itself. The thing as it would be outside the knowing relationship.
- The thing as perceived. The epistemological object via perception.
- The thing as conceived. The epistemological object via conception.
- The consciousness of the thing. The consciousness as consciousness of the ontological object.

The epistemic goal of Eastern thought:

- The consciousness of the thing as conceived. The consciousness of the epistemological object.
- The consciousness of the self as knower.
- The self-in-itself. The self as it would be outside the knowing relationship. Pure consciousness, i.e., the principle of awareness that constitutes the essence of an individual. Consciousness, not as a consciousness *of* anything, but as consciousness per se. This is known in Indian philosophy as the *sākṣin* (the witnessing self).

Philosophers both in the West and in the East seek to attain an ideal epistemological goal that cannot be reached. Neither the knower nor the known can be known outside the knowing relationship. A second-century Buddhist philosopher saw this clearly: "Certainly there is no self-existence of existing things in conditioned causes and if no self-existence exists, neither does 'other-existence.'"[20]

The epistemic goal of Western thought, that is, knowing an object within the knowing relationship as it would be outside the knowing relationship, may be compared to seeing a mirror without a reflection of the seer in the mirror. The object known is believed to be the same as the object unknown. Immanuel Kant was the first Western philosopher to challenge this belief. He wrote in 1787, "Hitherto it has been assumed that all our knowledge must conform to objects. But all attempts to extend our knowledge of objects by establishing something in regard to them *a priori*, by means of concepts, have, on this assumption, ended in failure. We must therefore make trial whether we may not have more success in the tasks of metaphysics, if we suppose that objects must conform to our knowledge. This would agree better with what is desired, namely, that it should be possible to have knowledge of objects *a priori*, determining something in regard to them prior to their being given. We should then be proceeding precisely on the lines of Copernicus' primary hypothesis. Failing of satisfactory progress in explaining the movements of the heavenly bodies on the supposition that they all revolved round the spectator, he tried whether he might not have better success if he made the spectator to revolve and the stars to remain at rest."[21] The impossibility of discovering anything as it would be in an undiscovered condition has been called *the egocentric predicament*.[22] Western philosophers overcome the predicament by defining the object-in-itself as *the object-as-perceived* and/or *the object-as-known*. In other words, the Western knower in fact, whatever he may claim in theory, confuses the object-in-itself with a postulated object-in-itself. In his obsession for objectivity he treats the epistemological object-in-itself as though it were the ontological object-in-itself. For example, the Western astronomer seeks to know the moon by building a collection of concepts that will accurately and completely represent the moon as it is apart from the collection of concepts. "Moon reality" is translated into the known reality of the moon. Moon-as-known becomes equivalent to moon-as-moon.

The West has the will and capacity to confer on anything the shape and existence of an epistemological object. Thus it creates its own antagonists. The West moves on ever discovering and creating new epistemological objects. All this is alien to the East. The Eastern mind is not interested in shaping the nonsubject into the other. In place of the hostile antagonisms of opposites that we find in the West, the East sees the sovereignty of polarities. The West seeks a principle that will neutralize the opposite on a higher plane, but the East sees the polarities working together like a magnet, that is, working opposed to, but not against, each other. The real in the East is the point at which the polarities neutralize each other. The real absorbs the polarities into one, rather than conciliating the opposites at a higher plane. The juxtaposed polarities are absorbed into the identity of the real. Whereas the West seeks to transcend dynamic antagonisms by a higher principle, the East absorbs the juxtaposed polarities into a unity. One model is the amazing manner in which the Chinese have been able to assimilate Confucianism and Taoism within the same culture.

The West holds that conceptual thought can penetrate the depths of experience; the East holds that conceptual thought cannot penetrate to these depths. The West holds that the higher is to be understood by the lower; the East holds that the lower is to be understood by the higher. The West looks for the parts; the East seeks the whole. The East is anxious that the wholeness of the phenomenon be preserved, that it not be altered for the sake of cognition. Knowing Eastern style requires that the consciousness undergo a change, not that the phenomenon change. The mind must be empty so it can know.

Tradition and custom function in the East as do rational theories in the West. The East attempts to follow Nature—"Nature" being that which "has always been done." The West attempts to follow Reason—"Reason" being the free creative exercise of the mind in the solving of problems. This difference comes to expression in the difference the West and the East hold with regard to change. The East tends to move within a given framework. It improves the given, reforms the given, shapes the given. Existing conditions are assumed to be the essential structure of things. They may be modified, but the traditional structure remains. By contrast the West tends to think of improvement or progress in terms of revolutionary acts that change the structure. The West commonly looks to the overthrow of the established frame as the heart of improvement.

Wing-tsit Chan speaks of the affinity of Oriental metaphysics, epistemology, and ethics: "They are interdependent, and one exists for, and leads to, another. The unity of knowledge and conduct in Oriental philosophy is almost proverbial. So is the insistence on the close relationship between the realization of human nature and the realization of reality. This explains the absence of knowledge for its own sake in the Orient. This also explains why philosophy and life in the Orient are closely related and why Oriental philosophy appears extremely ethical."[23] He adds: "the first and last problem of Oriental philosophy in general is human perfection and freedom."[24]

Chan calls for "a properly balanced synthesis" of the Western tendencies—"scientific . . . rational . . . positive . . . affirmative with regard to the particular"—and of the Eastern tendencies—"emphasis on intuition, monism, the harmony between man and nature, the transmutation of evil by human effort, the tranquillity of mind, the ethics of simplicity, contentment, nonviolence, and noninjury, and above all, the concept of the undifferentiated continuum or the 'field.'"[25] But what is "a properly balanced synthesis"? Chan says "a world philosophy must be evolved." My view is that hopes for a world or global philosophy are unrealistic, and that such a philosophy, even if possible, is undesirable. But recognition of the limitation of both the Eastern and the Western traditions is a necessary step toward an adequate philosophy in East and West. Chan, writing in 1949, reflected the post-World War II dreams of world unity expressed, for example, in Wendell Wilkie's *One World*. What is needed, in my opinion, is not a world of one philosophy but a world that appreciates diversity, a world in which philosophers in each culture have knowledge of and appreciation of other philosophies, a world in which there is the willingness to respect, to understand, and in some instances to assimilate ways of thinking and acting of other peoples. Philosophy both in the West and in the East has suffered from two assumptions: (1) the assumption that philosophy should reflect rather than mold society, and (2) the assumption that the pursuit of knowledge is self-validating. These assumptions have encouraged philosophers to disengage themselves from the society in which they live. They have looked down from ivory towers at the efforts of politicians, economists, and social workers to change society. They have sometimes justified their discipline on the ground that some members of society must clarify, analyze, and integrate the cultural achievements of mankind. But in a world of potential genocide we must ask if philosophers should rethink their role. Do we need new engineering skills, or do we need new controls of the skills we have? Do we need new moral systems, or do we need the will to apply existing moralities to the problems of hunger, crime, overpopulation, and war? Do we need new ideas, or do we need new ways to implement the ideas we have? Can philosophers claim the immunity of seers, or must philosophers become kings? Plato warned that unless philosophical wisdom is merged with political power, cities will have no rest from their ills.

7. Eastern Philosophy

I would modify Haas's argument that the East introduces *philousía* in place of *philosophía* by saying that the East puts *philosophía* within *philousía*, that is, the pursuit of wisdom is situated within a framework that pursues realization, liberation, and fulfillment. Hinduism seeks *mokṣa*, Buddhism seeks *nirvāṇa*, and Confucianism seeks the ideal known as *chün-tzu* (Sage Man). According to Buddhism all life is transitory and filled with suffering *(duḥkha)*, but the suffering can be arrested *(nirodha)*. The way to accomplish this is known as *duḥkha-nirodha-mārga* (the suffering-elimination-way.) The Chinese use the term *t'i-jen* (Personally Realizing Truth) for the whole within which philosophy, as it is defined in the West, is placed. *T'i-jen* implies personal experience, intuition as an addition to rational thinking, and a unity of knowledge and conduct. The Sanskrit word most closely related to *t'i-jen* is *sādhanā*. This term may be defined as a human discipline aimed toward the realization of ideal goals. *Sādhanā* has two parts—the intellectual and the soteriological. The former is what things are in the context of the human search for knowledge; the latter is what things mean in the context of the human search for significance. "In India," writes one Western student, "philosophy is considered a spiritual activity higher than religion and eminently practical. For Indians, philosophy begins not in wonder but in suffering. It is not a speculative theory which may or may not have practical applications, but is essentially practical, though it may be considered abstractly as pure theory."[26] An Indian philosopher adds that philosophy that is only intellectual, which contains no soteriological elements, is "mere argumentative philosophy."[27] Mircea Eliade observes, "In India, truth is not precious in itself; it becomes precious by virtue of its soteriological function."[28] Hence in *sādhanā*, *duḥkha-nirodha-mārga*, and *t'i-jen* the essentialistic is subsumed within the existentialistic, thinking within living, speculating within valuing, "being a philosopher" within "being human."

Existentialism puts philosophy within the context of the fulfillment of humanism, as Frederick Copleston indicates in his definition of existentialism as "the form taken in a particular historical epoch by the recurrent protest of the free individual against all that threatens or seems to threaten his unique position as an ex-sistent subject, that is to say, as a free subject, who though a being in the world and so a part of nature, at the same time stands out from the background of nature."[29]

The locating of philosophy—as known in the West—within *duḥkha-nirodha-mārga* or *t'i-jen* or *sādhanā* indicates that Eastern philosophy is something to which to be committed. Even those who are aware of the *sādhanā* character of Indian philosophy sometimes err in their conception of the relation of philosophy and *sādhanā*. For example, Agehananda Bharati distinguishes the two, but, rather than describing the relationship as the inclusion of philosophy within *sādhanā*, refers to the relationship as polar opposition. "Tantric literature," he says, "is not of the philosophical genre: the stress is on *sādhanā*."[30] He refers to "conceptual and intuitive polarization."[31] Again he says that ". . . taking *sādhanā* seriously means regarding it as more important, though not necessarily more interesting, than philosophy"[32]—again implying that *sādhanā* and philosophy are mutually exclusive.

William Ernest Hocking, one of America's great idealistic philosophers of this century, may not have been aware of *sādhanā* or *t'i-jen*, but he was much impressed by the pragmatic significance of Eastern metaphysics: "If you ask the average Westerner what life means, he is dumb. He is satisfied to live, and to let somebody else think about it. The Oriental is wiser; his philosophy is always at work. He has no philosophy and no religion which is not at work. His reflections are kept in close connection with his actions. We have to learn from the Orient the practical significance of metaphysics. A race of people who could beget so jejune a scheme of thought as logical positivism, which declared metaphysical problems meaningless, has every reason to listen quietly to the mind of the Orient."[33]

This brings us back to the relationship between philosophy and religion in the East. There is danger in identifying them, as some authorities tend to do, because the reader is apt to add mentally "as understood in the West" to both the words *philosophy* and *religion*. But to affirm that the East integrates theory and practice is a weak statement. So we might conclude that in the East philosophy is religious and religion is philosophical. Two opinions—one from a Chinese philosopher and one from a Japanese philosopher—may help clarify the issue. Wing-tsit Chan calls attention to seven connections of Oriental philosophy and religion:

1. Oriental philosophy and Oriental religion have a close historical connection, but not necessarily a philosophical connection.
2. Oriental religion often contains nature worship, alchemy, and charms. Oriental philosophy shuns such.
3. The religious element is present in many Oriental philosophical systems, but not in all.
4. Oriental philosophy may be regarded as usually nonreligious in the sense of nondependence upon the supernatural for salvation and knowledge.
5. Oriental religions accept dreams and revelations; Oriental philosophy as a rule does not (except in the case of the *Vedas*).
6. Oriental philosophies often conceive of deity in terms of a universal principle, rather than as a supernatural being. Many Oriental philosophies try to disprove God.
7. Oriental philosophy is religious in the sense that it affirms intimacy between man and reality. This explains why in the Orient religions often grew out of a philosophy, e.g., Buddhism.[34]

Junjiro Takakusu finds no distinction between Buddhist philosophy and Buddhist religion: "In Buddhist systems, investigation by oneself and argument with others, meditation by oneself and teaching to others, all go together. When the Life-view is formed it is at once applied to Life-culture, aiming at a realization of the Life-ideal. Accordingly, it is philosophy but at the same time religion; there is, in fact, no distinction between the two. One ought not to think that these two are not as yet differentiated in Buddhism, because Buddhism holds that these two should not be divided. Otherwise it will end either in a philosophical amusement or a superstitious belief. Some Buddhist ideas may seem to be purely theoretical, but no Buddhist theory, however negative or passive, will be without an application to actual life. . . . no negative principle or passive view will remain negative or passive when it is applied to Life-culture. All tends toward the realization of the Life-ideal."[35]

8. Indian Philosophy

The term *Indian Philosophy* usually denotes Hindu philosophy, but a comprehensive study of the philosophy of the Indian people would need to include not only the philosophy associated with Hinduism but also that associated with Islam, Zoroastrianism, Sikhism, Jainism, and many other ethnic, cultural, and religious groups that live or have lived in South Asia, including such tribal and forest people as the Nāgā, Muṇḍ, Santāl, Goṇḍ, Oraon, Adī, Bīrhor, Mallār, Kariā, Kādar, Savara, Juāṅg, Shānār, Bhīl, and Toḍa. K. M. Sen in *Hinduism*[36] says it is a pity that most modern treatments of Indian philosophy deal only with the life and thought of the elite aspects of Indian culture. This would be a valid criticism of a cultural study of India, but in a volume on philosophy, as has already been indicated, a distinction must be made between *professional* philosophy and *everyone* philosophy. Sen calls attention to many non-Vedic aspects of Hinduism, for example, worship of rivers, mountains, trees, and animals; the gods Śiva, Kālī, and Geneśa; phallic symbols *(liṅga)*; the prayer-worship known as *pūjā*; and many tantric practices. He singles out the Bāul singers of Bengal as a group that ought to be considered when one studies Indian philosophy. These fascinating troubadours who seek through song to worship the god whom they call "the Man of my heart," who reject all temples and all scriptures, who refuse to record their own history on the grounds of the harmony of past-present-future *(trikāla-yoga)*, and who stress simplicity and naturalness *(sahaj)*, should definitely be studied in an anthropological, sociological, and/or cultural study of India. But a "philosophy" that remains only in an oral tradition, that is not in a publicly sharable state, that is, in some written form, can be classified as an everyone philosophy rather than the sort of philosophy we are studying in this volume.

The Indian philosophy that I am considering in this volume—the Vedic-Upaniṣadic tradition—is indeed part of the Hindu way of life. It is far more than an academic discipline of colleges and universities. Professors of philosophy in Indian universities have difficulty confining their subject matter in a monadic department. An Indian philosopher confesses, "The Indian philosopher, with his synoptic insight into the soul of things, does not make any hard and fast distinction between departments of knowledge like metaphysics, psychology, ethics, and religion. He is more interested in the synthetic grasp of the underlying principles of all knowledge than in the analytic method of discovering distinctions."[37]

Indian philosophy as a way of life is quite unlike the restraint that was an important part of the Greek pattern of life and thought. As Nirad C. Chaudhuri has said, "There is nothing an Indian understands less in his unvarnished Indianness than the Greek notion of *sophrosyne,* which, to quote Sir Richard Livingstone, stands for self-control, balance, sanity, and reasonableness; avoidance of extremes of actions, speech, and thought; a rightness of mind which brings harmony into a personality or life. The Indian swings from pole to pole. . . . Thus to ask an Indian to be balanced among a number of things, each good in its way, is to ask him, not to be effective in his varied loyalties, but to be futile in all of them. . . . He is and can be driven only by his impulses and emotions, fixed into impulsive and emotional habits, and these impulses and emotions cannot be checked in their natural course without bringing about, as a result of the check, an atrophy of the whole motive power of effort."[38] Hence, it is not surprising that Indian philosophy nurtures devotees and disciples rather than scholars, even among Westerners. Schopenhauer, one of the first Europeans to study the *Upaniṣads,* set the pattern of uncritical enthusiasm in his remark in the preface to *Welt als Wille und Verstellung:* "It has been the solace of my life, it will be the solace of my death." Chauduri may have been too caustic when he wrote, "There are few characters more painfully unattractive than the Hinduizing Occidental,"[39] but, in my opinion, he was not far off the mark. Donning an ocher robe does not make one a Hindu!

Although there is no Sanskrit term equivalent to the Greek *philosophía,* there is an abundance of related terms. The more important are the following: *dṛṣṭi* (having an opinion), *darśana* (having a point of view), *tattva-jñāna* (true knowing of the essence of things), *viveka-jñāna* (discriminative knowledge), *ānvīkṣakī* (thinking about thinking), *adhyātma-vidyā* (knowing the inner nature of things), *ātma-vidyā* (knowing the self), *prajñá* (direct knowing of things), *bodhā* (the understanding that accompanies the self-awakening experience), *sādhanā* (the total discipline designed to accomplish the full development of man), *anu-īkṣakī* (the survey of all things), *para-vidyā* (higher knowledge), *mokṣa-śāstra* (science of liberation), and *mata* (doctrine). Indian philosophy first began in the subcontinent of Asia as a soteriological technique; hence, the terms *sādhanā* and *mokṣa-śāstra* (treatise on liberation) were both appropriate. But as Indian philosophers became more self-critical and defensive, their philosophies became thought systems defended by reason. This is best designated by the term *darsána* (a point of view). Indian philosophy as tolerant viewpoints is interestingly depicted in a volume written in the seventh century A.D. describing the visit of a king to a forest university. According to the *Harsha Charita* of Bana, the king saw "Buddhists from various provinces perched on pillows, seated on rocks, dwelling in bowers of creepers, lying in thickets or in the shadow of branches, or squatting on the roots of trees—devotees dead to all passions; Jains in white robes, mendicants, ascetics; followers of Kapila, Lokayatikas, followers of Kanada, followers of Upanishads, students of legal institutions, students of the Puranas, adepts in rituals, adepts in grammar, followers of Panchatantra, and others besides, all diligently following their own tenets, pondering, urging objections, raising doubts, resolving them, expounding etymologies and disputing, discussing and explaining many points."[40]

Indian philosophy must be studied as situated within Hinduism much in the manner in which the philosophy of the Middle Ages in the West was situated within Christianity. Just as the medieval philosophers found authoritative ideas and values in the Bible and the Church Fathers, so the intellectuals in India found the basic assumptions of their culture in the collection of ancient prayers and poems known as the *Vedas* and in the later collections of speculations known as the *Upaniṣads*. One feature of Indian philosophy that differentiates it from Western philosophy is that with the exception of Buddhism and Jainism it has remained scholastic with respect to its tradition, whereas Western philosophy has not. Indian philosophy tends to conservatism and continuity. "Conformism is a fundamental characteristic of the Indian mind and there seems to have been no wish to deviate from tradition."[41] Western philosophers are frequently exasperated when, in discussion with Indian philosophers, they are informed that a certain idea is true because it is found in the *Ṛg Veda*. Indian philosophers defend this methodology on the ground that truth is timeless. But Western philosophers reply that whereas the Greeks believed in a past Golden Age, modern Western philosophers, due to such factors as Christian eschatology, the Renaissance, the Enlightenment, the scientific revolution, and the discovery and colonization of the American continents, look to the future for more important truths and values. Westerners rejoice in change, development, evolution, and progress. Hindus seek sameness, stability, continuity, and permanence. Richard Lannoy has expressed the Indian attitude toward change in these words: "Change does not increase the good; there is no such thing here as progress; value lies in sameness, in the repeated pattern of the known, not in novelty. What is good in life is exact identity with all past experience, and all mythical experience. . . . In the West we see our history climactically; we plan our future experiences climactically, leading up to future satisfaction or meaning, and to fulfillment through pursuing a career. In India, action is a series of anti-climactic masquerades."[42] Twentieth-century Indians often have difficulty in harmonizing East and West in themselves. Some, like Nehru, become Europeanized, finding their Hindu roots an embarrassment; others like Gandhi, remain as closely as possible to the traditional Hindu patterns of life and thought. East and West remain in conflict in India.

Indian philosophy as a *sādhanā* is primarily concerned with the freedom of human beings from anything that stands in the way of the full realization of their potentialities. Knowing is secondary to becoming. Science is ancillary to humanism. Epistemology, cosmology, anthropology, and axiology are important to the extent that they aid in self-realization. The centrality of man is stressed throughout the development of Indian philosophy. For example, in the great epic of India, the *Mahābhārata,* the dying Bhīṣma discloses "the secret and supreme doctrines," namely, "There is nothing in the universe higher than man."[43] In the other epic of India, the *Rāmāyaṇa,* we are informed that the devotee of Rāma is greater than Rāma, that is, man is greater than God. Indian philosophy, declared one Indian scholar, "is a running commentary on the text, 'Thanks that I am man.'"[44]

9. Chinese Philosophy

The Chinese language is either admirably qualified or hopelessly unqualified for philosophical expression, depending upon whether one favors terms that have a nimbus of nuances or terms that are unmistakably clear and distinct. D. T. Suzuki observed, "One thing at least that prevented the Chinese from making headway in their philosophy is their use of ideological characters. Not only are the characters themselves intractable and clumsy, but their grammatical construction is extremely loose. The verbs are not subject to conjugation, the nouns are indeclinable, no tense-relations are grammatically expressible. . . . When we cannot wield the tool as we will, the material on which we work fails to produce the effect we desire; and the reader is at a loss to understand the meaning which was intended by the author." Suzuki concluded that the Chinese language is "an inconvenience, and even a hindrance, to philosophical writing."[45] Wing-tsit Chan conjectured, "No two translators of Chinese terms will ever agree entirely on their translations."[46] The result is that a great deal of scholarship in Chinese philosophy is philology, that is, controversy over the meaning of words. The Chinese language as the outgrowth of pictographs cannot express abstract ideas easily. Hence the Chinese language suggests rather than articulates. A translation is really an interpretation. The literature of China is often in the form of simple stories whose external simplicity hides an inner profundity. Three Chinese words related to philosophy as it is practiced in the West are *cheng-ming, ko-chih,* and *t'i-jen. Cheng-ming* (Rectification of Names) was what Confucius said he would put first on his agenda were he ever to become the prime minister of a state. Only when terms are correctly used and understood can reality be properly described and human relationships correctly observed. Confucius believed that the right terms to be used in human relationships are those which call people to the realization of the ideal. *Cheng-ming* might be called semantics within the context of pragmatics. *Ko-chih* is often translated as "Investigation of Things and Achievement of Knowledge." It refers to both inductive investigation and deductive validity, but like *cheng-ming,* its connotation is too humanistic to be equated with the objective scientific methods used in the West. *T'i-jen* (Personally Realizing Truth) has already been noted in this chapter. The intuitive nature of Chinese thought is also indicated in the related term *chih hsing ho-i* (Unity of Knowing and Doing), which stresses knowing as dynamic rather than static and as relative rather than absolute. *Cheng-ming, ko-chih,* and *t'i-jen* may be regarded as the three basic methodologies of Chinese philosophy—and the third one is decidedly favored. In other words, Chinese philosophy is humanistically oriented. Knowledge is valued for what it does to and for human beings: "No ontological speculation, no cosmological hypothesis, no abstract ethical theory, seemed worthy of their serious contemplation, unless it had a direct bearing upon practical morality."[47] In traditional China it was through philosophy that a man became an "Inner Sage," accomplished great deeds in the world as an "Outer King," and sometimes became both "Inner Sage and Outer King," that is, the Chinese equivalent of Plato's Philosopher King. Three other terms have ontological-axiological connotations: *li, tao,* and *jen.* *Li,* the basic concept in modern Chinese philosophy, is not to be confused with *li* (Ceremony) and *li* (Profit). The context will indicate which *li* is intended. *Li* is variously translated as Reason, Eternal Principle, Rational Principle, Law, and Truth. For the Neoconfucians *li* is the rational principle of existence, and *ch'i* is the material principle. *Li* is comparable to the *lógos* is Greek thought. It is the *li* of things that makes them one in reality, and that gives man the authority for referring to the plethora of things as constituting a Universe. *Tao* (Way, Principle, Cosmic Order, Nature) has different meanings, depending on whether it is used within Taoism or Confucianism. If within Taoism, it is an ontological term for the first principle of totality. If within Confucianism, it is a moral principle—the way to live, the way of moral order, and only secondarily a metaphysical principle. The Neoconfucians, who reintroduced metaphysical considerations into Confucianism, meant by *tao* the way man should live when he follows the reason in things. *Jen* is the term used in Confucianism for virtue in general. *Active Human Heartedness, True Humanity, Goodness, The Moral Ideal of the Superior Man,* and even *Love* are some of the translations. Context indicates whether it is the fundamental virtue of human life or whether it signifies the sum total of all virtues.

Chinese philosophy does not lend itself easily to tidy systems. Unlike Indian philosophy, Chinese philosophy is usually associated with specific individuals rather than particular systems. Philosophy in China is not a special study for people of special interests. Rather it is a study that enables any man to become a full man. E. R. Hughes in the introduction to his *Chinese Philosophy in Classical Times* writes, "There is something particularly appropriate about an 'Everyman' volume on Chinese Philosophy, for the Chinese people and their tradition have been impregnated with a sense of Everyman."[48]

Chinese philosophy has no strong tradition of revealed and authoritative writings. While Chinese philosophical writings became the ideology of Chinese civilization, these writings were never prized as more than human records. One could disagree with the literature without being a heretic. Chinese philosophy is humanistic. Confucius set the general pattern in

Chinese philosophy in being concerned about human life. Those who were interested in nature for the most part studied nature in order to learn how human beings ought to live. The end sought was the tranquil state of mind. Chinese philosophy is this-worldly, yet it does not neglect otherworldliness. The aim of philosophy in China is the achievement of the good life in the earthly society. Otherworldly concerns are chiefly about how to treat the manes. But while ethical concerns are uppermost, one must not suppose that therefore metaphysics is neglected. Chinese philosophy is political philosophy; but, insofar as a view of the world affects the practical solutions of everyday problems, a Chinese philosopher can also be very much interested in metaphysics. However, this interest is only in respect to the extent to which metaphysical studies contribute to self-cultivation. Chinese philosophy is characterized by what might be called a "dialectical movement." That is, it seeks a reconciliation of conflicting entities or forces into a whole, for example, *yin* and *yang* into *tao*, Heaven and Earth into Man. There is great emphasis on harmony of opposites. This harmony is metaphysical, ethical, and logical.

There is little epistemology in Chinese philosophy. Fung Yu-lan says this is because the Chinese never clearly separated the subject and the object, the ego and the non-ego. Knowledge is not valued for itself but for what it can do for man. Hence the writing of books is not taken seriously. According to traditional Chinese values what a man is (that is, his moral qualities) is important; what one has (that is, material possessions and knowledge as displayed in writings) is of little worth.

The ideal life according to Fung Yu-Lan consists of activity in four spheres.[49] The first two are the outcome of things left as they are; the latter two are the products of cultivation. The first two are the gifts of nature; the latter two are the creation of man. The spheres are the natural, the utilitarian, the moral, and the transcendent. The natural sphere is the sphere of human innocence. In it man acts without understanding the meaning of his action. He merely follows his own tendencies and the customs of his society. In the utilitarian sphere man becomes aware of himself as distinct from others. He seeks his own greatest advantage, his good reputation, and his own property and position. In the moral sphere man becomes aware of society. He seeks to discharge his debt to others. He rejoices in his society's joys, and grieves in its sorrows. In the transcendent sphere man becomes aware of the universe. He rejoices in the joy of the Great Whole, but he will not grieve because the Great Whole has nothing over which to grieve. The function of philosophy, according to Fung, is to enable man to reach the moral and transcendent spheres. It is not enough to be moral, for man must possess an understanding of moral rules and must have an awareness of the nature of his actions. He must know why there are moral principles, and he must know why he should act in accord with the moral principles. He must neither act without knowing, nor know without acting. The same is true for the transcendent sphere. It is not enough to know the reality of the transcendent sphere. He must also be in the transcendent sphere, that is, he must have "knowledge of Heaven," give "service to Heaven," "rejoice in Heaven," and experience "identification with Heaven." These four are strikingly similar to the four *mārgas* (ways) in Hinduism—the way of knowledge *(jñāna mārga)*, the way of works *(karma mārga)*, the way of devotion *(bhakti mārga)*, and the way of union *(yoga mārga)*, but, whereas in Hinduism each must select one way and stay with it, in the Chinese goals of life all four ways are integrated in the life of the Great Man. The difference is that whereas in India, as Kṛṣṇa tells Arjuna in the *Bhagavad Gītā*, each is to follow the path he chooses[50] and stay with it,[51] the four paths in China are stages on the single path of the Sage.

10. A Schema for the Study of Philosophy East and West

How can philosophy East and West be studied such that the study will be fair to both East and West? At this point I think that the West must make a concession. If philosophy were to be studied as language analysis or as the metaphysics of objective reality, this would be unfair to the East. Eastern philosophers have not been unconcerned about language nor about the natural world, but that has not been their focus. The Eastern focus has been on the human effort to understand itself. W. H. Werkmeister has observed, "The most striking feature of Oriental philosophy, it seems to me, is its concern with the status of man in this world (China) and with man's ultimate goal (India)."[52] Max Müller believed that Western peoples might derive from India "that correction which is wanted in order to make our inner life more perfect, more comprehensive, more universal, in fact, more truly human."[53] Keshub Chunder Sen said Hinduism is "Human Catholic Religion."[54] Rammohun Roy called it "Universal Humanism."[55] Nobuo Haneda in a recent article says, "As the core of Buddhism is self-examination, Buddhism simply cannot exist without it. The Japanese Zen Master Dogen (1200–1253) said that 'learning Buddhism is learning the self.' And it is only through self-examination that we can understand the truths taught in Buddhism and awaken to our ignorance."[56]

Wing-tsit Chan writes, "If one word could characterize the entire history of Chinese philosophy, that word would be humanism—not the humanism that denies or slights a Supreme Power, but one that professes the unity of man and Heaven. In this sense, humanism has dominated Chinese thought from the dawn of its history."[57]

The study of the human self is significant in the history of Western philosophy. Yet, especially since the scientific revolution, the greater emphasis has been on exploring—and exploiting—the external world. Perhaps the time has arrived in which there should be a change of focus. An Indian philosopher, writing in 1950, warned, "The discovery of man is the principal necessity of modern times just as the discovery of nature was of earlier centuries."[58]

Copleston, in the epilogue of *Philosophies and Cultures,* summarizes, "Different peoples have their different traditions, customs, religious beliefs and social and political institutions. But they all consist of human beings. And the question, what is man? is important for them all. . . . How we think about man is not a trivial matter. All efforts at social engineering, all attacks on social engineering, presuppose ideas of man, even if these ideas are not made fully explicit. Further, such ideas can have world-wide repercussions. There is need, therefore, for inter-cultural dialogue, in which philosophers can and should play a part."[59]

Alois Dempf in *Selbstkritik der Philosophie* (Vienna, 1947) argues that philosophical thought within each culture develops through three stages: (1) philosophy originates as an effort to justify traditional views and values at the time of a cultural crisis; (2) philosophy later attempts to provide a cosmology as a wider framework for the cultural tradition; (3) when a time of relativism and skepticism arises, due to a clash of world views, philosophy centers reflection on man himself. Dempf supports his view of the three stages of development by appeal to thirteen historical periods in which philosophy, both Eastern and Western, has exhibited these stages. Dempf's indebtedness to his fellow countryman Auguste Comte, who a few generations earlier developed a law of three stages governing the history of man—religious, metaphysical, and scientific—may be surmised, but his support for his own thesis seems forced. However, one point of his theory is impressive and significant for an approach to Eastern and Western philosophies, namely, as philosophers become less parochial culturally due to the awareness of other philosophical traditions, they center their study on anthropological and personal issues. Hence it is the plan of this volume to analyze, compare, and contrast philosophies in the West, India, China, and Japan from the point of view of the human being. This means that we shall not begin with questions like "What is the state?" or "What is time?" or "What is God?" but rather with questions like "What is man's relation to the state?" or "What is the human experience of time?" or "What do human life and thought indicate about the possible reality and nature of God?" Robert Rossow, Jr., put the issue correctly when he wrote, "Never has the world so needed a new philosophy, a new way to conceptualize the nature of man and of his relation to his social and physical environment."[60]

One of the possible ways to conceive of the human being and his environment is to begin with the recognition that each lives in and is a part of three worlds: (1) the natural world of space and time, (2) the social world of family, community, state, and nation, (3) the creative world of art and religion. Each is a body in the physical world, a person in the social world, and a creator in the creative world. Totality, the universe or all that is, is the natural world including man, the social world including man, and the creative world including man. The human being is the universe become self-aware.

In the philosophical admonition "Know thyself" the natural-social-creative self is the self to be known—the epistemological object. But there is another self—the self that does the knowing—the epistemological subject. This I shall call the self-as-knower to distinguish it from the self-as-known. This is the "I" in such statements as "I know myself," "I like myself," "I hate myself," "I want to improve myself," and "I do not know what to do about myself." The self-as-knower differentiates the human from other animals and makes the human being a transcender of animality. No animal-qua-animal ever thinks "I am an animal." No animal-qua-animal is a philosopher.

The philosophical quest may now be stated as a fivefold attempt to know the self:

1. "Who am I as a self-knower?"
2. "Who am I as a self in the natural world?"
3. "Who am I as a self in the social world?"
4. "Who am I as a self in the creative world?"
5. "Who am I as a self-realizer?"

The human being as self-realizer takes on his own evolution, his own development. In the light of his own understanding of human nature and its total environment the human being determines his own goals. The human is both what he was and what he is to be. The human is the time-binding being for whom both memories and aspirations are part of the present.

In Western philosophy the quest for self-knowledge has often ended in puzzlement. Augustine announced as his starting point *Nosce te ipsum* (Know yourself), but he later confessed *Quaestio mihi factus sum* (A question have I become for myself).[61] Augustine's confession may be translated, "My physical-social-creative self, that is, myself-as-known has become a problem for myself-as-knower." Perhaps the most persistent and thorough effort to know the self in Western thought was that of David Hume. After completing his *Treatise on Human Nature* he wrote an appendix as, he said, "an opportunity of confessing my errors." He wrote that "upon a strict review of the section concerning personal identity, I find myself involved in such a labyrinth that, I must confess, I neither know how to correct my former opinions, nor how to render them consistent. . . . I must plead the privilege of a sceptic, and confess that this difficulty is too hard for my understanding."

In Eastern thought the Hindu tradition centers on the relationship of the true self *(Ātman)* and totality (Brahman). A. C. Mukerji observes that "the problem of the self is the one problem in discussing which Indian genius has showed itself at its best."⁶² The Buddhist tradition has long argued over the original insight of the Buddha that the self is an *an-ātman* (non-self). How can *karma* operate without a carrier of *karma*? Should one engage in self-salvation (the *arhat* ideal) or in the salvation of others (the *bodhisattva* ideal)? Are there indeed other selves to be saved? Is the self empty (Mādhyamika), or is there an overpersonal consciousness (Yogācára)? In Confucianism and Taoism the stress is on self-transformation *(tu hua)*. This pragmatic character of Chinese thought was formulated in *The Great Learning:* "The ancients who wished to manifest their clear character to the world would first bring order to their states. Those who wished to bring order to their states would first regulate their families. Those who wished to regulate their families would first cultivate their personal lives. Those who wished to cultivate their personal lives would first rectify their minds. Those who wished to rectify their minds would first make their wills sincere. Those who wished to make their wills sincere would first extend their knowledge. The extension of knowledge consists in the investigation of things. When things are investigated, knowledge is extended; when knowledge is extended, the will becomes sincere; when the will is sincere, the mind is rectified; when the mind is rectified, the personal life is cultivated; when the personal life is cultivated, the family will be regulated; when the family is regulated, the state will be in order; and when the state is in order, there will be peace throughout the world."⁶³

11. *The Future of Philosophy*

The future of philosophy is assured, since philosophy is the only study in which reflection upon it is part of itself. To ask what philosophy is is to philosophize. To argue for the death of philosophy is to philosophize. Philosophy will continue as long as human beings remain finite rational animals. As long as humans create knowledge and values, some will be concerned about clear statements and sound values. Some will weigh the merits of articulate uncertainty and inarticulate certainty.

Today there are movements—both conscious and unconscious—toward a uniform human culture. Asian and African peoples are imitating the West, and many in the West are experimenting in Eastern forms of meditation. Modern means of communication and transportation make cultural exchanges easy. Some desire and some fear that a uniform world philosophy may be created. One Western philosopher has expressed his own displeasure with the movements toward a world philosophy: "We are cultivating uniformity amidst unyielding political differences; the hope of the world, as I see it, lies in exactly the reverse: a political unity within which cultural and individual differences can flourish. I do not look forward to a state of society in which all men espouse one world philosophy, but rather to a state in which each man espouses his own philosophy, but one in which he can live at peace with all the world."[64] The world philosophy we need includes a recognition of the value of the plurality of philosophies that guarantee the right to differ, of intercultural understanding and appreciation rather than cultural imitations and cultural dominations. Radhakrishnan has said, "The need of philosophy today is for a world perspective which will include the philosophical insights of all the world's great traditions."[65] But is it not utopian and unrealistic to think that all the philosophical insights can be included in any system? Surely the most that can be expected is that the fundamental principles of the great traditions be given a hearing. René Guenon said that if the West is to make itself "bearable," "it must give up 'assimilation' and practice instead 'association.'"[66]

In April 1959 Arnold Toynbee and Raghavan Iyer recorded a discussion for the radio division of UNESCO in which they introduced a new image for the East-West separation. They said that the "iron curtain" that separates Russia and the West is political and military, and that there is an ideological and psychological "glass curtain" that separates East and West. Toynbee said that were it possible to condition the whole world so that all lived in the same climate and had the same income, the glass curtain would remain. At one close of the discussion Iyer said that a "widely prevalent illusion today is that somehow through a study of art and literature, we can automatically destroy the curtain." But he added, "I think there is no substitute in the end for understanding religious and philosophical conceptions in the East and in the West. . . . There is a basis both in East and West for a new humanism."[67]

The agreement of Iyer and Toynbee that East and West need to learn from each other and jointly develop a new humanism is taken for granted by many Westerners today, but this was not the case in the West in the years between the two World Wars. Charles Eliot wrote in 1921, "Let me confess that I cannot share the confidence in the superiority of Europeans and their ways which is prevalent in the West. . . . In fact European civilization is not satisfying and Asia can still offer something more attractive to many who are far from Asiatic in spirit. Yet though most who have spent even a passing visit to the East felt its charm, the history, art and literature of Asia are still treated with ignorant indifference in cultured circles."[68] William Ralph Inge, a leader in the Anglican Church, confessed, "It is a reproach to us that with our unique opportunities of entering into sympathetic relations with Indian thought, we have made few attempts to do so. . . . I am not suggesting that we should become Buddhists or Hindus, but I believe that we have almost as much to learn from them as they have from us."[69]

Is philosophy a passing phase in the life of mankind? Will the human race reach a stage in which philosophy will not be needed? Philosophy has its detractors. St. Paul warned, "Beware lest any man spoil you through philosophy."[70] Cicero criticized philosophers for their defense of unusual ideas: "There is nothing so strange or so little credible that it has not been maintained by one philosopher or another."[71] John Calvin thought philosophers were showmen: "The philosophers, being ambitious men, have sedulously affected an exquisite perspicuity of method in order to make an ostentatious display of their ingenious dexterity."[72] John Milton reserved a special corner of hell for philosophers:

> Others apart sat on a Hill retired,
> In thoughts more elevate, and reason'd high
> In providence, Foreknowledge, Will, and Fate,
> Fixt Fate, free will, foreknowledge absolute,
> And found no end, in wand'ring mazes lost.
> Of good and evil much they argu'd then,
> Of happiness and final misery,
> Passion and Apathy, and glory and shame,
> Vain wisdom all, and false Philosophie.[73]

The philosophic task may discourage even the philosopher; for example, "Philosophy is a child striving to hold water in its fist."[74] Yet, as long as the human being remains a finite, self-aware creature, the effort to understand and evaluate the self and the total environment will not cease. In the words of Thomas Merton: "If the world is to survive and if civilization is to endure or rather perhaps weather its present crisis and recover its dimension of 'wisdom,' we must hope for a new world culture that takes account of all civilized philosophies."[75]

2
The Human Being as Speaker

Did the human being create language, or did language create the human being? In the well-known Uncle Remus story Brer Rabbit would not tolerate silence in the Tar-Baby: "I'm gwine ter larn you how ter talk ter 'spectubble folks ef hit's de las' act. . . . 'Ef you don't tak off that hat en tell me howdy, I'm gwine ter bus' you wide open." If Tar-Baby were a self, it must speak. In the absence of language, there is no self.

Language is a system of signs. A sign is an object, sound, gesture, or condition that stands for something other than itself. Kierkegaard once entered a shop in Copenhagen to ask the shopkeeper what he was selling. There was a For Sale sign in the window but nothing else. The proprietor told him that the sign did not point to anything that was for sale since it was the sign itself that was for sale. If the shopkeeper had been precise, he might have said, "I am selling pieces of cardboard with the words 'For Sale' printed on them to people who may wish to use them to denote something they wish to sell. As they appear in my window they are not For Sale signs since a For Sale 'sign' that does not signify something for sale is not a For Sale sign."

A sign involves three entities: the user of the sign, the receiver of the sign, and the object indicated by the sign. Signs are products of sociality, although one can communicate with one's self through signs, for instance, a solitary hiker in the woods may make marks on trees to remind himself of the route he has taken. The signs usually used by human beings are auditory or visual, although the remarkable life of Helen Keller demonstrated the possibility of human communication through tactual and kinesthetic sensations. Aldous Huxley described in *Brave New World* an amusement house known as the "feelies," which displaced the movies. Perfume manufacturers advertise their products as means of communication. The sense of smell is an important means of communication in the Arab world. Edward T. Hall, in his fascinating study of social distance writes, "Olfaction occupies a prominent place in Arab life. Not only is it one of the distance-setting mechanisms, but it is a vital part of a complex system of behavior. Arabs consistently breathe on people when they talk. However, this habit is more than a matter of different manners. To the Arab good smells are pleasing and a way of being involved with each other. To smell one's friend is not nice but desirable, for to deny him your breath is to act ashamed. . . . When couples are being matched for marriage, the man's go-between will sometimes ask to smell the girl, who may be turned down if she doesn't 'smell nice.' Arabs recognize that smell and disposition may be linked."[1] Hall points out that business is conducted at a distance of about two feet in Arab countries, in accordance with the belief that persons emit different odors when lying and when telling the truth. Janet L. Hopson has studied odor signs. She claims that not only does each race of man have a distinctive odor but also that each human being has a unique odor.[2]

Lower animals use signs. Signals of warning, pain, affection, and sexual readiness are found among reptiles, insects, birds, and mammals. George Schwidetzky in *Do You Speak Chimpanzee?*[3] speculates that the first communication is oral, and that the oldest sound is hissing. He has classified even speech sounds that serve as communication links among simians: (1) the tongue-click, (2) the lip-crack, i.e., *p* produced by the rapid opening of the lips, (3) the lip-click, i.e., a sound between *p* and *f*, (4) the indrawn *hl*, (5) the *ngah* or *hkak* of young chimpanzees, (6) the *purr*, and (7) the *ururur* of the lemur.

1. The Origin of Human Speech

The study of the origin of human speech has until recently been based only on the imagination of the theorizer. This tendency to fashion *a priori* theories has given the study a bad reputation. Max Müller gave unacademic names to the theories, which made the theories easy to remember. There is the Pooh-Pooh theory, which contends that interjections such as "oh," "ow," "ah," "oof," and "whee" were the first speech elements. These are uncontrolled, instinctive ejaculations accompanying pain, exhaustion, surprise, fear, and other intense feelings. Another theory is that the first human sounds were imitations of the sounds made by lower animals. Müller christened this the Bow-Wow theory. This theory is not very flattering to human beings, holding that they were silent before noting that the lower animals were making sounds. The Yo-he-ho theory, which was presented by Ludwig Noire, associated the earliest audible signs with communal labor. Otto Jespersen criticized this theory on the grounds that speech originated in merry play and hilarity rather than in serious activities. Some think the first human sounds were made when a male tried to attract the attention of a female. Others suppose the first sounds were those of a mother lulling her infant. Charles Darwin sponsored the Ta-Ta theory, that is, the theory that speech in its origin is mouth-pantomine, that the vocal cords unconsciously attempted to mimic gestures made by the hands. Max Müller added a theory of his own, which he called the Ding-Dong theory. Müller, contending that every substance has its peculiar ring, reasoned that speech in human beings might be compared to the sound of a bell when struck with a gong. Richard Paget added a theory similar to Darwin's, based on his observation that bodily movements predominate in primitive communication. Human beings first gave signals with hands, feet, and head. When hands were busy, they gestured with tongue, lips, and jaw. Then they found they could communicate more effectively by blowing air through nostrils and mouth. The first oral sounds were probably *st, ps, sch,* and *brr*. This theory has been called the Wig-Wag theory.

Modern linguists are usually more interested in examining how sounds and words acquire meaning and significance than in determining beginnings of language. They agree that language was first a means of expressing feeling, and much later became a way of expressing thought. Jespersen compared modern languages with the older languages from which they had developed—English with Old English, Danish with Old Norse, French and Italian with Latin, Hindi with Sanskrit, and so on—and on the basis of such studies attempted to find a system of lines reaching beyond history to determine a direction of linguistic evolution: "The evolution of language shows a progressive tendency from inseparable irregular conglomerations to freely and regularly combinable short elements."[4] Primitive speakers were babblers. Sounds were fun to make—and only later, much later, were they used as a way to communicate thoughts. Jespersen gave as evidence lines from the Old Norse *Edda:*

>No dimber, dambler angler, dancer,
>Prig of cacker, prig of prancer;
>No swigman, swaddler, clapper-dudgeon,
>Cadge-gloak, curtal, or curmudgeon;
>No whip-jack, palliard, patrico;
>No jarkman, be he high or low;
>No dummerar or romany . . .
>Nor any other will I suffer.[5]

Primitive man, claimed Jespersen, came to attach meaning to rambling sequences of sounds much as children come to attach meaning to words spoken by elders. The human infant does not come quietly into the world outside the womb. Crying is a normal part of the life of the infant. Parents are worried if their child is silent—and with good reason, since silence in young children may be a sign of Mongolism. The normal child is a chatterer. Anyone who has watched elementary school children on the playground at recess time knows this. Susanne Langer contends that language develops from a purposeless "lalling instinct," which lasts in the human infant for about twelve years.[6] This unlearned tendency to produce sound serves "to bring things into their minds, not into their hands,"[7] that is, childhood babbling has aesthetic rather than utilitarian functions. The mutism of the great ape is in striking contrast to human chattering: "He [the ape] does not play with his mouth and his breath as human infants do. . . . Consequently there are no sounds and syllables that please or frighten him by their sheer aesthetic character."[8] Langer's argument is that the origin and essence of language are "the formulation and expression of conceptions rather than the communication of natural wants."[9] Connotation preceded denotation. She writes that "only long habit can fix an association so securely that the word and the object are felt to belong together, so that the one is always a reminder of the other. But when this point is reached, the humanoid creature will undoubtedly utter the sound in sport, and thus move the object into nearer and clearer prominence in his mind, until he may be said to grasp a conception of it by means of the sound; and now the sound is a word."[10]

Another view of the origin and function of speech is the view that human speech is a form of sound magic; for example, the author of an unsigned article in *India News,* 17 July 1978, states, "The Vedas are sound vibrations in space." He argues that the ancient Indians, through the repeated vocalization of the Vedic hymns and mantras, were able to influence the combination of the natural elements, and even realize atomic energy! Without any documentation he adds, "This has now been accepted by the modern world."

The human is the being who puts the word between his reception of things and his reaction to things. Before he can react to outward stimuli he must name it, whether that thing be a star, a flower, a planet, a disease, and so on. According to the Hebrew story of creation, God presented the created world to man for his naming: "So out of the ground the Lord God formed every beast of the field and every bird of the air, and brought them to the man to see what he would call them; and whatever the man called every living creature, that was its name."[11] The human reaction to reality is not an organic reaction. It is a delayed reaction. In the Hebrew story man's dominion over the beasts of the field and the birds of the air appears to be sequential to his naming, talking about, and knowing.

2. *Signs and Their Functions*

Some signs are artificial in that the relationship between the sign and that to which it points is established by convention, for example, the octagonal stop sign, the circular slow sign, and the X sign for a railway crossing. Other signs are natural in that they, unlike the artificial signs, participate or share in some manner with the object they represent. The sharing may be an instance of causality, as smoke is a sign of fire, or it may be an instance of similarity, as a photograph is a sign of a person. A word is a sign, but a word is not always a sign, that is, a word may be treated as a sign or it may be treated as only a word. Consider the word *dog*. *Dog* may be considered as black marks on white paper; as the placing in juxtaposition from left to right the fourth, fifteenth, and seventh letters of the English alphabet; as the word *god* spelled backward; as a sound that rhymes with *fog* and *bog;* and as the English equivalent of the German *Hund*, the French *chien*, and the Latin *canus*. *Dog* as a sign may be used as a means for calling up an image of a four-legged animal that barks, as a way to express how one feels ("I feel like a dog today"), and as a technique for arousing anger in another ("You dog!"). In the last three examples the sign has appeared in its three uses: (1) as a symbol that represents an object, known as its referent; (2) as a symptom that expresses a condition of the sender; (3) as a signal appealing to the receiver. The three uses of signs can be diagramed as follows:

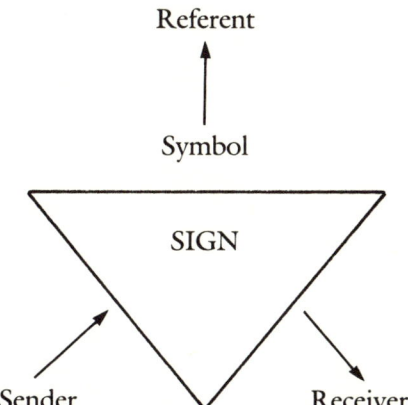

The functioning of signs is more complex than the representation-expression-appeal analysis suggests. Representation is a dual use of signs. The referent may be a thing or the characteristics of a thing. The former may be called the denotation or extension of a sign. The latter may be called the designation of the sign. For example, a married man who refers to "Mary, my wife and friend" uses these words to denote one woman and to designate two characteristics of her. Or again, an astronomer who says "Venus is the morning star and the evening star" denotes one star and designates two characteristics of that star. Expression-appeal, on the other hand, may be considered as a single functioning known as connotation or intension. This is the sense the sign has for sender and for receiver. Communication may misfire when connotations differ. For example, I was assured once in a hotel in Mysore (India) that a certain item on the menu was "Not hot," but I found it to be very hot. "Not hot" had vastly different connotations for the waiter and for me!

There are many ways to study signs. One way is to study them as objects used in communicative contexts. For example, an accoustical engineer designing a lecture hall does not usually need to know what will be the subject matter of the lectures to be given in the hall, or the language to be spoken, or the sex of senders or receivers; but he may need to know if special sounds will be used; for example, if ornithology is to be the topic discussed in the hall, and if the lecturer is going to illustrate the high pitches of certain bird calls, the engineer may need to provide special accoustical materials. A traffic control specialist considering the merits of red, green, and yellow colors, and of octagonal, round, and square shapes in the traffic signs of a city is studying traffic signs qua traffic signs. Typography as the study of the size, style, arrangements, and appearance of type for a book is another example of the study of signs as signs. Another is sigillography, the study of seals, that is, personal marks made on a soft material by means of a hard engraved negative to establish authenticity and also to insure that the document has not been interfered with after being executed.

A second way to study signs is to limit the study to the senders of signs. The physical, attitudinal, emotional, and psychological aspects of the human senders may be highly relevant to the understanding of the signs. The religion, politics, economics, social standing, vocation, and general health of the sender affect the selection and presentation of signs. The job of a drama critic is to evaluate the sender as sender.

Again the study can be limited to the receivers of signs. If one were planning to make a speech, one would want to know the composition of the audience. A lecture on educational goals would be very different if the audience is a class of fourth grade children, a labor union, the faculty of a high school, the administrators of a university, a Rotary Club, or the PTA in a racially mixed elementary school.

A fourth study of signs is the very important examination of the relation of senders and receivers of signs. This is known as pragmatics. It is a study of the origin, use, and effectiveness of signs to express a symptom of the sender in such a manner that it appeals to the receiver and produces the result that the sender intends. For example, one might evaluate the relative effectiveness of sending a written memo, making a telephone call, or making a personal visit as a way of asking one's employer for a raise in salary. One of the serious problems in international communication is the selecting of signs that have the same meaning and significance for both senders and receivers. Americans and Englishmen—two people separated by a common language!—often have humorous misunderstandings because of their different usages of the same sign. For example, in England it is highly complimentary to describe a woman as "homely," that is, home-loving.[12] Confucius stressed the importance of the relationships of signs between senders and receivers, and also of signs to referents. When he was asked what he would do first were he to become a prime minister, he replied that he would rectify all terms: "If names are not rectified [corrected], then language will not be in accord with truth. If language is not in accord with truth, then things cannot be accomplished. If things cannot be accomplished, then ceremonies and music will not flourish. If ceremonies and music do not flourish, then punishment will not be just. If punishments are not just, then the people will not know how to move hand or foot. Therefore, the superior man will give only names that can be described in speech and say only what can be carried out in practice."[13] Wing-tsit Chan, in commenting on this passage, writes, "This means not only that a name must correspond to its actuality, but also that rank, duties, and functions must be clearly defined and fully translated into action. Only then can a name be considered to be correct or rectified."[14]

A fifth study of signs deals with the relation between signs and the things, events, actions, states of affairs, and so on, to which the signs refer. This is called *semantics,* the study of the symbolic aspect of signs. There is some confusion about the meaning of sign and symbol, particularly in the field of religion, because of the propensity of interpreters of sacred scriptures to distinguish between a literal interpretation and a symbolic interpretation; for example, among Jews and Christians some treat the creation stories literally and some symbolically, and among Hindus some treat the Rāma and Sītā stories in the *Rāmāyaṇa* literally and some symbolically. In the *Upaniṣads* the innocent-looking word *iva* (as it were) appears frequently,[15] reminding the reader that the statement made must be taken symbolically. For example, a seer, speaking of sleep, says

> Now, as it were [*iva*], enjoying pleasure with women,
> Now, as it were [*iva*], laughing, and even beholding fearful sights.[16]

Eastern peoples seem to have fewer problems than Westerners in the symbolic interpretation of religious literature. The Christian theologian Paul Tillich fought a lifelong battle trying to get his fellow Christians to interpret the doctrine of God symbolically rather than literally. He wrote that "everything religion has to say about God, including his qualities, actions, and manifestations, has a symbolic character . . . the meaning of 'God' is completely missed if one takes the symbolic language literally."[17] "God is a being" is a symbolic statement. (The *Upaniṣads* would put this "God is *iva* a being.") "God is being-itself is a non-symbolic statement. It does not point beyond itself."[18] Confusion can be avoided by remembering that a sign in its symbolic aspect may represent the referent either literally or nonliterally. In either case it remains a sign. For example, a Christian who saw  on the wall of a house in Rome in the second century had to decide whether to interpret the sign literally or symbolically. In the first interpretation it probably indicated the location of a fish market; but according to the second interpretation it symbolized Christianity, since the letters of the Greek word for fish *(ichthús)* were an acronym for "Jesus Christ—God, Son, and Savior."

Paul Tillich made a sharp distinction between sign and symbol. According to him both sign and symbol point beyond themselves to something else; but whereas symbols participate in the reality to which they point, signs do not. Tillich's example of a symbol is a nation's flag. He wrote that "the flag participates in the power and dignity of the nation for which it stands. Therefore, it cannot be replaced except after an historic catastrophe that changes the reality of the nation which it symbolizes. An attack on the flag is felt as an attack on the majesty of the group in which it is acknowledged. Such an attack is considered blasphemy."[19] The defacement of a highway sign is illegal, but such an act is not considered blasphemous.

Suzanne Langer drew a different distinction between sign and symbol.[20] According to her, a sign announces an object to a receiver, whereas a symbol leads the receiver to conceive of the object. Since the symbol-object relationship requires that the receiver be a conceiving agent, we can assume that animals lower than the human can grasp signs but cannot grasp symbols. The word *James* may be a sign for a dog. Upon hearing *James* the dog whose owner is named James may begin looking for its master; but the dog cannot ask, "What about *James*?" as he could were the dog a symbolizing animal. But what is *James* as sound before it is sign or symbol? Langer said it is a "call-name." This seems a bit inelegant and cumbersome. I prefer to refer to a sign-word as a word with three dimensions or uses: symbol, signal, and symptom. The sign *James* and the sign *JAMES* are two signs qua signs, but only one sign qua symbol. Langer's analysis does call attention to the fact that a sign can function in many ways in its symbolic aspect; for example, *James* may symbolize the presence of the man named James. That is, one can use the term merely to call the attention of the man to what one wants to say, as in "James. Please come here," or one can use the term to call a third party's attention to the presence of James. But the sign can also be used in more complex manners in which it symbolizes a wide range of characteristics. For example, James's wife might say, "James, you are not James today." In this instance the first use of *James* symbolizes the presence of her husband, and the second use of *James* symbolizes the entire spectrum of moral, social, religious, physical, psychological, artistic, creative, et cetera, characteristics that she and he associate with the word *James* when it is applied to this person. Part of the problem of sophisticated communication is that every sign has unique symbolization for each sender and each receiver. This is a serious problem in cross-cultural philosophical dialogue. We should never assume that because Western and Eastern philosophers use the same terms, for example, *self, cause,*

God, freedom, law, time, and so on, they are communicating. Of course, this is found within a culture, but it must especially be watched when comparing Eastern and Western philosophies.

A sign in its symbolic aspect is an effort to represent an immediate experience; but all symbolism, in the words of Cassirer "harbors the curse of mediacy," and thus "it is bound to obscure what it seeks to reveal." This is true of both the inner and the outer world: "When speaks the soul, alas, the *soul* no longer speaks."[21]

A sixth study of signs considers the formal relations among signs in linguistic constructions. This is known as syntactics. When syntactics is applied to a theoretical language including formal logic, it is called logical syntax. Logical syntax analyzes such problems as the differences of statements like "X is," "X is real," "X is existent," and "X is factual."

When signs are studied properly, they are studied completely, that is, they are studied in all their dimensions. This comprehensive study is known as the general theory of signs, semiotics, semasiology, or sematology.

The early students of language debated whether words were directly connected with the objects signified or whether they were the result of arbitrary creation. Those who held the former view were called analogists; those who held the latter view were called anomalists. Today signs are sometimes classified as indexical, iconic, or conventional. Indexical signs acquire their symbolic function through causal connections. The sign is caused by, or constantly associated with, an object such that the presence of the sign is an indication of the presence of the object; for example, smoke accompanies fire, so when one sees smoke one assumes that there is fire. Smoke is therefore the sign of fire. Iconic signs acquire their symbolic function through similarity to an object; for example, in Christianity the image of a cross is a sign of this religion because of the similarity in appearance of the visual image to the Roman form of execution by which Jesus was put to death. Many of these signs have been stylized so that they have rather remote relations to the wooden cross, for example,

Some of the Chinese characters are iconic; for example, the character for man 人 is the remnant of an original pictogram of man 𠂉 . Some words are iconic with respect to sound. These are onomatopoeic words like *murmur, cuckoo,* and *whippoorwill*. Since 人 does not stand for the sound *jen*, it is possible for Japanese to use the same sign with the same symbol and pronounce it *hito*. Conventional signs acquire their symbolic function through use. Perhaps some of the conventional signs once had indexical or iconic characteristics, but they have been lost. Whereas we know why the Chinese character ⼈ represents the human being, we do not know why *man* and *homo* represent the human being in English and Latin. Most of the words in the 5,000 to 6,000 languages spoken on this globe are conventional by use. However, there are languages in which the words are conventional by design. These are artificial languages developed usually by linguists. One of the earliest of the artificial languages was developed by George Dalgarno, a Scottish student of languages, who wrote a book in 1661 entitled *Ars Signorum, or Universal Character and Philosophical Language*. Dalgarno divided all knowledge into seventeen categories, each indicated by a consonant. Subclasses were labeled by vowels, thus elephant *(Nηka)*, horse *(Nηkη)*, donkey *(Nηke)*, and mule *(Nηko)*. Many other artificial languages have been created, each offering different forms of conventional signs, for example, Volapuk (1880), Bopal Esperanto (1887), Spelin (1888), Dil (1893), Balta (1893), Veltparl (1896), Langue Bleue (1899), Mundolingue (1890), Idion Neutral (1903), Interlingua (1903), Ido (1907), and Novial (1928). Others include Little English created by Jane Renkin Aiken, Basic English by C. K. Ogden, and Iret by H. E. Palmer of the Institute for Research in English Teaching in Tokyo. In many cultures and subcultures there are conventional signs; for example, among the hoboes in America the following conventional signs are marked on gates or fences: ◯ (good for a handout), ● (cranky woman or bad dog), ⌀ (not generous), and ⦶ (stay away). The conventional signs of society are numerous: traffic signs, proofreaders' signs, hitchhikers' signs, signs of the policeman directing traffic, signs in athletic contests, signs among truck drivers, railway signs, auctioneering signs, sign language of the deaf, stockbroker signs, and so on. Consider, for example, the signs in professional baseball: signs of the umpire to indicate strikes and balls; signs from the coach in the dugout; signs from the third base coach to the batters and base runners; and signs from catcher to pitcher. Travelers are often struck by the differences in conventional signs in different cultures. In the West assent is indicated by nodding the head, but in India it is indicated by moving the head horizontally. The sign for "Come here" in the West is made with the palm of the hand up, but in India it is made with the palm of the hand down. Most families develop signs that are understood only by members of the family; for example, in some families it is understood that when one makes a statement with fingers crossed the statement is a lie.

Words are constantly changing. The following cataloguing of twelve types of changes is only suggestive:

1. Some words change when they are coupled with other words, for example, *shipyard, playground, housewife,* and *warehouse. Horse* designates four-leggedness in a mammal, but not when *horse* is coupled with *sea* to become *seahorse*.

2. Some words change their denotation. For example, the word *chair* until very recent years denoted "a piece of furniture upon which one can sit"; but, because of objections that the word *chairman* has been interpreted as "the male *(vir)* provided with a chair" (while others sat on benches) rather than "the person *(homo)* provided with a chair," some people—and some institutions—insist that the word *chairman* be dropped and that the person who presides at a meeting shall be addressed as *Chair*.

3. Some words change in designation. For example, the word *democracy* meant for Plato the rule of the many who happen to be poor, but in various times and places since Plato it has had many other designations, such as equality for all, civil liberties, general welfare, free enterprise, one vote for every adult, and the like.

4. Some words change in both denotation and designation; for example, the word *God* is changed by some modern theologians from the representation of a being with infinite attributes to the representation of a belief that values are objective.

5. Some words change in connotation. For example, the connotation of *Nazi* is very different today from what it was in 1930.

6. Some words change in physical shape. An obvious change is comparing English and American spelling, for example, *theatre-theater, honour-honor*. All modern speakers of English have difficulty in comprehending the earliest English lyric:

> Sumer is icumen in,
> Lhude sing cuccu!
> Groweth sed, and bloweth med,
> And springth the wude nu.
> Sing cuccu!

Some words become shortened, for example, *dormitory-dorm, cafeteria-cafe, promenade-prom*.

7. Some words change in pronunciation, for example, the words *schedule, tomato,* and *aluminum* in the United Kingdom and in the United States of America.

8. Some words are dropped from the vocabulary, for example, the following English words are no longer used by English-speaking people: *oxter* (armpit), *pingle* (fight), *yerk* (hit), *sdeign* (disdain), *daw* (fool), *yuke* (itch), and *begeck* (cheat).

9. Some words are created. The following have been recently created, but not all of them are generally accepted: *inducation, iffy, proto-god, slanguage, muliverse,* and *googol* (the one-hundreth power of ten!)

10. Some words shift from one part of speech to another. For example, the word *horse,* which is a noun denoting a certain kind of animal, has become

in American slang a verb representing a form of activity that is aimless and hedonic, for example, "We were just horsing around last night." Again the noun *party* has in recent years on college campuses shifted to a verb, for example, "Where shall we party tonight?" An interesting example of adjectives' shifting to nouns is to note how adjectives for colored objects become nounal, for example, *White* (Caucasian), *Black* (Negro), and *Red* (a communist).

3. The Uses of Language

Philosophers are often surprisingly unimaginative in their analyses of the functions of language. John Locke said language has three uses: (1) to convey ideas to one another; (2) to convey ideas quickly; (3) to convey the knowledge of things.[22] Surely Locke must have known that conversation in a British pub does more than convey knowledge of things quickly to one another. A London pub at five o'clock each weekday afternoon is filled with men and women enjoying conversation before taking the bus or tube home. The topics discussed may not be momentous, since the enjoyment of talking is the motivation. Speech has hedonic values.

Four important uses of language may be called the constative, the directive, the emotive, and the performative. The term *constative* comes from the verb *to constate,* meaning to state as certain or to assert positively. To assert, however, does not necessarily mean that the assertion must be true. One may state positively that which happens to be false, as, for example, "Canton is a city in Germany." One may make an assertion that cannot be false or true because under the common understanding of the words it is meaningless, for example, "Calcutta is north of a sneeze." A meaningless sentence such as this is a constative sentence, but it is not a proposition or statement, since the terms *proposition* and *statement* in philosophy are limited to meaningful sentences, that is sentences that may be either true or false. Great care must be exercised in characterizing sentences as meaningless; for example, a poem like the "Jabberwocky" has meaning when the strange terminology is explained. That which is predicated of a subject may be metaphorical, imaginative, or pictorial as well as literal. For example, "Leonard is a fox" is a constative use of language both in the case in which Leonard is indeed a bush-tailed mammal and also in the case in which Leonard is a sly, crafty businessman. Language as the means for conveying knowledge is far from infallible. George Berkeley stated the problem well in *A Treatise Concerning the Principles of Human Knowledge:* "It cannot be denied that words are of excellent use, in that by their means all that stock of knowledge which has been purchased by the joint labours of inquisitive men in all ages and nations may be drawn into the view and made the possession of one single person. But most parts of knowledge have been strangely perplexed and darkened by the abuse of words, and general ways of speech wherein they are delivered, that it may almost be made a question whether language has contributed more to the hindrance or advancement of the sciences."[23] In his *Commonplace Book* he observed that endeavoring to express abstract philosophic thoughts by words unavoidably runs into difficulties.

The directive or motivative use of language is, as the terms imply, used to guide behavior, thoughts, attitudes, and so forth, and also to encourage, discourage, arouse, stimulate, and the like. "Take the bus to 84th Street and walk three blocks north" does not give any information about 84th Street, but it illustrates a very important and necessary use of language. Cookbooks, builders' manuals, handbooks for automobile operation, and rules for card games are only a few of the many instances of directives.

The emotive or affective use of language is the expression of feelings and attitudes toward objects. "I like mangoes," "I do not care for boiled cabbage," "Ouch," and "I love you" are examples. The separation of the affective or emotive use from other uses is not easy. For example, an exclamation like "Look out" is both an expression of emotion and a directive. In fact, "I like mangoes" and "I love you" are statements of fact (presumably)—and therefore constatives—and also expressions of emotion. It can even be maintained that all constative statements have an element of emotion; for example, "13 plus 24 equals 37" has various emotional overtones depending upon whether one uses the sentence in helping a timid child with a mathematical problem, or whether one is correcting a shop clerk whom one suspects of having deliberately overcharged.

The performative use of language is an extremely important use that until quite recently was missed in language studies.[24] A performative sentence is one in which the utterance is the performing of an action. It does not say something, does not describe or report, and is not true or false. Many performative sentences are contractual; for example, to say "I bet," "I promise," or "I agree," is to bet, to promise, or to agree. When the judge says "I sentence you to 30 days in jail," or the clergyman says "I pronounce you husband and wife," they are not using language hedonically, constatively, directively, or emotionally. The saying is the doing. "I sentence" sentences: "I pronounce you husband and wife" weds. But there are subtle differences between sentences like "I thank," "I feel grateful," and "I am grateful." The first is performative. "I thank" is to thank. The second is constative. "I feel grateful" describes one's state of feelings. "I am grateful" is a sentence in which one is both expressing one's gratitude and also describing one's state of gratitude. Varieties of performative sentences are verdictives, which deliver a verdict, for instance, "I acquit . . ."; exercitives, which exercise power, for instance, "I order . . ."; commissives, which commit the self in some manner, for instance, "I promise . . ."; behabitives, which evidence a state of behavior, for instance, "I apologize . . ."; and expositives, which perform an act by exposition, for instance, "I argue. . . ."

The uses of language thus far considered must not be thought of as separate, nonoverlapping, nor exhaustive. Additional uses are the mystificational, obscurantist, imaginative, pictorial, illustrative, metaphorical, analogical, anagogical, interrogative, descriptive, prescriptive, occultist, ceremonial, evaluative, vituperative, persuasive, moral, soteriological, intentional, decisional, hortative, determinational, reportative, and—no doubt—many more.

Possibly each language is unique for some form of communication. For example, English is ideal for drawing up business contracts, German for writing theology, Sanskrit for psychoanalyzing, Hopi for presenting process philosophy, Chinese for understanding Buddhism, and French for making love!

Linguists have used three methods to develop a taxonomy of languages into families: (1) Word similarity. Languages are examined for similarities in personal pronouns, in verbs expressing basic activities such as come and go, give and take, live and die; in adjectives denoting qualities such as big and small, young and old; and in terms for parts of the human body, and for basic blood relationships such as father, mother, sister, brother. (2) Agreement in grammatical construction. Similarities in the definite article, agreements in the forming of the tenses of the verb, and agreements in the gender of nouns are studied. (3) Consistent differences in words of similar meaning, for example, the English words *to, tongue,* and *tin* with the German equivalents *zu, Zunge,* and *Zin.*

According to the ancient Greeks all who did not speak Greek engaged in incomprehensible muttering, which to Greek ears sounded like "bar-bar-bar," and from this parochial evaluation we derive the word *barbarian*. The ancient Hebrews heard foreign tongues as "ba-bel," and from this we get our word *babble,* to make meaningless sounds. We know now that the language of primitive peoples is not necessarily primitive. A nonliterate or semiliterate people may develop very complex words to express subtle nuances of experience; for example, the Eskimos have dozens of terms for different kinds of snow, and the ancient Chinese developed designations for familial relations not even recognized by Western peoples.

4. Language and Thought

What is the relation of speaking and thinking? European languages stress the ontological. They imply that the referent is a substance. Abstract concepts are reified. Words like *fist* and *lap* are illustrative. An English-speaking person ordinarily thinks that *fist* and *lap* refer to entities; yet this cannot be the case, since a fist vanishes when one unclenches a hand, and a lap disappears upon arising. A fist is a hand "fisted"; and lap is legs "lapped." *Fist* and *lap* are process terms, not substantive terms. Serious problems of misunderstanding arise when a process philosophy like A. N. Whitehead's is expressed in English. Such problems do not arise when a process philosophy like Mahāyāna Buddhism is expressed in Chinese. The Japanese Buddhologist Hajime Nakamura has studied Eastern languages as clues to the understanding of Eastern ways of thinking.[25] He claims that Indian languages stress universals, negatives, static qualities, and the subjective; the Chinese language stresses the concrete, the particular, the practical, and the harmonizing; the Tibetan language stresses the individual, the absolute, and the magical; and the Japanese language stresses the phenomenal, social relationships, and the nonrational. Nakamura's interesting study leaves unanswered the question of the mutual relations of language and thought. For example, did Sanskrit develop an abundance of terms for psychological entities and for interpersonal behavior because the users of Sanskrit were an introspective people, or did they become an introspective people because of the language they used? According to Jerrold J. Katz "the basic premise of the philosophy of language is that there is a strong relation between the form and content of language and the form and content of conceptualization."[26]

Language—the powerful tool by means of which the human being stores knowledge, instructs the next generation, preserves culture, expresses emotions, entertains, and conducts dialogue that transcends time—has many defects and limitations. Speaking is a means of confusing as well as clarifying, of impressing as well as expressing. The language of jargon, which George Orwell called "doublespeak," is widespread in modern life, especially among politicians who, because of the opportunities offered by radio and television, are encouraged to speak when they have little to say. As Aldous Huxley has said, "Never before, thanks to the techniques of mass communication, have so many listeners been so completely at the mercy of so few speakers."[27] The desire of politicians to make a statement that will express thought in a few memorable lines often backfires. A classic example was the defense of the United States armed forces in Vietnam offered by President L. B. Johnson: "We will continue fighting in Vietnam until the violence stops." The jargon of politics, bureaucracy, and professions is developed, observes Henry A. Barnes, "from the needs of lesser men to make their lives easier, shield their shortcomings, or cover the drabness of their operations with some tawdry gloss."[28] Fritz Güttinger has argued that the German language accommodates political jargon with greater facility than any other language.[29]

Philosophers in the West have always been interested in the problems of language. Traditionally the study has been about the valid use of terms to represent the referent of signs. William P. Alston has noted, "Language is the chief tool of the philosopher. Philosophy is a much more purely verbal activity than any of the sciences: verbal discussion is the laboratory in which the philosopher puts his ideas to the test."[30] Ludwig Wittgenstein in the 1940s wrote an important book entitled *Philosophical Investigations,* in which he claimed that philosophy should be limited to how words are used. Words, he said, have many uses in addition to the stating of facts. They are like "tools in a tool-box; there is a hammer, pliers, a saw, a screwdriver, a rule, a glue-pot, glue, nails and screws. The function of words is as diverse as the functions of these objects."[31] There are many rules, functions, and meanings governing the use of words. Language is a game undertaken in concrete contexts under definite guidelines. Philosophy is the study of the rules of the game. The problems with which philosophers deal are the problems resulting "when language goes on holiday."[32] Presumably there would be no philosophy if people used language correctly: "Philosophy is the battle against the bewitchment of our intelligence by means of language."[33] "The results of philosophy are the uncovering of one or another piece of plain nonsense and of bumps that the understanding has got by running its head up against the limits of language."[34] All philosophy, according to Wittgenstein, is a "critique of language."[35] "Philosophy is not a body of doctrine but an activity. A philosophy does not result in 'philosophical propositions,' but rather in the clarification of propositions."[36] Wittgenstein's critics accused him of turning philosophy into philology. His desire for clarity of expression was almost pathological. Western philosophy from its beginnings has been split between those who, like Plato, believe that what one has to say is so important that one must not omit any way of saying it, and those who, like Aristotle, believe that what one has to say is so important that one must not say it if it cannot be stated clearly.

If Wittgenstein was the modern Western philosopher of clarity, Alfred North Whitehead was the modern Western philosopher of significance. He split with Bertrand Russell after their co-authorship of *Principia Mathematics* on the grounds that meaning is of greater value than exactness. In a lecture on 8 November 1924 Whitehead said, "The dilemma of metaphysics is that either you are clear, and leave much out, or else you are adequate—and muddled. . . . You come to a point where clearness is impossible."[37] His last words of his last lecture at Harvard University were: "The exactness of logic is a fake."[38]

Professional philosophers are not the only ones who have problems with language. The average English-speaking person flavors his speech with expressions like "you know," "you know what I mean," "I hope you understand what I'm saying," "on the other hand," and "as a way of speaking" partly as verbal hesitation in order to put thoughts in order and partly because of the inadequacy of speech itself. Often speakers supplement speaking with hand gestures. While it is a malicious exaggeration to assert that certain peoples of the Middle East cannot communicate in the dark because they cannot see each other's hands, there is a kernel of truth in the statement. Try describing a spiral staircase without using your hands! The classroom blackboard is a reminder that university professors sometimes find charts, diagrams, and cartoons necessary to supplement their lectures.[39]

The experience of many is that some things are true provided they are not spoken. The profound love of a devoted husband and wife seems diminished in "I love you." Sympathy may sometimes be better expressed by a gesture than a word. Eliphaz, Bildad, and Zophar gave Job more comfort through sitting silently with him for seven days and seven nights than through their verbal offerings. Victor E. Frankl, a psychiatrist who survived Nazi concentration camps, reports, "The opportunities for collective psychotherapy were naturally limited in camp. The right example was more effective than words could ever be. The senior block warden who did not side with the authorities had, by his just and encouraging behavior, a thousand opportunities to exert a far-reaching moral influence on those under his jurisdiction. The immediate influence of behavior is always more effective than that of words."[40]

5. The Case for Silence

Philosophers can be divided into three classes depending upon what they assume about language. Some assume that all thoughts which are important and true can be stated and stated well. Others assume that not all thoughts that are important and true can be stated well, but the importance of expressing the thoughts is such that an effort must be made to state them, however poor the statement. Still others assume that not all thoughts that are important and true can be stated, and therefore in such cases the path of wisdom is silence. For them not to speak is preferable to speaking inadequately.

Silence has been defended in both Eastern and Western philosophical traditions. The Pythagoreans, contending that there is both ordinary silence and extraordinary silence, required their initiates to "hold their peace" on the grounds that "the utterance of all things to all men" be discouraged.[41] Euripides recommended silence, because as he said, ". . . the tongue is not to be trusted: it can criticize another's faults, but on its own possessor it brings a thousand troubles."[42] According to the author of the Letter of James in the *New Testament,* "The tongue is a fire. The tongue is an unrighteous world among our members, staining the whole body, setting on fire the cycle of nature, and set on fire by hell. For every kind of beast and bird, of reptile and sea creature, can be tamed and has been tamed by humankind, but no human being can tame the tongue—a restless evil, full of deadly poison."[43]

The classical Greek language had a marvelous provision for silence in two words for a first principle of reality. One word—*lógos*—symbolized a first principle that could be expressed; but a second word—*archē*—symbolized a first principle that might not be capable of being put into human language. An *archē* is a basic truth; a *lógos* is a speakable truth. Aristotle reports that Cratylus, an early teacher of Plato, became so impressed by the inadequacy of language that he "finally did not think it right to say anything but only moved his finger."[44]

Plato, in a letter to his former pupil Dionysius the Younger, reminded him that the teaching he had given was "not something that can be put into words like other sciences; but after long-continued intercourse between teacher and pupil, in joint pursuit of the subject, suddenly, like light flashing forth when a fire is kindled, it is born in the soul and straightway nourishes itself."[45] Some regard this as one of the foundations of mysticism. But the appeal to mystic silence is not welcomed by many modern Western philosophers; for example, Arthur O. Lovejoy called it an example of "the pathos of the esoteric." Lovejoy wrote, "How exciting and how welcome is the sense of initiation into hidden mysteries! And how effectively have certain philosophers—notably Schelling and Hegel a century ago, and Bergson in our own generation—satisfied the human craving for this experience, by representing the central insight of their philosophy as a thing to be reached, not through a consecutive progress of thought guided by the ordinary logic available to every man, but through a sudden leap whereby one rises to a plane of insight wholly different in its principles from the level of the mere understanding."[46]

Modern Western physicists may be more sympathetic than are modern Western philosophers to the notion of ideas that cannot be expressed. How can one describe light as both wave and particle? How can one explain why one must choose between velocity and position when describing subatomic particles? According to Robert H. March, "The normal reaction to a first exposure to relativity is: 'I think I understand it; I just don't believe it.' . . . Normally it takes a physicist about five years of contact with the ideas of relativity before he feels comfortable with them—not because they are complex or obscure, but just terribly strange. . . . So the reader is implored to have faith, in the hope that all will turn out self-consistent in the end."[47] Robert Oppenheimer says that the physicist must learn to understand that the electron is neither at rest nor in motion.[48]

Thomas Aquinas resorted to silence when words failed to convey his meaning. When he came to the University of Paris he was nicknamed "The Dumb Ox" because of his silences. His best-known silence was the result of an experience he had at Mass on the feast of Saint Nicolas in the year 1274. Josef Pieper in *The Silence of St. Thomas,* writes that "as Thomas turned back to his work after Holy Mass, he was strangely altered. He remained steadily silent; he did not write; he dictated nothing. He laid aside the *Summa Theologica* on which he had been working. . . . Reginald, his friend, asks him, troubled: 'Father, how can you want to stop such a great work?' Thomas answers only, 'I can write no more.' "[49] The *Summa Theologica* remains to this day an unfinished masterpiece.

Meister Eckhart had similar experiences. He wrote that "the best life and the loftiest is to be silent and to let God speak and act through one."[50] "God despises ideas."[51] "The moment you get [one of your own] ideas, God fades out and the Godhead too. It is when the idea is gone that God gets in."[52] "It is in the stillness, in the silence, that the word of God is to be heard. There is no better avenue of approach to this Word than through stillness, through silence."[53] In Trappist monasteries the silent monks communicate by the use of four hundred nonverbal gestures.

In the West the scholastics often chose the *via negativa* (the way of negation) to describe God, that is, since one cannot say what God is, then one attempts to say what God is not. This procedure is also found in Hinduism: in order not to be silent about the Brahman the way of *neti, neti* (not this, not that) is followed. As a modern Vedāntist writes, "The intuition of Brahman transcends the limits of the logical intellect, though it is the fulfilment of logical thinking."[54] Although a vow of silence is sometimes practiced by Hindu holy men, the philosophers of India have not commonly praised silence. According to *The Nyāya Sūtras* of Gotama,[55] one who is silent after an opponent has repeated a proposition to him three times is to be publicly rebuked.

Taoism, on the other hand, advocates silence, particularly when the object of thought is Ultimate Reality. Silence is recommended in the *Tao Te Ching*:

> The Tao that can be told of is not the eternal Tao;
> The name that can be named is not the eternal name.
> The Nameless is the origin of Heaven and Earth;
> The Named is the mother of all things.[56]

Ultimate Reality cannot be expressed in words. "Heaven and Earth" (which probably means all things that are) originate in nonbeing *(wu-ming)*, a simplicity that cannot be put into words. The sage who understands the nature of the Tao "manages affairs without action, and spreads doctrines without words."[57] "Much talk will of course come to a dead end."[58] "Nature says few words."[59] "The Tao is hidden and nameless."[60] "He who knows does not speak. He who speaks does not know."[61] "Close the mouth . . . and to the end of life there will be (peace) without toil. Open the mouth . . . and to the end of life there will be no salvation."[62]

Buddhism also holds that the real world is inexpressible in words. According to the *Avataṁsaka Sūtra:* "Reality itself has neither form nor no-form; like space it is beyond knowledge and understanding; it is too subtle to be expressed in words and letters. Why? Because it is beyond the realm of letters, words, speeches, mere talk, discriminative intellection, inquiring and speculative reflection; and again it is beyond the realm of the understanding which belongs to the ignorant, beyond all evil doings which are in accordance with evil desires. Because it is neither this nor that, it is beyond all mentation."[63] One of the sermons of the Buddha was a sermon without words. The Buddha stood before the *sangha* holding a flower in his hands. When one of the monks smiled and nodded in understanding, the Buddha handed him the flower and walked out of the assembly hall saying nothing. The tradition of silence has continued in Buddhism. The artist Liang K'ai portrayed in one of his paintings the Patriarch Hui-nēng tearing up the Sūtras since wisdom is to be found within the person, not in books. The artist Yin-i'o-lo portrayed Shih-tē laughing as he holds up a blank sheet of paper to show that the true doctrine is not to be found in scriptures. A ninth-century poem by an unknown Buddhist advises

> The whole world is tormented by words
> And there is no one who does without words.
> But in so far as one is free from words
> Does one really understand words.[64]

The eleventh-century Buddhist Ssū-hsin Wu-hsin advised, "Do not waste your time with words and phrases, or by searching for the truth of Zen in books; for the truth is not to be found there."[65] In the present century the great Buddhist teacher D. T. Suzuki insisted on the "distinction between mere learning or mere philosophy and self-realization, between what is taught and teachable in words and what altogether transcends one's verbal expressions."[66]

Mahāyāna Buddhism contends that words are fingers that point to the moon, and warns that one must not confuse the finger with the moon. According to the *Laṅkāvatāra Sūtra* the ignorant are those who cling to names, signs, and ideas. Words can be placed in four different classes, and all are to be avoided: (1) Some words separate individuals where there are in fact no individuals, for instance, the words *I* and *mine*. (2) Other words are linked with memories, which are filled with unrealities. (3) There are many words linked with the mental processes that give separate reality to things that do not in fact have separate reality, for instance, *mind, self,* and *soul*. (4) And there are words growing out of inherited prejudices based on false imaginations and speculations. Many of these are words associated with the concept of God. Words are artificial creations. They cannot express the highest Reality. The *Laṅkāvatāra* warns, "Therefore, let every disciple take good heed not to become attached to words as being in perfect conformity with meaning, because Truth is not in the letters. When a man with his finger-tip points to something, the finger-tip may be mistaken for the thing pointed at; in like manner the ignorant and simple-minded, like children, are unable even to the day of their death to abandon the idea that in the finger-tip of words there is the meaning itself. They cannot realise Ultimate Reality because of their intent clinging to words which were intended to be no more than a pointing finger."[67]

The Mādhyamika philosophy is a very ancient system within Buddhism. The school was founded in India in the second century A.D. by Nāgārjuna. Nāgārjuna, as a typical Eastern philosopher, was concerned for both language clarification and spiritual realization. This philosophy is sometimes called Śūnyavāda (Emptiness Doctrine), since it holds that the wheel of causation is a chain of dependent origination without any substantial entities. In Mādhyamika the Middle Path, which for the Buddha must have been a path between self-denial of the Jains and self-indulgence of the Cārvākas, becomes a path avoiding affirming or denying. Thus, it is not right to say "I am," for this affirms the existence of a self; and it is not right to say "I am not," for this denies the existence of a self, and to deny existence is to imply that the notion of self is an intelligible notion. So in Mādhyamika the self can neither be affirmed nor denied, since the "self" is an empty notion. Mādhyamika would reform the chart of symptom-signal-symbol to deny that words are symbolic. Words are practical tools of human life that operate between senders and receivers. They are ways to get things done, not ways to symbolize reality. There is no reality independent of the language system; so, in the words of Wittgenstein, "Whereof one cannot speak, thereof one must be silent."[68] Philosophers, according to Wittgenstein, should "bring words back from their metaphysical to their everyday use."[69] *Śūnyatā* (emptiness) is not a term for an inexpressible Ultimate Reality, as would be the case in the framework of the Absolute brand of Hinduism associated with Śaṅkara, nor is it an affirmation of a nothingness (nihilism). Rather it is a reminder that in Buddhism intellectual discussion starts with the human situation of incompleteness and frustration rather than with the assumption that God does or does not exist. The Mādhyamika destroys reason in order that intuition may take over. It eliminates speech and words in order that becoming may displace talking. Three assumptions are made: (1) There is no factor in existence that has a permanent quality about it. There is no being that is absolute, a thing in itself, independent, and immutable. All is radical becoming. The world *becomes* continually. It *is* nothing. (2) Knowledge and becoming are coextensive. One becomes what one knows. This is similar to the English word *realize,* which has two elements in it: knowing and becoming. Knowledge should not lead to a wisdom that is an end in itself, but to a wisdom that is a means to liberation. (3) There are two kinds of truth: conventional and ultimate. Conventional truth considers the objects of knowledge—the referents symbolized by signs—to have fixed, determinate, and self-existing nature. Ultimate truth is the recognition that the referents are empty. The former truth is satisfactory for practical living, for example, for eating, sleeping, speaking, and so on; but if one is to realize *Nirvāṇa,* one must perceive "things" in a different manner, that is, as mental fabrications.

Zen Buddhism is the practical application of Mādhyamika principles. In Zen all philosophy is terminated. Knowing and speaking are transmuted into techniques to destroy knowing and speaking. In the words of Bodhidharma, who brought Buddhism from India to China, Zen is:

> A special transmission outside the scriptures;
> No dependence upon words and letters;
> Direct pointing at the soul of man;
> Seeing into one's nature and the attainment of Buddhahood.[70]

The goal of seeing directly into one's nature is the enlightenment experience, which Zen calls *satori*. *Satori* is that slant on the commonplace which D. T. Suzuki sometimes whimsically said was just like everyday experiences except about two inches off the ground. In our terminology it may be adumbrated by calling it the awareness of having the experience while having the experience. *Satori* is the experience *per se,* not the experience *of.* Sonaku Ogata in *Zen for the West* says it was the *satori* experience which Eckhart described as "disinterest" in contrast to "experience."[71] According to Eckhart, "Experience must always be an experience of something, but disinterest comes so close to zero that nothing but God is rarefied enough to get into it, to enter the disinterested heart.... Every person experiences things in his own way and thus every distinguishable thing is seen and understood according to the approach of the beholder and not, as it might be, from its own point of view."[72]

The *koans*—questions and problems that cannot be answered nor resolved by the rational mind—are instruments used in Zen instruction to drive the student back to the raw data of his own experience. They are designed to end all speech, to force the pupil into profound silence. Silence is not a permanent condition of the human, but only a reminder that when speaking man should find the sign which best expresses his symptom, represents the object, and appeals as he wishes to the receiver. Sometimes silence is the best sign. According to one Zen *mondo* (story) a master asked his student what he would do in a certain situation. As an answer the student rose, placed his sandals on his head, and silently left the room. The master cheered this as the proper response. Another *mondo* points out that even Zen monks have difficulty in their silences. Four pupils promised one another to observe seven days of silence. On the first day all were silent, but when night came and the oil lamps grew dim one said to a servant, "Fix those lamps." The second pupil, surprised to hear the first talk, remonstrated, "You were not supposed to say a word." Whereupon the third remarked, "You two are stupid. Why did you talk?" "I am the only one who has not talked," concluded the fourth pupil.[73] The human animal is a chatterer. He finds great difficulty in being silent. His problem is the quality of his speaking. The *Mahābhārata* offers excellent advice: "Silence is better than speech. To speak the truth is better than silence. Again to speak truth that is connected with righteousness is better than to speak the truth. To speak that which, besides being true and righteous, is agreeable, is better than to speak truth connected with righteousness."[74]

3
The Human Being as Knower

The self is a knower. But what does it mean to know? Knowing is notoriously ambiguous. The following sampling of sentences using the verb *to know* is illustrative:

1. "I know there is a pencil in my hand." (I apprehend immediately through my senses the presence of a pencil in my hand.)
2. "I know the taste of ripe olives." (I recall having tasted a ripe olive.)
3. "I know that the whole is greater than the part." (I understand directly without going through a process of thinking that the whole of anything is greater than the part of that thing.)
4. "I know the solution to that puzzle because I worked it out last week." (I solved that puzzle last week, and I now recall the solution.)
5. "I know a cyclotron when I see one." (I am able to recognize the physical appearance of the thing called "cyclotron.")
6. "I know my own mind with respect to that issue." (I have mentally considered that issue, and I have arrived at a personal position with respect to it.)
7. "I know I have a toothache." (I have a direct unsharable experience of pain in my tooth.)
8. "I know him to be an honest man." (I have had sufficient contact with this man to arrive at the judgment that he is an honest person.)
9. "I know him slightly." (I am acquainted with him.)
10. "I know I left my glasses on the table." (I am psychologically convinced that I left my glasses on the table.)
11. "I know how to swim." (I have acquired proficiency in the activity known as swimming.)
12. "I know the meaning of *misology*." (I am able to express the word *misology* in simple terms that constitute a definition not inconsistent with the definition one might find in a standard dictionary.)
13. "I know this cafe, having eaten here about a year ago." (I recall having eaten in this cafe about a year ago.)

14. "I knew the man before he spoke." (I recognized the man on the basis of previous observation before he spoke.)
15. "He knew great happiness in his third marriage." (He experienced great hedonic satisfactions in his third marriage.)
16. "I know the twenty-third psalm." (I have memorized the twenty-third psalm, and I am able to recite it from memory.)
17. "I know exactly how you feel." (I empathize with your feelings.)
18. "I know . . . I know." (I am listening to what you are saying and I am comprehending the ideas and the emotions you are expressing.)
19. "I know that my Redeemer liveth." (I have religious faith that one known as "The Redeemer" is operative in my life.)
20. "Adam knew his wife Eve; and she conceived and bore Cain." (Adam and Eve had sexual relations resulting in the birth of Cain.)

A cursory examination of these twenty uses of *to know* reveals that, while most of the sentences deal with knowing *that* such and such is the case, a few deal with knowing *how* to do something. Number 11 is clearly a "know how" statement: "I know how to swim." Number 17 is indirectly a "know how" statement: "I know exactly how you feel." I experience my own swimming directly, but I experience another's feelings only metonymically. The distinction between knowing *that* and knowing *how* is crucial for an understanding of the difference between Eastern and Western philosophy. Western philosophy is chiefly concerned with human efforts to understand intellectually the universe and the human place in the universe. Western philosophy, according to both Plato and Aristotle, originates in human wondering about the nature of things. Western philosophy seeks to arrive at knowledge *that* such and such is the case. Eastern philosophy has its genesis, not in intellectual wonder, but in suffering, that is, in all that is fraught with unpleasantness and pain. The ultimate telos of Eastern philosophizing, therefore, is not to arrive at statements *that* such and such is the case but at therapies to reduce and ultimately eliminate the sufferings of humanity. Philosophical knowledge in the East is knowing *how* to deal with human life. Philosophical knowledge in the West is knowing *that* such and such is the nature of things.

This is a first evaluation. It is an overall approximation. To classify all Western philosophy as theory and all Eastern philosophy as therapy would be too facile. Some Western philosophers have sought to apply philosophy to the practical needs of human beings, and intellectual wondering has been incorporated into *sādhanā*, *t'i-jen*, and *duḥkha-nirodha-mārga*.

Theoretical knowledge is divided both in the East and in the West into "knowledge about" and "knowledge of." Knowledge about is designated by such terms as *knowledge by description, indirect knowledge, secondary knowledge, propositional knowledge,* and *relative knowledge*. Knowledge of is designated by such terms as *knowledge by acquaintance, intuitive knowledge, direct knowledge, primary knowledge, ineffable knowledge,* and *absolute knowledge*. One may be said to know London after one has read about the city in an encyclopedia, listened to travelers who have been there, studied the history of the city, consulted maps, and so on. One may also be said to know London after one has lived in the city for many years, traveled its subways, visited its museums and churches, wandered its streets, attended plays and concerts in the West End, et cetera. The temptation to say that one is real knowledge and the other is merely experience should be resisted. Nor are they two degrees of knowledge. Rather they are two kinds of knowledge.

In China a distinction between "experiences while awake" and "experiences while asleep" should be noted. Chuang Tzu made the distinction—and then blurred it: "Once I, Chuang Chou, dreamed I was a butterfly and was happy as a butterfly. I was conscious that I was quite pleased with myself, but I did not know that I was Chou. Suddenly I woke, and there I was, visibly Chou. I do not know whether it was Chou dreaming that he was a butterfly or the butterfly dreaming it was Chou."[1]

Descartes also classified human experiences into dreaming and waking experiences, but he, unlike Chuang Tzu, believed that there is a method for distinguishing the two: "How do we know that the experiences occurring in our dream are any more illusory than the others? They are often no less lively and distinct. And if the best minds study the question as much as they like, I think they will find no adequate grounds for removing this doubt, if they do not presuppose the existence of God. . . . But if we did not know that all truth and reality in us proceeds from a perfect and infinite being, then, however clear and distinct our ideas might be, we should have no reason to be certain that they had the perfection of truth."[2] Descartes, having distinguished clear and distinct ideas that do not proceed from God (relative knowledge), and clear and distinct ideas that do proceed from God (absolute knowledge), concluded that only the latter have "the perfection of truth." In the absence of any test for determining which ideas proceed from God and which do not, Chuang Tzu's puzzle remains. The Indian view is found in Śaṅkara's distinction bewteen *parā vidyā* (a knowing in which there is a oneness of knower and known) and *aparā vidyā* (an inferior form of knowing in which the world is presented and misrepresented in accord with the limitations of human sensation).

Knowledge is the raw material from which wisdom may be fashioned. Any sort of knowledge, any concept, any thought, any idea can conceivably be the starting point of philosophical reflection resulting in wisdom. This reflection proceeds through four operations:

1. Analysis. "What are the elements of the idea?"
2. Clarification. "How can the idea be defined in terms of these elements?"
3. Interpretation. "How is the defined idea related to other ideas?"
4. Evaluation. "What is the worth of the idea when put into life situations?"

To illustrate how philosophizing transmogrifies knowledge into wisdom, let us take the idea of home. Every English-speaking person has some notion of the meaning of this word. For one person it denotes a vine-covered cottage, for another an isolated farm, for another a few rooms in a crowded apartment house. For one it brings nostalgic memories of a happy childhood, for another it arouses memories of a tragedy, for another it calls to mind parental responsibilities. In philosophical reflections we first ignore these individual conceptions and attempt to decide what the elements are that make up the idea of home. Probably we would agree that the elements include a place of shelter, at least two generations usually connected by blood lines, and a legal status. In the second operation we clarify the concept by redefining it in terms of the elements. A home, we might say, is a social organization in which people of at least two generations reside in the same dwelling, the members of this organization being bound to each other either by blood or by marriage. In the third operation we would probably examine the relation of the home to the school, the church, the community, and the nation. We might also consider the different conceptions of the home in other periods of history and in other cultures. Finally, we would try to express the worth of the home in terms of child development, self-expression, moral improvement, economics, political status, happiness, and so on. Here we would allow the nimbus of emotion to cluster around the bare bones of the intellectualized concept. If, after having gone through these processes, we are also able to apply this knowledge and realize these values in our own experience, we may be said to be wise with respect to the home. This last step is most important. The hiatus sometimes said to exist necessarily between thought and action is one of the most revealing signs of foolishness. Theory that stops short of practice is truncated theory. Application is an aspect of evaluation.

1. *The Ways of Knowing*

Thus far we have been considering that knowledge is. Next we shall consider how knowledge is acquired. Knowing how we know is probably more significant than knowing what we know, for when we know how we know we are aware of the ways in which our knowledge can be clarified, expanded, and improved.

Let us assume that during the course of an evening's conversation we have jolted down eight statements that other people in the room have made:

1. "The Republican party is always more conservative than the Democratic party."
2. "Columbus discovered America in 1492."
3. "London is larger than Moscow."

4. "A colored thing is a spatial thing."
5. "I have a headache."
6. "The solution was acid."
7. "The Golden Rule is a sound business principle."
8. "God created man."

During a lull in the conversation we call the attention of the group to our list, and ask the author of each statement to name the source of the information. We shall assume that the replies to the question are these:

1. "How do I know that the Republican party is always more conservative than the Democratic party? Why, I've always believed that. I certainly don't see any reason for changing my belief now."
2. "How do I know that Columbus discovered America in 1492? I got that from a dependable volume on the history of America."
3. "How do I know that London is larger than Moscow? Well, I know that Paris is larger than Moscow, and I know that London is larger than Paris, so it follows that London is larger than Moscow."
4. "How do I know that anything that is colored is spatial? Now, look—if you understand what color means, then you see at once that a colored thing is a spatial thing."
5. "How do I know that I have a headache? Because I feel it. It's my head that aches, and I can't make you feel it. You just have to take my word for it."
6. "How do I know that the solution was acid? I tested it with litmus paper. If you will come around to the laboratory in the morning, you too can apply the litmus paper test."
7. "How do I know that the Golden Rule is a sound business principle? Well, I have conducted my business on this principle for forty years, and during those years I have prospered financially and I have made many good friends."
8. "How do I know that man was created by God? Because I read that in the Bible."

Eight different ways of knowing have been utilized by these people: tenacity, authority, rationalism, self-evidence, intuition, empiricism, pragmatism, and revelation.

a. Tenacity

Tenacity as a way of knowing consists of two operations: (1) repetition of an idea, and (2) refusal to entertain alternative ideas. Tenacity smacks of dogmatism and narrow-mindedness. Not many of us are willing to admit that we possess knowledge on this basis. Yet we must remember that many ideas have been entertained simply because people did not bother to question them. For example, the sun rises and sets, the earth is flat, heaven is above the earth, a heavy object falls faster than a light object. The wisdom of proverbs and folk tales is wisdom acquired through repetition. Emile Coué (1857–1926) advised men and women to improve themselves by frequent repetition of the formula: "Every day, and in every way, I am becoming better and better." Adolf Hitler said that an idea repeated often enough will become an accepted idea. In Aldous Huxley's *Brave New World* the children acquire "Elementary Class Consciousness" through hypnopaedia (sleep teaching); for example, the Beta children as they sleep are exposed to the recorded words, "I'm so glad I'm a Beta. Gammas are stupid, and Epsilons are still worse." C. S. Peirce said he once was entreated not to read a certain newspaper lest it change his opinion on free trade. It is a great comfort to possess a few beliefs that one does not doubt. In times of insecurity such intellectual foundations seem particularly desirable. Lincoln Steffens told of a business executive who begged Steffens not to remind him of his past miscalculations because he could not act if he at the same time were to question his judgments. To doubt one's first principles may be, as Oliver Wendell Holmes, Jr., declared, the sign of a civilized man, but is it a characteristic of a leader of men? Which do people prefer in their leaders—continual examination of their own ideas, or ideas held with tenacity? Franklin Delano Roosevelt, the most charismatic of the presidents of the United States, acted with complete confidence in the rightness of his policies. Many people refuse to examine their beliefs lest they be disclosed as faulty. Some refuse a physical examination, fearing the revelation of a serious illness. David L. Costill reports that after a talk to the Indiana Track Coaches Association in which he stated that tests indicated that vitamin supplements were not necessary for one who followed a balanced diet, one coach challenged him: "You're wrong about vitamins. I've been taking them for years and can really feel the difference." Costill adds, "In the end I was unable to convince the coach that he was wasting his money. He needed no scientific facts; experience told him he was right and I was wrong. It was hard to argue facts against fixed beliefs and perceptions of experience."[3] Some Christians refuse to examine the *Koran;* some Communists will not study democratic principles; and some capitalists will not read Karl Marx. Of course, we must not hastily throw away that which has stood the test of many years of experience, but when we refrain from examining other ideas simply for fear of losing our cherished concepts, philosophy becomes, in the words of W. K. Clifford, "the still small voice that murmurs 'fiddlesticks.'"

b. Authority

The way of authority appeals to the testimony of others. One may know that Columbus discovered America in 1492 because one found that statement in a reliable history book. It would be impossible to compute how much of what one knows has come from authorities. Certainly it is a large percentage. Parents are usually the first authorities. Later the child is enlightened by playmates, teachers, schoolbooks, and religious leaders. The first knowledge is received without questioning the reliability of its source. Later some authorities are discovered to be undependable, and some thought to be dependable are found to disagree with each other. Most young people in their early teens go through a "storm and stress" period in which they rebel against all authority. They would learn everything for themselves. Some subject matters can be known through experience, yet it would be foolish not to accept knowledge that can be gained through authorities. One could test the contents of the bottle in the medicine chest marked "Poison," but it is wiser to accept it at face value. Even if one had the equipment and the information necessary for calculating the speed of light and the acceleration of falling bodies, one might better accept the conclusions of the reliable scientists in such matters. Life is too short to gain all knowledge by personal experience. Human supremacy among the animals is partly the result of an ability to learn from history. Anatole France said that man is the animal that writes history and tells lies. A. H. S. Korzybski and that man is the time-binding animal. The human events that antedated one's birth can be discovered only by appealing to the authority of elders, or of written history, or of primary sources, or through artifacts left by predecessors. Even one's birth must be established by authority. Many people have had the curious experience of hunting for a birth certificate, a doctor's record, or the record in a family Bible to establish the legal status of their birth.

The rebellion that is often felt against authorities may originate in the discovery of the frequent misuse of authority. Many "infallible authorities" have proved to be errant. The Kalif Omar ordered the destruction of the great library of ancient Alexandria on the grounds that if the books agreed with the *Koran* they were useless and need not be preserved, and if they disagreed with the *Koran* they were pernicious and ought to be destroyed. Thus by appeal to a supposedly infallible authority, humanity suffered one of the greatest losses of scholarly records. Aristotle was for several centuries treated as an infallible authority on all questions about the natural world. In the middle of the fourteenth century the Inceptor in Arts at the University of Paris was asked to swear that he would teach nothing inconsistent with Aristotle. In 1624 the Parliament of Paris passed a decree threatening with death anyone who held or taught anything contrary to Aristotle.[4] But to reject all authorities because some authority has been misused is to fail to distinguish between dogmatic authorities and scientific authorities. The former claim finality; the latter are always open to further testing and refining. George Boas clearly distinguishes the two kinds of authorities as follows: "The progress of science is due above all to the scientists' willingness to consider all authorities on trial. They serve until they are superannuated. Their proponents must submit to dethronement at any time regardless of their status as great authorities. What authorities say in science is not true because they are authorities, but they are authorities because what they say is true."[5] Dogmatic authority in Christianity was supported by Cardinal Newman: "Ecclesiastical authority, not argument, is the supreme rule and the appropriate guide for Catholics in matters of religion."[6] Billy Sunday said the same—but less elegantly: "When the word of God says one thing and scholarship says another, scholarship can go to hell!"[7] When authorities disagree or when authority as a source of knowing is doubted, other sources of information must be consulted.

c. Reason

The rationalist starts with ideas known to be true, and argues consistently to a conclusion. If one knows that London is larger than Paris, and that Paris is larger than Moscow, then one knows by appeal to the logical principle of relational transfer that London is larger than Moscow. But how did one know the relative sizes of London and Paris and of Paris and Moscow? This information probably came from a reliable authority. Thus rationalism is a method of thinking without error once we have axiomatic truths. For this reason rationalism has been regarded by some philosophers as a secondary, rather than a primary, source of knowledge. Some item must be known on some other basis than reason. So in rationalism the basic information cannot itself be established by rationalism. Geometry begins with axioms, which are the bases of all proofs in the system. But the axioms are not proved. Descartes used the rational method to establish the existence of himself, but he began with the nonsharable experience of his own activity of thinking: "I think." He reasoned from that experience to the affirmation of his own existence: "I think. Whatever thinks must exist. So I exist." Rationalism elucidates what follows from axioms. Some philosophers think that it is a way of conceptualizing what must from given statements, and deny that it is a source of knowledge. They think that reason can establish validity of argument but not the truth of sentences. For example, we know that the circumference of a circle is equal to its diameter times 3.14159, and we know that the figure we are considering is a circle, so are we giving new information when we draw the conclusion that the circumference of this figure is equal to its diameter times 3.14159? (Actually we know that the circumference of a circle is not equal to its diameter times 3.14159. Pi has been calculated by modern computers to 100,000 decimal places.) The conclusion of a rational argument is not new knowledge, contend these philosophers; it may be psychologically new, but it is not informationally new.

On the other hand there is the long and living tradition of rationalism. The rationalists believe that by the manipulation of ideas true propositions about a real world can be established. Do not suppose that a rationalist is one who never uses his sense organs or that within his rational argument no use is made of sensed experience. When Aristotle argued from the movements he saw around him to the existence of an Unmoved Mover that was the primary source of all movement, he was arguing rationally, although some of the data of his argument were sense experiences. Another example of a rational argument is Anselm's ontological argument for God: we know that God exists, because we have an idea of a being than which nothing greater can be conceived, and this greatest idea must include the idea of existence of it is to be the greatest idea. All rational arguments make a big assumption about the real world, namely, that the world is capable of being grasped by man's rational powers and of being expressed in rational words. This is a tremendous act of faith on the part of the rationalists. Yet are we not lost indeed if we cannot believe in the knowability of the world? The irrationalist can taunt us with the reminder that we live in a world in which the ratio between the diameter and the circumference of a circle cannot be expressed in a rational number.

d. Self-Evidence

One way by which premises can be established is the way of self-evidence. There are some ideas whose truth is so apparent that any intelligent person who understands the meaning of the idea must accept it as true. Our example was "A colored thing is a spatial thing." The truth of the sentence is self-evident since the idea of a colored thing is that of something spread out in space, that is, spatial. How about the self-evident truth in the Declaration of Independence: "We hold these truths to be self-evident . . . all men are created equal . . . they are endowed by their Creator with certain unalienable Rights, that among these are Life, Liberty, and the Pursuit of Happiness"? Self-evidence in this context means ideas that any reasonable person will recognize and accept. Some ideas are self-evident because they are universal, but others are relative to a particular people; some appear to be discovered, others to be agreed upon. The former can be described as axiomatic self-evidence, the latter as postulated self-evidence. Color is obviously spatial, but in the United States Constitution men are declared to possess unalienable rights. A proposition may be said to be established by self-evidence, we may conclude, either by discovering that the predicate term is necessarily implied in the subject term or by an agreement to treat the proposition as an axiom.

e. Intuition

The fifth way of knowing we have called the way of intuition. The man who has a headache knows he has a headache. He has direct experience of pain. Anyone who has ever had a headache knows the sort of pain he is suffering, but no one other than the one having the headache can actually feel *this* headache. While all knowing is a relationship between a subject and an object, in an intuition the object known is in some way a part of the subject. In sumi-e painting, according to Suzuki, "What we see before us is the painter himself, and not the form of the subject which he is imagined to have painted."[8] The Chinese artist Yu-K'o is said to have mediated upon a bamboo grove so long and so intently before he painted that he became "transformed into bamboo." Jorge Tyller, an outstanding Mexican dancer, performs a traditional Yaqui deer dance in which according to critics he "does not interpret the deer . . . he is the deer." Immediacy and certainty make knowledge gained in this manner seem peculiarly reliable to the one who has the intuition. The physician may tell the man with a headache that he has no physiological reason for having a headache, but the physician will have great difficulty in convincing the patient that he does not have a headache. The esoteric character of an intuition, which makes it psychologically certain to the one having the experience, also implies that the experiencer cannot convey to another his own knowledge. Intuitive knowledge is nonsharable knowledge. There are important cautions about intuitive knowledge: (1) The psychological certainty of intuition should not in itself convince one of the truth of intuition. (2) The unsharable nature of intuitions should not convince one of the falsity of intuitions. An intuition is a belief that one is convinced is true, yet one cannot give convincing reasons for holding it. For example, one may be thoroughly convinced that another person is lying; but, realizing that one cannot defend the conviction by saying, "He is lying because he hesitated before replying, he did not look me in the eyes, and he drooped the left side of his mouth," one says instead, "I have a hunch he is lying." Those who prefer the sharable techniques of reason and experience often distrust the intuitions of poets, artists, musicians, and mystics. But the intuitionists counter that life is more than that which can be measured by computers. Pierre Teilhard de Chardin, who was both a scientist and a mystic, wrote as follows in defense of intuition: "Minds that are exclusively accustomed to looking in everything for the rational explanation and the consciously appreciated causes, are at a loss when they are presented with these turbulent awakenings and obscure tendencies. At first, their curiosity is aroused, but they soon turn away, shocked or with a smile. They feel that such phenomena are too erratic to detain the historian, too wayward to merit the attention of the serious thinker." Teilhard concludes, "Such people understand nothing of the mystery of life."[9] Perhaps the nonintuitionism that Teilhard attacked is not so prevalent as he thought, for it is generally acknowledged that hunches, insights, guesses, hypotheses, and trial-and-error experiments are important elements of the methods used in the sciences. But frequently scientists attempt to cover up this aspect of their quest for knowledge as not consistent with their claim to objectivity. Robert Jastrow writes that "scientists have permitted (and occasionally encouraged) the development of a public image of science as an impersonal and dehumanized field of work, unintelligible and inaccessible to all but a gifted few. This stereotype portrays the scientist as a man who starts with a premise of established fact, proceeds by a formal reasoning, and arrives in this way at an incontestable conclusion. It represents the scientist as a logically perfect but alien being, dealing in facts and truths, a man who works like a machine." Jastrow continues, "This is a false image because a scientist goes about his business in the same manner as everyone else, relying heavily on subjective and intuitive judgments. However, when he has reached a significant result, he covers up his tracks and replaces his intuitive reasoning by a formal discussion designed to convince his colleagues. These traditional methods of presentation in the scientific literature, which conceal the intuitive element in scientific discovery, serve to alienate the general public."[10]

f. Experience

Knowledge that is gained through experiences that can be shared with other people is called empirical knowledge. It can always be put to the public test. If a certain solution is established as acid by the litmus paper test, its acidity can be tested by other people. Empiricists are well aware that sense organs vary among human beings, that the keenness of the sense organs varies within the life span of each individual, and that people often make perceptual errors; yet empiricists believe that the most dependable sort of knowledge is that gained through the use of sight, hearing, small, taste, and touch. They point out that in the method of authority confidence is placed in someone else's experience, that the rationalist must start from principles that have probably been reached empirically, and that intuitions are reliable only when there is some empirical evidence that other persons have similar intuitions. Therefore, empiricism is said to be the primary source of all knowledge.

Empiricism is the heart of the method used in the sciences. Although empirical knowledge is knowledge that is always open to the public test, that which makes it true is not general agreement but the conviction that empirical knowledge represents things as they are. Things-as-they-are is contrasted with things-as-they-are-known-to-be. This creates for the empiricist a curious problem. He knows that things-as-they-are-known-to-be can never be identical with things-as-they-are, yet this is the unverifiable and unprovable assumption on which his theory of knowledge rests. The epistemological character of the object of knowledge shifts to the ontological character of the object outside the knowing relationship. This is in conflict with the empiricist's theory of knowledge. It can even be described as a form of falsification, inasmuch as it is a claim that the object of knowledge is in fact the object outside the knowing relationship. Huston Smith argues that it is a form of violence: "The Western hunt for knowledge, analytic and objective to its core, has violence built into it. For to know analytically is to reduce the object of knowledge, however vital, however complex, to precisely this: an object."[11]

The turning point in Western thinking is often said to have been the change from the Ptolemaic to the Copernican view of the world. The Copernican Revolution—the shift from an earth-centered perspective to a solar-centered perspective—has been interpreted as a radical change from an anthropomorphic to a nonanthropomorphic view. But this is not the case. The Copernican view is still anthropomorphic, except that, for the Copernican, celestial phenomena are viewed from the sun rather than from the earth. Knowledge requires both knower and known. As Stephen Pepper has said, "There are not many facts that do not depend upon a point of view. What is a chair to us, is something quite different to a dog. And when we try to 'reduce' the chair to facts that would be identical both for us and the dog, there is not much left of the chair. Physics has persistently sought such invariant facts, and the result has been to strip the world of most of its character and to offer us instead pointer readings. Even these are not quite free from a point of view, for a man must be educated to read a scale and tell off numbers."[12] It is empirical nonsense to claim that the world-as-known is identical with the world-apart-from-being-known. The object of knowledge is the "real object" analyzed, categorized, dissected, truncated, and so on. For example, when one says "I see a cube," one is in no sense speaking exactly, since a cube must have six surfaces, and it is impossible to see more than three surfaces simultaneously. Empiricists do not like to be reminded of this feature of human knowing. Bishop Berkeley's claim "To be is to be perceived" prompted Samuel Johnson to kick a stone in refutation of Berkeley. According to Berkeley this "refutation" was a failure, since the only reality Johnson experienced in his kick was the pain in his toe!

In the early part of the twentieth century a vigorous battle was fought among American philosophers about the mind-dependence or mind-independence of the objects of sense experience. The new realists were panobjectivists, holding that sense data are fully objective. The convergent railroad tracks that one sees and the parallel railroad tracks over which the trains run are both objective in the sense that both are independent of being sensed. But obviously there is a difference. This was explained by affirming that there are two sorts of being or "istence." Some things have *ex*istence, for example, the parallel tracks, and some things have *sub*sistence, for example, the convergent tracks. The minority of things exist; the vast majority subsist. The new realists had difficulty in establishing a criterion for subsistence that allowed reality to all possible objects of perception and rejected impossible objects such as a square circle. Their objective world became a world in which few perceptual errors were possible. In some manner everything was objectively real in all the ways in which everything could be experienced. The critical realists rejected an epistemological monism that identified things-as-they-are and things-as-they-are-experienced. They argued for an epistemological dualism. According to them human beings experience the world not directly but by means of mediating entities, which are the logical essences of both ideas in the mind and physical objects. Physical objects exist but are not experienced directly. Their existence is established by what some members of this school called "animal faith." Essences are the joint product of mind and object, and by means of essences one becomes aware of an external objective world. This ingenuous speculation was an effort to bridge the hiatus between epistemological idealism, which holds that one can experience only one's ideas, and naïve realism, which holds that objective reality is experienced directly. But the indirect form of perception offered by the critical realists cut perceivers off from direct experience of an objective world. The difference between realists and idealists may be clarified by an illustration: a realistic baseball umpire would say, "I call them as they are," but an unrealistic baseball umpire would say, "I call them as I see them." The new realists tried to locate in the objective world the strikes that the umpire called "balls" and the balls that he called "strikes." Indeed, their panobjective world would contain the following:

1. Strikes not called anything by the umpire.
2. Balls not called anything by the umpire.
3. Strikes called balls by the umpire.
4. Balls called strikes by the umpire.
5. Strikes called strikes by the umpire.
6. Balls called balls by the umpire.
7. Nothing thrown by the pitcher, yet the umpire called a strike.
8. Nothing thrown by the pitcher, yet the umpire called a ball.

The existentialist revolt in the West associated with Kierkegaard, Heidegger, Jaspers, Sartre, and others claims that the worth of knowledge is not in the intrinsic value of knowledge as the rationalists claim, nor in the power of knowledge to utilize nature for human ends, nor in the improvement of social conditions. Knowledge, according to existentialists, makes the human being by means of choices made. The distinction between a mind-independent objective world and a mind-dependent subjective world has no interest for existentialists. An existentialistic baseball umpire would say, "Why all this foolishness about strikes, balls, called strikes, and called balls? There are no strikes or balls until I call them."

Another feature of empiricism that embarrasses empiricists is the relationship between sensing and believing. One of the empiricists' claims, "I'll believe it when I see it," can in fact be converted to "I'll see it when I believe it," since what one senses is limited to what one believes to be real. The one who sees ghosts is the one who believes in ghosts—generally. A well-known American philosopher of science once confessed to me that strange things were happening in his home that could only be accounted for as the work of a poltergeist—yet he did not believe in poltergeists. He finally sold the house and moved, to escape events that could not be explained by his ontological assumptions.

Until the nineteenth century Western philosophy was a battleground between the rationalists and the empiricists. The rationalists contended all that can be known must be known through the intellect, and almost nothing can be known through the physical senses. The empiricists held that all knowledge is rooted in the physical senses, and that apart from sensation knowledge floats into unbridled speculation. Sensations keep human beings in touch with the real world. These different methodologies are congruent with the different conceptions of what it is mankind is able to know according to the rationalists and the empiricists. The former held that human beings can know whatever is eternal, necessary, immutable, and universal. Plato, the founder of this view of knowledge, regarded mathematics as the paradigm of all knowing. He located these ideal objects in an independent realm of universals which he called Forms. When Platonism became Christianized in Augustine, the ideal objects of knowledge became ideas in the mind of God. The other way of locating the rational objects of knowledge was to position them somehow either in the nature of things or in the minds of men and women. Empiricists have regarded knowledge as human construction based on the data given through sense organs. Many philosophers insist that the argument has been over the emphases of the two approaches. The rationalist needs to use sense organs to establish some of the ideas from which he starts, and the empiricist needs to use reason to relate his sense experiences. This was the recognition Kant had in mind in his oft-quoted statement: "Thoughts without content are empty, intuitions without concepts are blind."[13]

Today most Western philosophers doubt that fully objective empirical knowledge is possible. Michael Polanyi states it well: "For, as human beings, we must inevitably see the universe from a centre lying within ourselves and speak about it in terms of a human language shaped by the exigencies of human intercourse. Any attempt rigorously to eliminate our human perspective from our picture of the world must lead to absurdity."[14]

Empiricism yields probabilities rather than the logical certainties of rationalism or the psychological certainties of intuitionism. Albert Einstein once said, "No amount of experimentation can ever prove me right. A single experiment may at any time prove me wrong." If rationalists contend that no foundation firm enough to yield a logically certain conclusion can be established by using only empirical procedures, empiricists counter that no foundation based on logical certitude alone can refer to reality. When considered from the point of view of establishing knowledge, rather than from the view of gaining knowledge, we can say that the rationalists would prove the truth of a sentence by appealing to abstract and universal principles assumed to be true, while the empiricists would make a sentence probably true by appealing to concrete and particular instances.

g. Pragmatic Results

The seventh way of knowing is called *pragmatism*. William James subtitled his volume on pragmatism "A New Name for Some Old Ways of Thinking." Folk wisdom is full of pragmatic observations, for example, "By their fruits you shall know them," "See how it works in practice," and "The proof of the pudding is in the eating." In our illustration the friend knows that the Golden Rule is a sound business principle because he has put it into practice for forty years and has found that during that time he has made both money and friends. While pragmatism as a school of philosophy is a twentieth-century creation, it is indeed a very old way of thinking. One cannot imagine a time in which human beings have not been inclined to accept as true, real, and valuable that which works well in practice. Knowledge may be acquired in the process of living as well as in passive reflection. The phrase *works well* and the illustration I have chosen of the Golden Rule as a "sound human principle" brings out an important factor in pragmatic knowing, namely, in pragmatism knowledge and value are closely related. It would not be fair to say of pragmatism that it is a way of knowing in which a sentence is known to be true merely if it is in accord with one's wishes; nevertheless, pragmatism is a way of knowing in which desires, wishes, hopes, volitions, and preferences are relevant to the knowing process. The Golden Rule, according to our wealthy businessman, is known to be sound because its application has produced valued results. The critics of pragmatism are quick to point out that false ideas may also produce desirable results, and that true ideas may produce undesirable results. Hence they affirm that the value of an idea when put into practice is not in itself a sufficient criterion for knowledge.

h. Revelation

Revelation—the last way of knowing on the list—connotes the uncovering of the previously hidden. There are two kinds: primary and secondary. Primary revelation is the direct experience of information from a supernatural source in a vision, dream, trance, or mystical state. Secondary revelation is the reported experience in a sacred book. The *Koran,* for example, is a secondary revelation for the Muslim, although it was a primary revelation for the Prophet Muhammad. In Judaism and Christianity revelation is linked with the conception of a personal God who is believed to act in historical times in the lives of persons and nations. The Bible is the record of both primary revelations—for example, the experiences of Moses on Mount Sinai and of Paul on the road to Damascus, and secondary revelations, that is, writers who speak with authority but not from a specific mystical experience. The prophets of the Old Testament sometimes prefaced their own observations with the certifying statement "Thus says the Lord," and Paul once admitted, "I have no command of the Lord, but I give my opinion as one who by the Lord's mercy is trustworthy."[15] Some Christians have assumed that the Bible is the infallible, inerrant, and final revelation of God to man. Dean Burgon, preaching in Christ Church Cathedral at Oxford University in 1861, said, "The Bible is the very utterance of the Eternal: as much God's own word as if high heaven were open and we heard God speaking to us with human voice.... The Bible is filled to overflowing with the Holy Spirit of God; the books of it and the words of it and the very letters of it."[16] One of the interesting aspects of the method of revelation is the search for more subtle hidden meanings. For example, in Revelation 13:18 reference is made to "the beast," whose number is 666. This may have been a sign to symbolize Nero Caesar, since the numerical equivalent of the Hebrew form (NRON KSR) is 666, that is, N (50) + R (200) + 0 (6) + N (50) + K (100) + S (60) + R (200) = 666. Later Christians, by other numerological manipulations, established that 666 denoted Napoleon.

In Hinduism the *Vedas* are said to be *śruti,* a term sometimes translated "revelation." This is not quite accurate. A literal translation would be "that which is heard." For some Hindus, *śruti* connotes authoritativeness by reason of great age; for others it means that which is revealed directly to ancient sages by God; and for still others it means having no beginning in time, that is, coming neither from the hand of man nor from God. "The whole Indian Philosophy is a vast commentary on the Vedas or on the sayings of the Great Buddha and Mahavira," claims R. C. Pandeya.[17] On the basis of this, Pandeya argues that nothing is completely new: "In the realm of thought novelty is possible only in explanation and interpretation of old facts and arguments."[18]

2. Meaning

Knowledge can be described simply as true sentences, and we have considered eight ways in which a sentence may be said to be true. But before determining if a sentence is true or false a decision must be made as to whether it is a meaningful sentence. Meaningless sentences are neither true nor false. For example, unless we suspect that the author of such sentences as

"Green is more identical than blue" or "A loud noise is wider than an itch" has used words in other than their usual meanings, we would be unwise to spend time and energy deciding whether they are true or false. In determining whether a sentence is true we must decide first whether the sentence has meaning, second, what is its meaning. We must decide what is the meaning of such sentences as "This is the will of God," "Music came from her heart," "My love is a red, red rose," "Nature is kind," and "Law imposes order" before we decide whether they are true. William James gave in his lectures on pragmatism a vivid example of the necessity of deciding what is the meaning of a sentence before deciding whether the sentence is true.[19] On a hunting trip he was asked by his friends to settle an argument. His hunting companions imagined a hunter trying to shoot a squirrel. The squirrel was on the trunk of a tree. As the hunter moved around the tree in a wide circle, the squirrel moved around the tree so that at all times the trunk of the tree was between the squirrel and the hunter. The men disagreed as to whether the hunter had circled both the tree and the squirrel. James contended that the problem could not be solved until the men agreed as to what was meant by the sentence "The hunter went around the squirrel." If this meant that the hunter went first north of the squirrel, then west, south, east, and north again, the answer was "Yes." But if this meant that the hunter first faced the belly of the squirrel, then one side, the back, the other side, and the belly again, the answer was "No." James says that his clarification pleased none of his companions, but he believed it made very good sense to determine meaning before determining truth or falsity.

Max Black reports that he once saw two distinguished linguists almost come to blows in public over whether "The master beat the peasant" has the same meaning as "The peasant was beaten by the master." Black observes, "Questions of meaning are apt to generate spectacular manifestations of *furor academicus*."[20]

Although a sentence must be meaningful to be true or false, not all meaningful sentences are true or false. Some sentences are factually meaningful. They state something about the nature of things—and hence are called "statements," or they propose something for our belief—and hence are called "propositions." Other sentences are expressively meaningful. They suggest, hint, intimate, adumbrate, and so on, an attitude, feeling, emotion, evaluation, and the like, of a person toward an object, an act, a set of conditions, or a concept. They are not statements or propositions. Responses to them are not "True" or "False," but "That approximates the way I feel" or "That does not do justice to my attitude." These sentences may be described as pictorial, imaginative, metaphorical, metonymical, and so forth. Wordsworth's lines "I wandered lonely as a cloud/ That floats on high o'er vales and hills" and "My heart leaps up when I behold/A rainbow in the sky" are not factually meaningful. I do not resemble a cloud that floats over vales and hills, and my heart does not leap! Yet these lines may convey the emotion I feel toward the natural world.

Efforts in Western philosophy to formulate a criterion of factual meaningfulness range from the looseness of pragmatism, that is, a statement has meaning if it makes a difference to someone somewhere sometime, for example, ". . . what concrete difference will its being true make in any one's actual life? . . . What experiences will be different from those which would obtain if the belief were false? What, in short, is the truth's cash-value in experiential terms?",[21] to the stringency of experimental verification, that is, a statement has meaning if it is capable of being tested scientifically.

The clearest and most provocative presentation of the empirical verification criterion of meaning is that of A. J. Ayer in *Language, Truth and Logic,* (1964). Perhaps its highest praise was Bertrand Russell's observation: "I should like to have written it myself." Ayer, taking his cue from David Hume, divided all genuine statements into two classes: (1) those dealing with "relations of ideas" and (2) those dealing with "matters of fact." The former are *a priori* statements, that is, they are based on reason alone. They are the statements of logic and mathematics. They are necessary and certain because they are analytic, that is, the conclusion calls attention to what is implied by the premises. For example, if A is greater than B, and if B is greater than C, the conclusion, A is greater than C, merely affirms what was already implicit. The conclusion affirms the implication. In other words, "relations of ideas" statements make no assertion about the empirical world, and therefore one does not appeal to sense experience to see if they are true. "Matters of fact" statements are *a posteriori* statements, that is, they are based on sense experience. They are the hypotheses of empirical sciences, and as such are probable and cannot be certain. It was for these that Ayer developed a criterion of meaningfulness. His criterion and its implications were stated as follows in the preface to the first edition of *Language, Truth and Logic:* "To test whether a sentence expresses a genuine empirical hypothesis, I adopt what may be called a modified verification principle. For I require of an empirical hypothesis, not indeed that it should be conclusively verifiable, but that some possible sense-experience should be relevant to the determination of its truth or falsehood. If a putative proposition fails to satisfy this principle, and is not a tautology, then I hold that it is metaphysical, and that, being metaphysical, it is neither true nor false but literally senseless. It will be found that much of what ordinarily passes for philosophy is metaphysical according to this criterion, and, in particular, that it can not be significantly asserted that there is a non-empirical world of values, or that men have immortal souls, or that there is a transcendent God."[22] In 1946 Ayer confessed, "In the ten years that have passed since *Language, Truth and Logic* was first published, I have come to see that the questions with which it deals are not in all respects so simple as it makes them appear; but I still believe that the point of view which it expresses is substantially correct. Being in every sense a young man's book, it was written with more passion than most philosophers allow themselves to show, at any rate in their published work, and while this probably helped to secure it a larger audience than it might have had otherwise, I think now that much of its argument would have been more persuasive if it had not been presented in so harsh a form."[23] Ayer therefore set forth at that time a more mellow criterion: ". . . a statement is verifiable, and therefore meaningful, . . . if some . . . observation-statement can be deduced from it in conjunction with certain other premises, without being deducible from those other premises alone."[24] The key term, *observation-statement,* he defined as a statement "which records an actual or possible observation."[25]

This criterion was used by the Viennese logical positivists, with whom Ayer was in close agreement, to demonstrate that all universal statements about the world are nonsense. They had in mind such statements as "All is love," "God is all," "The Absolute enters into all things, but is a part of nothing," "Everything is fated," "Everything that happens is according to God's will," "*Ātman* is Brahman," and "The Tao is everywhere." According to the logical positivists a statement like "The moon is made of green cheese" is meaningful only if there is a portion of the moon that is not made of green cheese—and therefore not all the moon is green cheese! "Everything increased ten times over night," can be meaningful only if one thing did not increase ten times during the night, by which the increase of everything else can be measured. The intent of these applications of the meaning principle is obvious: they challenge the knowledge claims of metaphysicians and theologians. However, if the meaning criterion proposed by the logical positivists applies to metaphysics and religion, it must also apply to such statements as "Everything is caused," "There are no uncaused events," and "There is no First Cause." When the empirical verification criterion is applied to causality, its defenders may find themselves in the embarrassing necessity of agreeing with medieval philosophers that the universality of the causal principle depends upon the reality of a First Uncaused Cause, which, in the words of St. Thomas, "everyone understands to be God." The logical positivists were anxious to eliminate many of the statements contained in traditional religions—as Ayer indicated in the preface to the first edition of *Language, Truth and Logic*—but they may not have given sufficient attention to the symbolic and mythological characteristics of religious language, nor were they fully appreciative of the human need to find meaning in the mystery of existence.

3. Truth

Philosophers traditionally distinguish three theories of the nature of truth: the correspondence theory, the coherence theory, and the pragmatic theory.

According to the correspondence theory of truth, a statement is true when the meaning of the statement correctly represents the real object or state of affairs. If we disagree whether a long black line on the opposite wall is a crack in the plaster, or a pencil mark, or a spider's web, we walk over to the wall and examine it more closely. We check it with another sense experience. If it can be moved with a finger, it is probably a web; if it cannot be moved with a finger and can be erased with a pencil eraser, it is probably a pencil mark; if it cannot be moved or erased and feels rough to the finger, it is probably a crack. The empiricists appeal to the correspondence theory of truth.

The rationalists appeal to the coherence theory of truth. According to them if a proposition is true it must be consistent with other propositions known to be true. Descartes established the truth of the proposition "I exist" by pointing out that it is the logical conclusion of two related propositions that are known to be true: "I think" (known intuitively) and "Whatever thinks must be an existing thing" (known self-evidently). The coherence theory is concerned only with the agreement of propositions, whereas the correspondence theory is concerned with the agreement of propositions and reality. The coherence theory of truth can best be stated negatively: a proposition that contradicts a proposition known to be true cannot itself be true. This view of truth requires that there be at least one proposition in the argument whose truth does not depend upon the truth of any other proposition. If no proposition were true independently of the other propositions in the argument, we might have a closed system of mutually dependent propositions, or we might have an unending series of dependent propositions. But in either case we would have no truth. Consistency alone is no guarantee of truth. A boy who comes home in the afternoon with wet hair and muddy clothes may give his mother a lengthy explanation consistent with his original profession of innocence, "I did not go swimming." But mothers do not need to be philosophers to know that a story consistent with the original proposition, "I did not go swimming," may be far from the truth. Everyone knows that a lawyer can present a coherent case for the defense of a guilty client. However, we would be doing grave injustice to the defenders of the coherence view of truth if we gave the impression that rationalists believe that coherent statements are true just because they cohere. Rather, according to the rationalists, propositions are true when they cohere with the widest system of coherent belief. Human knowledge constitutes a unified whole of true propositions. Truth is one. This noble conception of truth had to be challenged by the founders of modern science. Galileo distinguished studying philosophy and philosophizing. The former activity compares philosophical texts in order to find a synthesis of opinion on the grounds that all knowledge is in books. It is useful to study what has been investigated by others, but "a man will never become a philosopher by worrying forever about the writings of other men, without ever raising his own eyes to nature's works in the attempt to recognize there the truths already known and to investigate some of the infinite number that remain to be discovered."[26] In a letter to Kepler he complained that the philosophers in his university would not even look through his telescope.

The pragmatic theory of truth applies a utility test. The truth of an idea, according to James, is the satisfactory working of an idea. Each idea is "a plan for action." If the idea when put into action works out well, it may then be said to be true. Truth is not a static property of statements; it is an idea at work in the world. The test of ideas, like the test of puddings, is in putting them into the life situations for which they are intended. An example given by James is that of a man lost in the woods. He finds a cow path, and speculates that by following the path he will find his way out of the woods. The truth of the idea consists in the actual following of the path. The verification of an idea is the truth of the idea. This view of the way of testing the truth of statements has some relationship to the empirical test of truth in that in both cases a relationship is established between a statement and sensed reality. However, pragmatism establishes a relationship between a sentence and what the person may want. The theory has been constantly criticized as unnecessarily confusing truth and value. "Satisfactory results" was used by James to designate that which is emotionally satisfying, that which is ethically desirable, as well as that which is testable by sense experience. One of the most devastating questions that can be asked of a supporter of this theory of truth is "Is the pragmatic theory of truth only pragmatically true?" The assumption of the question is that the pragmatist will not be satisfied with a theory of the nature of truth that is true on pragmatic grounds.

4. *The Rules of Logic*

Logic is the study of what correctly follows from what in the order of thinking. This description might be expanded to the study of what conclusion is entailed in given premises. The premises are called assumptions or statements-taken-for-granted. But care must be taken, because the premises may be assumed in the West for the sake of argument, not always because they are believed to be true. The logician *qua* logician is not concerned about the truth of statements. The relationship between premises and conclusion is known as implication. The psychological process of drawing the conclusion is known as inference. When the inference drawn is implied by the premises, the inference is said to be valid. So logic can be tentatively defined as the science of valid inference.

A comprehensive definition of logic is difficult because of the two forms of reasoning: one independent of sensation, known as deductive, formal, or *a priori* logic; the other dependent on sensation, known as inductive, informal, or *a posteriori* logic. Deduction moves from premises, one of which must be a general or universal statement, to a necessary conclusion. Induction moves from particular observed facts to a probable general conclusion. Deductive logic is formal in that it is concerned solely with the form or structure of valid reasoning. Inductive logic is informal in that it is concerned with the content as well as the form of reasoning. Deduction identifies the conclusion that the premises enjoin. Induction seeks a conclusion that is likely true upon the basis of the data being considered. A deductive conclusion is a proof. An inductive conclusion is one for which there is a weight of evidence. In deduction it is nonsense to affirm the premises and deny the conclusion. But not so induction, since in induction the conclusion is not forced. The principle of induction has been succinctly stated as follows by an American philosopher: "Seek to achieve the maximum of order by logical operations upon elementary propositions. Generalize this order (whatever its form be: causal, statistical or other), with a minimum of arbitrariness, that is, according to the principle of simplicity."[27] The phrase *with a minimum of arbitrariness* indicates that the inductive principle is strikingly different from the logical requiredness of the relation between premises and conclusion in deduction. The distinction between deduction and induction—a distinction so clear and so dear to Western philosophers—is, according to some Eastern philsophers, rooted not in the nature of thought but in the nature of Western thought. They see in this distinction a dichotomy of life and thought that is untrue to the human condition. For example, Lin Yutang once wrote, "The logical man is always self-righteous and therefore inhuman and therefore wrong."[28] The denigration of logic has not always characterized Eastern thought. The Chinese pilgrim Hsiuan-tsag, who visited the Buddhist university of Nālandā in northern Indian in the seventh century A.D., reported as follows: "If one of the assembly distinguishes himself (in disputation) by refined language, subtle investigation, deep penetration, and severe logic, then he is mounted on an elephant covered with precious ornaments and conducted (in procession) by a numerous suite to the gates of the abbey. If, on the contrary, one of the members breaks down in his argument, or uses poor and inelegant phrases, or if he violates a rule in logic and adopts his words accordingly, they proceed to disfigure his face with red and white and cover his body with dust and dirt, and then carry him off to some deserted spot or dump him in a ditch."[29]

The separation of logic into formal and informal has not always characterized Western logic. Aristotle, the founder of logic in the West, made no such distinction. He formulated what has come to be known as the three Laws of Thought, but they were for him laws of both thought and being. Each law according to the Aristotelian analyses must appear therefore with its dual connotation, namely,

1. The Law of Identity. If any statement is true, it is true—and if any thing is A, it is A.

2. The Law of Noncontradiction. No statement can be both true and false—and no thing can be both A and not-A.
3. The Law of Excluded Middle. All statements must be either true or false, i.e., there is no middle between truth and falsity with respect to statements—and all things must be either A or not-A.

Aristotle also held that universal or general statements—statements beginning with the word *all* or a synonym of *all*—necessarily imply that they are members of the class. Thus in the syllogism

All M is P;
All S is M;
So all S is P,

we are to assume the existence of things that are M and things that are S. But modern logicians, contending that the validity of the conclusion does not depend on the truth of the general premise, point out that a general statement may refer to a null class, that is, a class that has no members. Therefore they interpret "All M is P" as "If all M is P" or "All M is P, but there may be no M." The writers of textbooks, as a way of warning students of the separation between validity and truth, may illustrate the syllogism by using nonsense sentences, for example,

All mombites are phlogons.
All sarbats are mombites.
So all sarbats are phlogons.

They may illustrate by deriving a valid and true conclusion from two false premises, for example,

If all stone is good to eat,
and if all bread is stone,
then all bread is good to eat.

What about logic in Eastern philosophy? Wing-tsit Chan acknowledges, "From the outset, we must declare that logic in Oriental philosophy does not attain the prominence we find in Western philosophy."[30] This is especially true of the Chinese. Suzuki says logic is "sadly lacking in the Chinese." The Chinese, he adds, "did not want to waste their mental energy on things which have apparently no practical and immediate bearings on their everyday life."[31] Chan, however, will not admit that Chinese philosophers are illogical: "Chinese thinkers . . . do not reason as methodically as Western philosophers, though none the less clearly and distinctly. There is no doubt that, compared with either the West or India, China lags far behind in systematic reasoning, in explanation, and in proof. Aside from the short-lived Neo-Mohist school of logic and the Buddhist logic that came in with Buddhist philosophy as a handmaid, there is hardly any formal system of logic in China."[32] Chan may be too modest in this statement, since the Ch'an form of Buddhism (generally known by its Japanese name, *Zen*) developed in China.

Logic and the principles of reasoning were developed in India largely because of the Hindu assessment of life, which can be stated syllogisticaly as follows:

> Man's chief problem is suffering *(duḥkha)*. *Duḥkha* is rooted in ignorance *(ajñāna)*. So man's chief problem is the elimination of *ajñāna*, i.e., the overcoming of *ajñāna* (binding ignorance) by means of *jñāna* (liberating knowledge) and hence the attainment of *mokṣa* (salvation).

Indian philosophy distinguished *vidyā* (learning in the sense of scientific knowledge) and *jñāna* (soteriological knowledge, which frees man from all that stands in the way of his perfecting.) But *jñāna* does not oppose nor exclude *vidyā*, and part of the inclusion is the analysis of logical reasoning. The ancient Indian philosophers arrived at a five-part syllogism that does not, to use an expression of Francis Bacon, let nature slip out of its hands. Its existentiality is established both by illustration and application. The five parts are:

1. *pratijñā* (proposition). A statement of the thesis to be established.
2. *hetu* (reason). A statement of the means for establishing the thesis.
3. *udāharaṇa* (explanatory example). A statement of the universal relation, accompanied by a concrete and familiar instance that shows that the reason does apply to reality.
4. *upanaya* (application). A statement indicating that the universal relation applies to the thesis to be established.
5. *nigamana* (conclusion). A statement of the original thesis now established.

An illustration often used is the following:

1. The hillside is on fire.
2. The hillside has smoke.
3. Whatever has smoke has fire, e.g., a fireplace.
4. The hillside has smoke that is accompanied by fire.
5. So the hillside is on fire.

Udāharaṇa links the argument to the major premise, thus making the argument valid by calling attention to a general rule that applies to another instance. The early Nyāya logicians debated whether *udāharaṇa* establishes or illustrates the universality of the argument. But modern Indian logicians commonly point out that the virtue of the third part of the syllogism is that it combines and harmonizes induction and deduction.[33] The informal aspect of the Indian syllogism is an instance of the Eastern view that a form of reasoning that does not deal with life situations is no more than mental gymnastics. Zen Buddhists, as we shall note later, not only reject formal logical reasoning but also ridicule it.

The principles of induction were formulated by John Stuart Mill in his *A System of Logic* in 1843. Mill distinguished four types of experiments, which he described as "the only possible modes of experimental inquiry—of direct induction *a posteriori,* as distinguished from deduction."[34] Mill thought his study systematized the best ideas promulgated by previous writers on induction, and fulfilled Bacon's plan for an inductive method that "leaves little to the acuteness and strength of wits, but places all wits and understandings nearly on a level."[35] All forms of inductive reasoning, according to Mill, are methods for determining the cause (or effect) of phenomena, and all methods can be classified as variations of four basic methods. The four are the following:

1. The Method of Agreement. "If two or more instances of the phenomenon under investigation have only one circumstance in common, the circumstance in which alone all the instances agree is the cause (or effect) of the given phenomenon."
2. The Method of Difference. "If an instance in which the phenomenon under investigation occurs, and an instance in which it does not occur, have every circumstance in common save one, that one occurring only in the former; the circumstance in which alone the two instances differ is the effect, or the cause, or an indispensable part of the cause, of the phenomenon."
3. The Method of Residues. "Subduct from any phenomenon such part as is known by previous inductions to be the effect of certain antecedents, and the residue of the phenomenon is the effect of the remaining antecedents."
4. The Method of Concomitant Variations. "Whatever phenomenon varies in any manner whenever another phenomenon varies in some particular manner, is either a cause or an effect of that phenomenon, or is connected with it through some fact of causation."

The ancient logicians of India arrived at a remarkably similar view of the methods of induction, which they called the *pañcha kāraṇī* (five steps). The five were described as ways to determine a relation known as *phalahetu* (literally "effect and cause"). Why the Indian logicians refer to the effect-cause relationship while the Western logicians refer to the cause-effect relationship is uncertain. Perhaps it is an indication that Westerners think temporally, whereas the Indians think ontologically. The *pāñcha kāraṇī* are the following:

1. No cause and no effect.
2. Cause appears.
3. Effect appears.
4. Cause disappears.
5. Effect disappears.

The *pāñcha kāraṇī* stated as a rule would be: If there is an entity called A and an entity called B, and if it is observed that where there is no A there is no B, that when A appears B appears, and that when A disappears B disappears, then A can be said to be the cause of B. The similarity of this analysis and Mill's analysis is still more obvious when it is noted that the Indian logicians referred to steps 2 and 3 as "agreement in presence," steps 4 and 5 as "agreement in absence," and steps 2, 3, 4, and 5 as "the method of double agreement." One striking difference between Mill's methods and the *pāñcha kāraṇī* is that the latter were formulated over two thousand years earlier!

5. Knowledge According to Indian Philosophy

Six orthodox systems of philosophy have developed in the classical Hindu tradition of life and thought. These may be regarded as commentaries, clarifications, and extensions of philosophical speculations recorded in the *Upaniṣads* between about 800 and 300 B.C. The six systems, known as *darśanas* (points of view), grew out of the desire of believers to defend the Upaniṣadic insights against heretical movements such as Buddhism and Jainism. The six are Sāṁkhya, Yoga, Nyāya, Vaiśeṣika, Mīmāṁsa, and Vedānta. The Nyāya is primarily a study of knowledge. The word *nyāya* means right or correct in the context of reasoning. The narrow use denotes syllogistic reasoning, but the wider use denotes the entire science of demonstration. The oldest and basic writings of the school, *The Nyāya Sūtras of Gotama* (third century B.C.),[36] begin by promising that through an understanding of the principles of knowledge the anguish of existence, the pain of rebirth, all defects of knowing, and all wrong notions will be annihilated, and the result will be the ultimate bliss of enlightened liberation *(mokṣa)*.

The factors of knowing according to the *Nyāya Sūtras* are four:

1. *pramātṛ*. The knower or subject.
2. *prameya*. The known or object.

3. *pramāṇa*. The knowing or process.
4. *pramiti*. The knowledge or state of knowing.

This analysis was accepted by the other schools, with the exception of the Vedānta school, the largest and most important of the schools, which did not and does not make the subject-object separation; for example, a twentieth-century Vedāntist writes, "The fundamental mistake of the Nyāya is the mistake of Locke, and other empirical thinkers who regard the individual as one natural unit and the world as another. This mechanical view, however legitimate for the limited purposes of daily life and psychology, is not ultimately defensible."[37]

The Nyāya logicians were especially concerned about *pramāṇa*, the means for the attaining of right knowledge. Their position was like Descartes' in that they were seeking to establish by rational means the old verities, which had formerly been made secure by appeal to reliable authorities. Faith alone could no longer check the general skepticism. So they set themselves to the task of examining the sources of knowledge in order to save inherited values and realities.

They recognized and defended four valid *pramāṇas*:

1. *pratyakṣa*. Perception.
2. *anumāna*. Inference.
3. *upamāna*. Analogy.
4. *śabda*. Authority.

This list of the *pramāṇas* might lead one to the assumption that the Indian logicians were concerned exclusively with the epistemological aspects of knowing. This was not the case, since *pramāṇa* was a discipline that included what Westerners would call linguistics, semantics, psychology, metaphysics, and debate as well as methodology. This is noticed in the amazing outline of what the *Nyāya Sūtras* cover in the first *sūtra*, namely, means of right knowledge, object of right knowledge, doubt, purpose, familiar instance, established tenet, members [of a syllogism], confutation, ascertainment, discussions, wrangling, cavil, fallacy, quibble, futility, and occasion for rebuke. Such a list of objectives indicates the disputatious intellectual atmosphere of the third century B.C.

Pratyakṣa is the most important kind of cognition, according to the Naiyāyikas (the followers of Nyāya), because when one has perceived directly one does not seek any other support for belief. A perception according to these Indian logicians is certain in the sense that we know *that* we sense but we may not know *what* it is that we sense. For example, when we hear a sound, we know that we hear but we may not know what caused the sound. This led the Naiyāyikas to make a distinction between two kinds or two stages of perception: (1) *nirvikalpa* (indeterminate) perception, that is, a bare sensation that is immediate, unanalyzed, unassociated with an object, and therefore inerrant; and (2) *savikalpa* (determinate) perception, that is, a sensation that is either correctly or incorrectly associated with an object. For example, what at first is seen only as a glob of color may upon nearer approach become identified as a cow.

The Nyāya logicians believed that perception involves the direct contact of a sense object on a sense organ. "*Pratyakṣa* is that knowledge which arises from the contact of a sense with its object."[38] This contact was believed to be actual rather than metaphorical. This, of course, is obvious for the senses of touch and taste. But according to the Nyāya theory there are also actual physical contacts in seeing, hearing, and smelling. Some thing comes in contact with the eye, ear, and nose in these forms of sense perception. The explanation offered is that there is in all forms of sensation a vibratory movement between the *prameya* and *pramatṛ*. Indeed, this physicalism is found not only in sensation but also in the awareness of universals, and even in the awareness of the nonexistence of sensed objects. The perceiver, according to this theory, perceives the orange and the color of the orange, and also the universal orange and the nonapple on the table. Surendranath Das Gupta summarized the Nyāya position as follows: "Sense-contact with the object is thus the primary and indispensable condition of all perceptions and not only can the senses be in contact with the objects, their qualities, and the universals associated with them but also with negation."[39]

The Nyāya philosophers also classified perceptions into the ordinary (*laukika*) and the extraordinary (*alaukika*). In ordinary perception there is a direct vibratory contact of sense object and sense organ, but in extraordinary perception the contact is indirect. Ordinary perceptions may be external or internal. The external ordinary perceptions are five, each utilizing a different material element as medium:

Sense organ	*Element*	*Object of sense*
nose	earth	smell
tongue	water	taste
eye	light	color
skin	air	touch
ear	ether (*ākāśa*)	sound

The internal ordinary perceptions are the activities of the mind *(manas)* in contact with psychical processes such as desiring, striving, enjoying pleasure, feeling pain, and so on. The objects of internal perception are activities and aspects of the psychic being rather than activities and aspects of the external world. This distinction is the same as that made by Leibniz, namely, between perception (the inner state as representing outer things) and apperception (the inner state as reflectively aware of itself); for example, to perceive is to see a cow, but to apperceive is to be aware that one is perceiving a cow.

There are three types of extraordinary perceptions: (1) perception of classes *(sāmānya-lakṣaṇa,* (2) complication *(jñāna-lakṣaṇa),* and (3) intuitive yogic perception *(yogaja).* According to the first type of extraordinary perception, each perception is dual: the object perceived is perceived both as the particular object and as the class perceived in and through the particular object. Socrates is perceived both as Socrates-qua-Socrates and as Socrates-qua-man. This means that, according to the Naiyāyikas, all universals have members. Complication as a type of extraordinary perception refers to the association of senses so they become integral parts in a single perception. For example, a statement like "The grass looks soft" implies that seeing can give a touch sensation as well as a sight sensation. Visual perception and touch perception can be the activity of the same sense organ. Aristotle, making a similar observation, concluded that all sensation is the result of one sense, the *sensus communis.* Yogic perception refers to the claims of some holy men that they possess unusual perceptual powers not possessed by ordinary men. For example, a living Bengali yogi has contended that he, while in Calcutta, can see objects in New Delhi hundreds of miles away.[40]

Anumāna is the second way of knowing according to the Indian analysis. The term is commonly translated *inference,* and it is defined as "knowledge which is preceded by perception."[41] Inference is what one does with that which is presented to the mind by the various forms of perception. Three kinds are listed: (1) *a priori,* (2) *a posteriori,* and (3) "commonly seen."[42] The *a priori* form is discussed in terms of the five-part syllogism already considered in this chapter. The five parts are defined as follows:

1. The proposition. ". . . the declaration of what is to be established."[43]
2. The reason. ". . . the means for establishing what is to be established through the homogeneous or affirmative character of the example."[44]
3. The example ". . . a familiar instance which is known to possess the property to be established, and which implies that this property is invariably contained in the reason given."[45]
4. The application or "re-affirmation." ". . . that which, on the strength of the instance, re-asserts the subject as being 'so' . . . or, as being 'not so.'"[46]
5. The conclusion. ". . . the re-stating of the proposition, after the reason has been mentioned."[47]

Śaṅkara distinguished, as already noted, two levels of thought: *aparā vidyā* (lower knowledge) and *parā vidyā* (higher knowledge). The former uses a logic of relativism appropriate to the pluralities of human experience; the latter uses a logic of absolutism appropriate to Totality. *Parā vidyā* is a logic of negation, since no positive statements can be made about the unfathomable Brahman. This logic is commonly known as "four-cornered negation." According to the logic of negation the only way to make a statement about the Absolute is to deny the four possible affirmations: S is P, S is not P, S is both P and not P, and S is neither P nor not P. This form of logic, we ought to note, is not a denial of the three Laws of Thought, but a recognition that the Absolute cannot be known relatively. The Absolute is that which contradicts or negates all relativities.

The Naiyāyikas stress that repeated and varied observation *(bhūyo-darśana)* is needed in the inductive aspect of *anumāna* to ferret out hidden essential conditions. The "commonly seen" form of *anumāna* is an inference that goes beyond perception because of past perceptions; for example, when seeing a horned animal we may infer that it has a tail, not because we see the tail but because it is "commonly seen" that horned animals have tails.

Upamāna is "the knowledge of a thing through its similarity to another thing previously well known."[48] This principle of analogy was clearly understood by the Indian logicians, namely, if X is like Y with respect to A, then X is like Y with respect to B. Some tried to use *upamāna* in a manner very much like American pragmatism; for example, if the theory of medicine propounded by the sages of old is found to be true in practice, then the science of spiritual freedom propounded by them must also be true. Analogy was recognized as a probable rather than a certain way of knowing. It was not fully accepted even in the third century B.C. This we know from Gotama's own words: "*Upamāna*, some say, is not a means of right knowledge, as it cannot be established either through complete or considerable or partial similarity. This objection does not hold good, for *upamāna* is established through similarity to a high degree."[49] The questions of what "a high degree" means and who determines the degree remain unanswered.

Śabda is defined as "the instructive assertion of a reliable person."[50] Even though the word *śabda* may be translated as testimony or authority, the literal translation is "sound," and in this context it means the spoken words of wise men. The *śruti* (revelation) of the *Vedas* was the verbalizations of ancient seers. Remembered recitations of wisdom literature is highly prized today—even in Indian universities. We know that Gotama had Vedic authority in mind in his presentation of *śabda* as a means of acquiring knowledge because he states, "The *Veda*, some say, is unreliable, as it involves . . . the faults of untruth, contradiction, and tautology."[51] The "some" to whom he refers and whom he refutes were the Cārvāka philosophers, ancient materialists who were active as early as the fifth century B.C. Gotama counters that the "untruth" in the *Vedas* "comes from some defect in the act, operator or materials of sacrifice."[52] The "contradiction" can be explained by taking into account the time frame.[53] The "tautology" may be only a reiteration for emphasis.[54] The reliability of the *Vedas* is "the reliability of their authors."[55]

The force of conviction is located in the wisdom of the sage, not in a holy word. Later Indian philosophers offered four caveats in the understanding of authorities: (1) Watch out for the conventional uses of words. (2) Be careful in identifying duplicate meanings. (3) Observe when words are repeated for effect. (4) Be sure the intention of the author is understood.[56]

Indian society remains to this day a highly traditional society. The voice of Vedic authority is still heard in the land. A sympathetic Western critic warns that *śabda* must be renounced if modern Hindu intellectuals wish to claim to be philosophers: "The Indian theologian will have to renounce *śabda* if he wants to be a philosopher. If he cannot dispense with it, he will remain in the old chair, he will remain a theologian."[57] Some Indians who have acquired a Western education turn upon their traditional culture. For example, Ramakant A. Sinari has written the following: "Generally, Indians are one of the most metaphysical, ambiguous and fuzzy-headed species on earth. And, therefore, apart from the fact that this characteristic has been and still is the main hindrance in the part of their success in practical life, it has acted as a fuel for their spontaneous and emotive representations in transcendentalism, mysticism, aestheticism, literature and poetry. Ambiguity is an inseparable accompaniment of the inward-seeing consciousness."[58] Sinari's charge of Indian fuzzy-headedness is paralleled by E. A. Burtt's similar charge. But there is an important difference. Whereas the Indians are said to be loose thinkers because of their introversion, Westerns are charged with being wishful thinkers because of their efforts to defend orthodoxy and refute heresy. Burtt writes that in his opinion the West has "an especially difficult struggle throughout its history with fuzzy and wishful thinking, arising in large part from the dogmatic intolerance of the Western mind."[59]

6. *Knowledge According to Buddhist Philosophy*

Buddhism agrees with Hinduism that the central problem of man is *duḥkha*. The word probably comes from *du* (unpleasant) and *kha* (hole), and hence has the connotation of painful emptiness. In attempting to express its meaning in English, words such as *suffering, impermanence, transitoriness, ephemera, incompleteness, fragmentation, imperfection, turmoil,* and *frustration* are used. The human being is a finite entity with infinite aspirations, a being whose reach exceeds his grasp, an animal who would be a god. But Buddhism disagrees with Hinduism as to the cause and cure of *duḥkha*. Whereas Hinduism locates the origin in ignorance of one's nature and the therapy in gnostic wisdom, Buddhism locates the origin in cleaving desires and the therapy in a path leading to the cessation of cleaving. Hinduism redefines god. Buddhism redirects aspirations. Hinduism developed a philosophical tradition. Buddhism's tradition may be described as psychological, soteriological, and even medicinal.

Edward Conze warns against a philosophical Buddhism: "Philosophy, as we understand it in Europe, is a creation of the Greeks. It is unknown to Buddhist tradition, which would regard the enquiry into reality, for the mere purpose of knowing more about it, as a waste of valuable time. The Buddha's teaching is exclusively concerned with showing the way to salvation. Any 'philosophy' there may be in the works of Buddhist authors is quite incidental. In the ample vocabulary of Buddhism we find no word to correspond to our term 'philosophy' . . . Buddhism as a 'philosophy' could . . . be described as a 'dialectical pragmatism' with a 'psychological' turn."[60] Yet two historical facts caused Buddhism to become a philosophy. One was the efforts of the Buddhists to propagate the doctrine. As Conze himself states, "A soteriological doctrine like Buddhism becomes a 'philosophy' when its intellectual content is explained to outsiders."[61] The other was that in order to survive in India the early Buddhists refuted the philosophical claims of Hinduism and in the process became philosophical themselves. Buddhists in later centuries offered interesting explanations for early philosophizing—even for the philosophizing of Gautama the Buddha. The defense was that philosophy consists of unreal and arbitrary conceptions which, after serving their function as techniques of liberation, are to be eliminated. "While the Tathāgata [honorific title for the Buddha], in his teaching, constantly makes use of conceptions and ideas about them, disciples should keep in mind the unreality of all such conceptions and ideas. They should recall that the Tathāgata, in making use of them in explaining the Dharma always uses them in the resemblance of a raft that is of use only to cross a river. As the raft is of no further use after the river is crossed, it should be discarded. So these arbitrary conceptions of things and about things should be wholly given up as one attains enlightenment."[62]

The pursuit of knowledge was believed to delay the attainment of salvation. For example, "When Ananda came into the presence of the Lord Buddha, he bowed down to the ground in great humility, blaming himself that he had not fully developed the potentialities of Enlightenment, because from the beginning of his previous lives, he had too much devoted himself to study and learning."[63] The indictment was that an essential ingredient of Enlightenment is spontaneity of mind, and learning mitigates spontaneity: "Ananda, if you are now desirous of more perfectly understanding Supreme Enlightenment and the enlightening nature of pure Mind-Essence, you must learn to answer questions spontaneously with no recourse to discriminating thinking."[64]

A fundamental Buddhist evaluation of knowledge is found in the *Laṅkavatāra Sūtra,* a work written in India that became important in the development of Ch'an Buddhism in China and Zen Buddhism in Japan. In this *sūtra* eight kinds of consciousness *(vijñāna)* are identified. The five sense and the awareness that one is sensing constitute the six sense-consciousnesses. They are the ways of contact with individual objects of the external world. At the extreme pole from sense-consciousnesses is universal-consciousness *(ālaya-vijñāna)*, also known as store-consciousness, foundation-consciousness, abiding-consciousness, and universal mind. According to the *Laṅkavatāra Sūtra* "*Ālaya-vijñāna* transcends all individuation and limits. *Ālaya-vijñāna* is thoroughly pure in its essential nature, subsisting unchanged and free from faults of impermanence, undisturbed by egoisms, unruffled by distinctions, desires, and aversions. *Ālaya-vijñāna* is like a great ocean, its surface ruffled by waves and surges but its depths remaining forever unmoved."[65] *Ālaya-vijñāna* is the inactive storehouse of experience—"the storage and clearing house of all the accumulated products of mentation and action since beginningless time."[66] It is "a permanent substratum of awareness." [67] In Buddhist metaphysics it is not a substance, but the resultant of actions. In Buddhist soteriology it is the *tathāgata-garbha*, the womb within which the Buddha is conceived, nourished, and matured. Between sense-consciousness and store-consciousnesses is *manovijñāna* (intermediate-consciousness, discriminating-consciousness, defiled-consciousness). *Manovijñāna* denotes the linking of sense-experience contributed by the senses and universal concepts contributed by *ālaya-vijñāna*. In the pictorial language of the *Laṅkavatāra Sūtra* the senses are described as "a dancer and a magician with the objective world as its stage." The intermediate-consciousness is "the wise jester who travels with the magician and reflects upon his emptiness and transciency." The store-consciousness "keeps the records and knows what must be and what may be."[68]

Buddhists have for the most part been spared one epistemological problem that plagues India and the West. This is the problem of religious authoritarianism. The Christian Bible, the Hebrew *Torah*, the Muslim *Koran*, and the Hindu *Vedas* and *Upaniṣads* have been—and in some cases still are—regarded as infallible sources of knowledge. Buddhists, by not having an authoritative scripture, have escaped the revolts against revealed truths and the heresy hunts that have marked and marred other cultures. Buddhists have generally been tolerant of other points of view. As Suzuki says ". . . wherever transplanted it [Buddhism] has allowed itself to establish a harmonious relationship with its new surroundings—moral, intellecutal, and spiritual. It has never been aggressive, nor arrogant, it has always been in readiness to propose new theories if neceesary to accommodate the old native beliefs already firmly established. Those who have come under the influence of Buddhism, therefore, always try to practice this spirit of generosity and of universal kindness even towards enemies."[69] E. A. Burtt praises the East, and especially Buddhism, for being "committed to the tolerant and generous principle that all sincerely championed viewpoints express some truth."[70] However, exceptions to the principle of tolerance can be found. One is the following statement of a Mahāyāna holy man, the Bhikshu Sangharakshita, made at the Indian Institute of World Culture in July 1954. The quotation is especially interesting since, in accusing the Theravādins of taking an attitude of scriptural infallibility toward the *Tripiṭaka,* the Bhikshu intimated a latent quarrel between the two forms of Buddhism. His words were: "Theravāda Buddhism on the whole resembles the tombs of the Egyptian kings; faithfully embalming against decay the outward forms of spiritual life, it has not succeeded in preserving that life itself; its boasted immutability is the settled and frozen immutability of death.... As for the modern Theravādins, their attitude is even more unintelligently conservative than was that of their forebears. Not only do they believe, in the face of even canonical evidence to the contrary, that every word of the Pali *Tripiṭaka* was uttered just as it stands today, by the Enlightened One Himself, but they vehemently insist that their form of Buddhism alone is orthodox, and that all other schools,—which nowadays they never study,—are corruptions and degenerations of the original Teaching.... Only an influx of Mahāyāna Buddhism as a living spiritual force will save the Theravāda countries from the stereotyped scholasticism that now passes for Doctrine and the rigid formalism that has taken the place of Method, and enable them fully to appreciate the real significance and true value even of their own tradition.... The Theravāda may be regarded as a quiet but stagnant backwater."[71] These uncharitable remarks might be accounted for by noting that the author is an English convert to Buddhism. Antagonistic arguing, name-calling, and belittling deface the history of Western philosophy and theology. A typical Eastern attitude was expressed by a Japanese Buddhist delegate at the close of the second East-West Philosophers' Conference (1949) at the University of Hawaii when he confessed that he did not know there were two forms of Buddhism before coming to the conference.

The wisdom loved and sought in Buddhism is *prajñā* (intuitive wisdom). This wisdom, rather than putting the world into categories to be understood by the knower, advances the knower on the *nirvāṇa* path of freedom from *duḥkha*. There are two ways of attaining this result. One is the way of intellectual analysis and clarification. This is the way of defining, analyzing, and classifying the *dharmas* (factors of existence). This way is known as the path of *abhidharma* (supplementary doctrine). The term comes from a collection of basic texts written in India before Buddhism began its pilgrimage to Eastern Asia. The total collection of writings is called the *Tripiṭaka* (Three Baskets). The three *Piṭakas* are the *Vinaya,* the *Sūtra,* and the *Abhidharma.* The *Vinaya* contains the canon law, with many details regulating life in the monasteries. The *Sūtra* contains discourses on doctrine directed chiefly to the laity. The *Abhidharma* deals with the same topics but in a more scholarly manner. Four methods are utilized in the *Abhidharma:* (1) analysis of words and meaning, (2) analysis of the theory of causation, (3) analysis of language and grammatical constructions, and (4) analysis of knowing from points of view both psychological and epistemological. This is indeed the way of intellectual analysis and clarification, but the way is followed in order to reach a state transcending analysis and clarification. The *Abhidharma* way is not pursued to attain knowledge. Its negative purpose is to eliminate illusions masquerading as knowledge. Its positive purposes is to assist in the struggle for release from attachment to apparent reality as each works out his own salvation and attains Buddahood. Knowledge is the raft to be abandoned upon reaching the other shore.

The other way is the way of contemplation *(dhyāna)*. *Dhyāna* repudiates and rejects the *abhidharma* way. "By merely listening to it, thinking of it, and intellectually understanding it, you will never come to the realization of any truth," declares the *Avataṁsaka Sūtra*.[72] The basic reality, according to Buddhist metaphysics, is *śūnyatā* (void or emptiness), and this can be understood only when the knower transcends the dualisms of subject-object, seer-seen, and knower-known. Buddhist intuition "has no words to express itself, no methods to reason itself out, no extended demonstrations of its own truth in logically convincing manner. If it expresses itself at all, it does so in symbols and images, and these are most puzzling to those who have not been initiated into them."[73] Intuition as interpreted by the Buddhists "requires pointers more than ideas to express itself, and these pointers are enigmatic and non-rational. They are shy of intellectual interpretation. They have a decided aversion towards circumlocution. They do not repeat, and brevity is their essence. They are like flashes of lightning. While your eyes blink, they are gone."[74] This way to *prajñā* is presented in a huge body of writings, dated between 100 B.C. and A.D. 1200, known as the *Prajñāpāramitā Sūtras* (Discourses on the Perfection of Wisdom). They are preserved in Sanskrit, Chinese, and Tibetan. Acccording to these discourses the wisdom that the *Abhidharma Sūtras* present as the rise and disappearance of *dharmas* is not a way to attain *nirvāna*. Perfect wisdom is the knowledge that there is no knowledge. Reality is *śūnyatā* (emptiness), and the proper expression of reality is silence. The *Prajñāpāramitā* does not make its case by reasoned arguments but by dogmatic affirmations. The *dharmas* are said to be empty, nonexistent, isolated, unrealm, unborn, illusory, nonproductive, without marks, and mere words. Paradoxical statements are offered to demonstrate that what is true from one standpoint is false from another. Thus arose what came to be known within Buddhism as "the two-truth theory." There are conventional or mundane truths adequate for practical living, and there are absolute or ultimate truths that lead to release from *duḥkha*. While Buddhism does not denigrate the role of sensation and conceptualization as ways to understand the physical universe—there is no conflict between science and religion in Buddhism—it does deny that empirical and rational forms of knowing are instrumental for human existential enlightenment. This is especially the case for Ch'an Buddhism, which began in China under the tutelage of Bodhidharma about A.D. 500. Ch'an was brought to Japan in the thirteenth century by Eisai and Dogen, where it was developed further and where it acquired a new name—Zen.[75] The opposition of Zen to discursive reason and verbal expression as techniques of Enlightenment may go back to an occasion in which Siddhartha Gautama stood before a gathering of monks and silently held a flower in his hand. This intuitive experience is known in Buddhism as *prajñā*. It leads to Enlightenment (*sambodhi* or *abhisamaya* in Sanskrit, *wu* in Chinese, *satori* in Japanese), a state described by the *Laṅkavatāra Sūtra* as "the state of consciousness in which Noble Wisdom realises its own inner nature,"[76] and by Chang Chen-Chi as "the transcendental experience of realizing universal Reality."[77]

The two-truth theory and practice in Buddhism have been carefully and fully presented by D. T. Suzuki in an article entitled "Reason and Intuition in Buddhist Philosophy."[78] "For 'intuition,' Buddhists generally use '*prajñā*' and for reason or discursive understanding, '*vijñāna*.'"[79] Suzuki's essay is a detailed listing of the relationship between *prajñā* and *vijñāna*, which in typical Zen manner he described as "contrasted,"[80] "diametrically opposed,"[81] "*prajñā* goes beyond *vijñāna*,"[82] "*vijñāna* is evolved out of *prajñā*,"[83] and "*prajñā* is *vijñāna* and *vijñāna* is *prajñā*."[84] We can gather from this that, whereas *prajñā* and *vijñāna* are contrasted when intellectually analyzed, they are an integral part of the total environment within which human beings exist. Thinking is within the context of living. To understand *prajñā* and *vijñāna* they must be contrasted despite the fact that existentially they are not contrasted. The highlights of the contrasts Suzuki describes can be indicated in two parallel columns that are either Suzuki's own words or paraphrases of them:

prajñā	*vijñāna*
Not based on senses and intellect.	Based on senses and intellect.
No opposition of subject and object.	Opposition of subject and object.
Self-knowledge of the whole.	Busies itself with parts.
An integrating principle.	Always analyzes.
A unifying principle.	A dividing principle.
Makes disconnected parts coherent, articulate, and significant.	Sees only disconnected parts.
A principle of wholeness.	A principle of differentiation.
Pure act, pure experience, intuitive act.	Uses intervening propositions.
Deliberation is absent.	Deliberation is present.

Has no definable object.	Has a definable object.
Goes beyond affirmation and negation.	Either affirms or denies.
Overrides definitions.	Wants everything clear-cut and well-defined.
Rejects principle of bifurcation.	Based on principle of bifurcation.
Deals with some things deeper than the world of relativities.	Deals with world of relativities.
A principle of immediacy.	A principle of conceptualization.
Makes paradoxical statements	Limited to intellectual statements.
Reality becoming self-conscious.	A way of talking about reality.
Has no methodology.	Has a methodology.
Unpredictable.	Predictable.
Does not elaborate.	Wordy.
Abhors abstractions.	Engages in abstractions.
Dynamic.	Passive.
Annihilates space and time.	Operates in space and time.
The activity itself.	A state of passivity.

The most controversial aspect of Buddhist *prajñā* is not listed above because it merits careful attention. This is its violation of the three Laws of Thought, which, as already noted, are almost deified in the West by the use of upper-case initial letters. A few quotations from Suzuki will indicate the seriousness of the Buddhist position: "Paradoxical statements are therefore characteristic of *prajñā*-intuition. As it transcends *vijñāna* or logic it does not mind contradicting itself; it knows that a contradiction is the outcome of differentiation, which is the work of *vijñāna*. *Prajñā* negates what it asserted before, and conversely; it has its own way of dealing with this world of dualities. The flower is red and not-red; the bridge flows and not the river; the wooden horse neighs; the stone maiden dances."[85] "When, therefore, *prajñā* violently breaks all the rules of ratiocination, we must take it as giving the intellect a sign of grave danger. When *vijñāna* sees this, *vijñāna* ought to heed it and try to examine itself thoroughly. It ought not go on with its 'rationalistic' way."[86] " 'A is not-A and therefore A is A.' This is the 'logic' of *prajñā*-intuition."[87] "Let me give a bit of logic here, hoping it will help clarify the nature of *prajñā* in this field. When we say that 'A is A' and that this law of identity is fundamental, we forget that there is a living synthesizing activity whereby the subject 'A' is linked to the object 'A.' It is *vijñāna* that analyzes the one 'A' into the subject 'A' and the object 'A'; and without *prajñā* this bifurcation cannot be replaced by the original unity or identity; without *prajñā* the divided 'A' remains isolated; however much the subject may desire to be united with the object, the desire can never be fulfilled without *prajñā*.

It is *prajñā*, indeed, that makes the law of identity work as an established self-evident truth requiring no objective evidence. The foundation of our thinking thus owes its functioning to *prajñā*. Buddhist philosophy is a system of the self-evolving and self-identifying *prajñā*."[88]

What is the point in rejecting the three Laws of Thought—and specifically, the law of noncontradiction? Aristotle said that if anyone claims that he rejects the law of noncontradiction, ask him to say something. If he says nothing, he is no better than a "vegetable."[89] If he says that something either is or is not, ask him to say something significant.[90] If he says, "I am a man," remind him that he is assuming the law of noncontradiction; for in affirming he is a man he is denying that he is a not-man. It is not possible to be a man and a not-man at the same time. Aristotle adds that "the point in question is not this, whether the same thing can at the same time be and not be a man in name, but whether it can in fact. Now if 'man' and 'not-man' mean nothing different, obviously 'not being a man' will mean nothing different from 'being a man'; so that 'being a man' will be 'not being a man'; for they will be one."[91] In other words, for Aristotle the Laws of Thought follow the nature of things. Things are not self-contradictory. Speaking and thinking are rooted in the laws of being.

This is exactly why the Zen Buddhist rejects the law of logical contradiction. He—contrary to Aristotle—believes that reality is self-contradictory. He can point to contradictory experiences; for example, love and hate on the surface seem to be impossible, but the only person one can really hate is the person one loves. Oxymorons are not unknown to western people, for example, *festina lente* (make haste slowly), "cruel kindness," "laborious idleness," "living death," "bittersweet experience," and "youthful age." Western psychologists sometimes describe behavior in which one person tries to manipulate another by refusing to cooperate as passive-aggressive behavior; Western botanists classify sycamore, poplar, and gum trees as soft hardwoods; and students of the American Indians describe a certain type of arrowhead as having an unfluted point. Oxymorons are common in Indian culture; for example, *bindu* means an inaudible sound. Indian philosophers often used oxymorons. For example, Śaṅkara in his commentary on *Vedānta Sūtra* II. i. 14 referred to "the whole real-unreal course of ordinary life," Āśmarathya taught a doctrine known as *bhedābhedavāda* (difference-nondifference), and Nimbarka's form of Vedānta is known as Dvaita-Advaita (dualistic-nondualism). Zen Buddhists have added a new and highly suggestive oxymoron when they say that to bring about *satori* the Zen master tries to create a "planned accident." Suzuki says that in Zen "A is not-A and therefore A is A."[92]

The universe itself is a great living, threatening *koan* [puzzle that has no rational solution] challenging a solution. The literature of Zen is filled with *koans* designed to shake the mind from its rational moorings. One of the best known is in the sermon of Basho, a ninth-century Korean monk: "If you have a staff, I will give you one; if you have none, I will take it away from you." Another is a poem by Fu Ta-shih, a Chinese monk of the sixth century:

> Empty-handed I go and yet the spade is in my hands;
> I walk on foot, and yet on the back of an ox I am riding:
> When I pass over the bridge,
> Lo, the water floweth not, but the bridge doth flow.

The intent is to escape being caught in the four possible propositions—"It is A," "It is not-A," "It is both A and not-A," and "It is neither A nor not-A"—through a denial of all four. To do this is to attain the state known as "no mind" *(wu hsin)*.

This is illustrated in a Zen story of a university professor who visited a Zen master to learn about Zen. When the master served tea, he filled the cup held by the professor and continued to pour. "Stop!" said the professor. "The cup is full. No more will go in." "Yes," replied the master. "You are full of your own opinions. How can I show you Zen unless you first empty your cup?" When one reaches the state of *wu hsin,* one will see that in the reality that is *śūnyatā* the statement "A is A and A is not-A" is true and the statement "A is A and A is not-A" is false. Suzuki's essay on *prajñā* and *vijñāna* is itself a very clever demonstration of the Zen method of pedagogy that is easily missed by the reader. In the second line of the article he states, "*Vijñāna* and *prajñā* are always contrasted."[93] A few pages later he observes that *"prajñā* is *vijñāna* and *vijñāna* is *prajñā."*[94] Anyone trained in the logic of the Laws of Thought must caution, "You can't have it both ways." But Suzuki, knowing what would be the reaction of his readers, added at once ". . . only this is to be 'immediately' apprehended and not after a tedious and elaborate and complicated process of dialectic,"[95] and still later he writes, "From *vijñāna*-thinking to *prajñā*-thinking there is no mediating concept, no room for intellection, no time for deliberation. So, the Buddhist master urges us to 'speak, quick, quick!' Immediacy, no interpretation, no explanatory apology—this is what constitutes *prajñā*-intuition."[96] Immanuel Kant set for himself the task of writing a metaphysic of *Reinen Vernunft* (Pure Reason), one which, soaring above the differences of cultural assumptions, prejudices, and methodologies, would be a theory of reality acceptable to pure rationalities whenever and wherever they are. To this Zen replies, "Very well. But when and where do you find these purely rational beings?"

It is not surprising that Zen Buddhists, having rejected reason as a principle of existence, also reject reason as a method to convince rational minds of the reasonableness of irrationality. In the eighth century Ma-tzu began to answer student questions by shouts and blows. In addition there has been treasured by the Zen masters a collection of hundreds of *koans,* for example, "What is the sound of one hand clapping?" and *mondos* (questions with meaningless answers), for example, "What is the fundamental teaching of the Buddha?" Answer: "There is enough breeze in this fan to keep me cool."

What should be the reaction of Western philosophers to the Eastern approach to the problems of knowledge? How can Western minds respond best to the Eastern view that knowledge is enlightenment rather than power to conquer and control the external environment? Should they write off the Hindu and Buddhist views as the products of minds not yet full exposed to the scientific revolutions? Should they shake their heads in puzzlement at the inscrutable East? Should they try to convert Eastern minds to the Western modes of thinking? Should they seriously examine the Eastern epistemologies and reform Western epistemologies where that seems advisable? One Western logician and philosopher of science who has carefully and sympathetically examined Indian and Buddhist modes of knowing has reminded his fellow western philosophers that "to the Eastern thinker a proposition or statement is not an objectivity entity, capable of being isolated from its living context and having properties by itself, as it is to a Western logician. It is something asserted by a human being, in some situation, for some purpose; it is an epistemic act, filling its role in a sequence or pattern of acts which he is performing in relation to certain objects and events. It must be understood therefore, in that setting. This means, among other things, that logical relationships are not examined in the purely implicative connections which they have with each other; no mathematical science of logical form as such seems to the typical Indian mind to serve any useful end. Even the most general principles of inference are considered in the context of their function in the search for knowledge or insight about man and his world."[97]

4
The Human Being as Self-Knower

Historians of philosophy assume that Western philosophy began when three Ionic Greeks in the sixth century B.C.—Thales, Anaximander, and Anaximenes—abandoning both the mythological explanations of natural phenomena and the popular view that all things are the mixture of earth, air, fire, and water, speculated that there is a single primordial substance, which is pluralized by natural causes to become the myriad objects of the natural world. Philosophy began as cosmogony. But within a generation it turned inward.

1. Philosophy as Self-Knowledge

Pythagoras (d. ca. 510 B.C.) was not only the Greek who created the word *philosophy*, but was also the one who changed the focus of philosophy from external reality to the self. He, holding that all living beings are akin, taught that the human soul can migrate into any of the manifold forms of life. Diogenes Laertius reported, "Once they say that he [Pythagoras] was passing by when a puppy was being whipped, and he took pity and said, 'Stop, do not beat it; for it is the soul of a friend that I recognized when I heard it giving tongue.'"[1] Pythagoras formulated a long list of abstinences and prohibitions to determine a desirable reincarnation: "Never approach butchers and huntsmen." "Do not eat living things—including beans." "Sacrifice only inanimate things." "Turn aside from highways and walk only on footpaths." "When you put on your shoes, start with the right foot; when washing your feet, start with the left foot."

Heraclitus, the second inward-directed philosopher, summed up his philosophy in one sentence: "I sought for myself." The similarity of this to the Delphic maxim "Know thyself" is obvious. But in Heraclitus self-knowing had a deeper meaning, since for him self-knowing is rooted in physical theories. All things happen according to the Logos, the formula of cosmic arrangement. Man's life is fused with the total environment. Wisdom consists in understanding this pattern and living harmoniously with it. In wisdom the active and fiery part of the soul makes contact with and becomes identified with the universal Logos. The individual becomes aware that all things are one. Sleep is a medial state between life and death in which man is sundered from his essential kinship with his natural surroundings. In sleep man is temporarily cut off from the Logos. Sextus Empiricus wrote that according to Heraclitus we become intelligent by drawing in this divine reason [logos] through breathing, and forgetful when asleep; but we regain our senses when we wake up again. "For in sleep, when the channels of perception are shut, our mind is sundered from its kinship with the surrounding, and breathing is the only point of attachment to be preserved, like a kind of root; being sundered, our mind casts off its former power of memory. But in the waking state it again peeps out through the channels of perception as though through a kind of window, and meeting with the surroundings it puts on its power of reason."[2] Euripides longed for a self that could know the self: "If I could only find another me to look me in the face and see my tears and all that I am suffering!"[3] Hindu philosophers by an alternative reasoning concluded that in *turīya*, a condition of pure intuitional consciousness that is described as beyond dreamless sleep and as a pure-objectless-knowing subjective condition, man becomes aware of his identity with all reality.

Socrates in autobiographical remarks confessed, "When I was a young man . . . I was most amazingly interested in the lore which they call natural philosophy. For I thought it magnificent to know the causes of everything, why it comes into being and why it is destroyed and why it exists; I kept turning myself upside down to consider things like the following: Is it when hot and cold get some fermentation in them, as some said, that living things are bred? Is it the blood by which we think, or air, or fire; or whether, it is none of these, but the brain is what provides the senses of hearing and sight and smell, and from these arise memory and opinion, and from memory and opinion in tranquility comes knowledge; again I considered the destructions of these things, and what happens about heaven and earth."[4] Socrates said he came to fear that by the study of natural phenomena he would lose "the eye of the soul" as those become blind who gaze long at an eclipse of the sun. He confessed that although natural science is "the invention of clever, industrious people," he had no time for the study: "I can't as yet 'know myself,' as the inscription at Delphi enjoins, and so long as that ignorance remains it seems to me ridiculous to inquire into extraneous matters. Consequently I don't bother about such things, but accept the current beliefs about them, and direct my inquiries, as I have just said, rather to myself, to discover whether I really am a more complex creature and more puffed up with pride than Typhon, or a simpler, gentler being whom heaven has blessed with a quiet, un-Typhonic nature."[5] Thus for Socrates "Know thyself" was a directive to become familiar with the goals of one's life rather than a command to seek out the metaphysical structure of the self. Values, not natures, were his quest. Plato and Aristotle disagreed with Socrates, holding that values are unreliable unless founded on realities.

Śaṅkara, who is generally regarded as India's greatest philosopher, described the life of man as a pilgrimage to his own self. The search, however, he said, is like searching for a necklace that the seeker is wearing on his neck. The science of the self *(adhātma śāstra)* is one of the common descriptions of the philosophy of India. A. C. Mukerji has written, "It is but common knowledge that the solution of the supreme problem in ancient India as well as Greece in the form of a command, namely, Know Thyself, was generally regarded as the *raison d'être* of philosophy."[6] N. C. Das, a philosopher from the University of Rangoon, said in a seminar on 8 September 1957, "The philosophic attempt to determine the nature of reality may start either from the thinking self or the objects of knowledge. In India the interest of philosophy is in the self or man—*Atmanam Viddhi*, i.e., 'Know thyself,' sums up the law and the prophets." Max Müller wrote that "in that study of ourselves, of our true selves, India occupies a place second to no other country."[7]

In China also philosophy began as self-examination. Confucius praised Tseng Ts'an for having said "Daily I examine myself."[8] Confucius advised, "When you see a man of the highest caliber, give thought to attain his stature. When you see one who is not, go home and conduct a self-examination."[9] Lao Tzu praised the knowledge of others, but reserved a higher encomium for knowledge of one's self:

> He who knows others is wise;
> He who knows himself is enlightened.[10]

The first business of philosophy in the East has always been "to train the inner consciousness so as to enable us to have an immediate perception of the self."[11]

Concern about the reality and nature of the self marked the opening of each of the major chronological divisions of Western philosophy. The ancient period began in earnest with Socrates' "Know yourself." The medieval period began with Augustine's cry "A question have I become for myself." The modern period began with Descartes' *Cogito ergo sum* (I think, therefore I am) and reached its zenith with Kant, who, adopting as his personal motto "Know thyself," concluded that the business of philosophy is to answer three questions: (1) What can I do? (2) What can I know? (3) What can I hope? Plato studied the self to help understand the city-state. Aristotle examined the self because, as he wrote, the study "contributes greatly to the advance of truth in general, and, above all, to our understanding of Nature."[12] Kant said of his *Critique of Pure Reason,* "It is a call to reason to undertake anew the most difficult of all its tasks, namely, that of self-knowledge."[13] Ernst Cassirer has written, "That self-knowledge is the highest aim of philosophical inquiry appears to be generally acknowledged. In all the conflicts between the different philosophical schools this objective remained invariable and unshaken: it proved to be the Archimedean point, the fixed and immovable center, of all thought."[14] The acknowledgment has not always resulted in action. Although the self has not been neglected in the West, there has been a tendency for philosophers, seduced by the success of the natural sciences, to become more occupied with the quest for knowledge of the external world than for knowledge of the self.

"Who am I?" and "What is man?" are related questions. "What is man?" is a scientific question asking about the relation of the human species to the inorganic world, to the world of plants and animals, and even to any higher beings that might exist. An instance of such a question is the psalmist's "What is man, that thou art mindful of him?"[15] "Who am I?" includes "What is the human being?" But in addition, "Who am I?" locates the individual person in the total environment of realities and values. Self-knowledge seeks both information about the human species and insight into the unique individual who asks the question.

One of the most illuminative quests for self-knowledge in the literature of Western philosophy was that of Descartes. He accepted the notion of a dual world of visible and invisible. His brief life was a bridge between the Middle and the Modern Ages. He wanted Scholastic certainty, but he could not accept scholastic methods. He wrote in his *Meditations,* "I know that I exist and that I am seeking to discover what I am, that 'I' that I know to be."[16] He meditated upon what he believed before beginning his pilgrimage of self-discovery: "What then have I previously believed myself to be? Clearly, I believed that I was a man. . . . I thought of myself first as having a face, hands, arms, and all this mechanism composed of [bone and flesh] (and members), just as it appears in a corpse, and which I designated by the name of 'body.' In addition, I thought of the fact that I consumed nourishment, that I walked, that I perceived and thought, and I ascribed all these actions to the soul."[17] But it is not a unique characteristic of man to consume nourishment and to walk, continued Descartes. Man knows he exists when not eating and walking, so these activities cannot be essential to his existence as a self. Then it occurred to Descartes that thinking is different: "Thought is an attribute that belongs to me; it alone is inseparable from my nature. I am, I exist—that is certain; but for how long do I exist? For as long as I think; for it might perhaps happen, if I totally ceased thinking, that I would at the same time completely cease to be. . . . I am therefore, to speak precisely, only a thinking being, that is to say, a mind, an understanding, or a reasoning being."[18] "I am not this assemblage of members which is called a human body; I am not a rarefied and penetrating air spread throughout all these members; I am not a wind, [a flame,] a breath, a vapor, or anything at all that I can imagine and picture to myself."[19] What is a thinking being?, asked Descartes. He answered, "It is a being which doubts, which understands, [which conceives,] which affirms, which denies, which wills, which rejects, which imagines also, and which perceives."[20] At this point Descartes reflected that even though he had established the reality of the self as mind, he could not eliminate from his thoughts that the body, and other corporeal things, are more distinctly known than the mind, "that indescribable part of myself which cannot be pictured by the imagination."[21] He took as an example a bit of wax that undergoes changes in taste, odor, color, shape, size, solidity, temperature, and so forth, as the wax is placed close to a fire. One's eyes suggest that there has been a complete change; there is no identity that refers both to the original bit of wax and to the stuff now by the fire, but the mind supports the terms of ordinary language that there is a sameness between the two phenomena. Perception is "solely an inspection by the mind."[22] All things external to the mind—wax, the physical world, and our own bodies—"are not properly known by the senses nor by the faculty of imagination, but by the understanding alone; and since they are not known in so far as they are seen or touched, but only in so far as they are understood by thinking, I see clearly that there is nothing easier for me to understand than my mind."[23]

In his next two meditations Descartes established the existence of God, and argued that God is the guarantor of the truth of the mind's ideas. God will not allow the human mind to have clear and distinct ideas that are untrue. Descartes, therefore, in his sixth and last meditation concluded that he and all mankind are not deceived in thinking "I have a body." The words are important: "I have a body," that is, "I *possess* a body," not "I *am* a body." He added, "I am not only residing in my body, as a pilot in his ship, but furthermore . . . I am intimately connected with it, and . . . [the mixture is] so blended (as it were) that [something like] a single whole is produced."[24] The body-ship analogy is later changed to body-machine: "the human body may be considered as a machine."[25] The difference between mind and body is that the former is "completely indivisible" and the latter "always divisible."[26] The mind as immaterial substance receives impressions "only from the brain, or perhaps even from one of its smallest parts—the one, namely, where the senses in common have their seat."[27] (Descartes was probably referring to the pineal gland.) He closed his meditations with an amazingly arrogant divine imprimatur: "For, from the fact that God is not a deceiver, it necessarily follows that in this matter I am not deceived."[28]

The modern period in Western philosophy came to an end when the World Wars of 1914–18 and 1941–45 brought about changes yet to be assimilated into human life and thought. For want of a better term the period since 1914 has sometimes been called "The Post-Modern Age." In the 1950s the New American Library published six volumes on Western philosophy titled *The Age of Belief* (medieval period), *The Age of Adventure* (Renaissance), *The Age of Reason* (seventeenth century), *The Age of Enlightenment* (eighteenth century), *The Age of Ideology* (nineteenth century), and *The Age of Analysis* (twentieth century). Perhaps a second volume is needed for the twentieth century, with the title *The Age of Anxiety*. Western man began to be aware of the fulfillment of the prophecies of the decline and fall of the West in the writings of Henry Adams, Oswald Spengler, Pitirim Sorokin, Arnold Toynbee, and Albert Schweitzer. The change has become particularly apparent in America with the closing of the frontier. Self-doubt displaces self-confidence. Anxiety displaces optimism. But not all is loss. As Rollo May says, "One of the few blessings of living in an age of anxiety is that we are forced to become aware of ourselves. When our society, in its time of upheaval in standards and values, can give us no clear picture of 'what we are and what we ought to be,' as Matthew Arnold put it, we are thrown back on the search for ourselves."[29] Emptiness and loneliness, adds May, are the two chief characteristics of people living in this age. Some Western scientists now realize the folly of knowing the external world while being ignorant of the self. For example, Erwin Schrödinger has stated, "It seems plain and self-evident, yet it needs to be said: the isolated knowledge obtained by a group of specialists in a narrow field has in itself no value whatsoever, but only in its synthesis with all the rest of knowledge and only inasmuch as it really contributes in this synthesis something toward answering the demand . . .' Who are we?'"[30] When contemporary man turns to Western philosophers for assistance in finding himself in this age of anxiety, he finds that most philosophers are either analysts or existentialists. According to the analytic philosophers clarification is the task of philosophy. The self is no problem. It is a meaningless reification. Moritz Schlick, the founder of logical positivism wrote, "Primitive experience, mere existence of ordered data, does not presuppose a 'subject,' or 'ego,' or 'Me,' or 'mind.'"[31] According to the existentialists the self is an objective reality. In the words of Jean-Paul Sartre, ". . .the ego is neither formally nor materially *in* consciousness; it is outside, *in the world*. It is a being of the world, like the ego of another."[32] The four periods of Western philosophy—ancient, medieval, modern, and contemporary—mark a movement from self-confidence to self-denial and/or self-questioning. Socrates advised men to examine the self; Augustine was distressed by inner conflicts; Descartes attempted to prove the reality of the self; Schlick denied the self as object; and Sartre denied the self as subject.

The quest for knowledge in the sciences was much the same. Astronomy, physiology, chemistry, geology, physics, and biology developed as separate branches of learning centuries before psychology became a separate science.

"We have gained the mastery of almost everything which exists on the surface of the earth, excepting ourselves," wrote Alexis Carrel in 1935.[33] He added, "The knowledge of ourselves will never attain the elegant simplicity, the abstractness, and the beauty of physics. The factors that have retarded its development are not likely to vanish. We must realize clearly that the science of man is the most difficult of all sciences. . . . Since the natural conditions of existence have been destroyed by modern civilization, the science of man has become the most necessary of all sciences."[34] The first man to walk on the moon characterized it as "a giant step" for humanity. It is time to make another "giant step"—a return to "Who am I?" The English astronomer A. S. Eddington wrote in 1920, "We have found a strange footprint on the shores of the unknown. We have devised profound theories, one after another, to account for its origin. At last, we have succeeded in reconstructing the creature that made the footprint. And Lo! It is our own."[35] But Eddington was far ahead of—or out of step with—his time. The West is still more interested in what it sees through the telescope than in the consciousness that designs the telescope and interprets what is seen through the telescope.

2. The Difficulty of Self-Knowledge

"How many different shades of meaning there are . . . in the famous 'Know thyself'! For Socrates, self-knowledge signifies dialectical examination and testing one's own opinions; for St. Augustine, it is a means of attaining knowledge of God by the image of the Trinity, which we find in ourselves; for Descartes, it is a kind of apprenticeship in certainty; in the Upanishads of India, it is knowledge of the identity of the self and the universal principle."[36] A basic problem in self-knowing is confusing the ontological quest and the axiological quest. The questions "What is the denotation and what are the designations of the word *I*?" are easily confused with the question "What are the values determining and controlling my life?" But both questions—"Who am I?" and "What should I value?"—are significant only when they are preceded by the existential realization "I am lost." José Ortega y Gasset warned, "He who does not really feel himself lost, is lost without remission; that is to say, he never finds himself, never comes up against his own reality."[37]

The difficulty of knowing the nature of the self is a common lament in both East and West. According to the *Pañchatāntra,* a collection of ancient Indian folk stories, "To know one's self is hard."[38] "I go perplexed, and bound in mind," adds one of the seers of the *Ṛg Veda.*[39] According to Aristotle, "The knowledge of the soul admittedly contributes greatly to the advance of truth in general,"[40] yet "To attain any assured knowledge about the soul is one of the most difficult things in the world."[41] Descartes held a contrary view. He titled the second meditation in his *Meditations on the First Philosophy:* "Of the Nature of the Human Mind; and that it is More Easily Known than the Body." Cassirer noted that the advance of psychological knowledge has not confirmed the Cartesian principle that "the evidence of our own being is impregnable and unassailable." He added, "The general tendency of thought is nowadays again directed toward the opposite pole. Few modern psychologists would admit or recommend a mere method of introspection. In general they tell us that such a method is very precarious. They are convinced that a strictly behavioristic attitude is the only possible approach to a scientific psychology. But a consistent and radical behaviorism fails to attain its end. It can warn us against possible methodological errors, but it cannot solve all the problems of human psychology. We may criticize or suspect the purely introspective view, but we cannot suppress or eliminate it. Without introspection, without an immediate awareness of feelings, emotions, perceptions, thoughts, we could not even define the field of human psychology."[42] Some claim that the twentieth century marks an all-time low in self-knowledge, as, for example, Martin Hiedegger, who writes: "No other epoch has accumulated so great a store of knowledge concerning man as the present one. No other epoch has succeeded in presenting its knowledge of man so forcibly and so captivatingly as ours, and no other has succeeded in making this knowledge so quickly and so easily accessible. But also, no epoch is less sure of its knowledge of what man is than the present one. In no other epoch has man appeared so mysterious as in ours."[43] Max Scheler made the same lament: "In no other time frame of human knowledge has the human been more of a problem to himself than in our own time. . . . We no longer have clear and consistent ideas of what it means to be human. The growing number of individual sciences that study the human being has still more confused and obscured rather than clarified what it means to be human."[44]

Alexis Carrel wrote, "Although we possess the treasure of the observations accumulated by the scientists, the philosophers, the poets, and the great mystics of all times, we have grasped only certain aspects of ourselves. We do not apprehend man as a whole."[45]

The quest for the self was well depicted by Rudyard Kipling in *Kim*. The young boy, Kim, squatting in the corner of the noisy waiting room of a railway station, thinks, "Nor am I alone—all alone. In all India is no one so alone as I! If I die to-day, who shall bring the news—and to whom? If I die and God is good, there will be a price upon my head, for I am a Son of the Charm—I, Kim." The author interrupts the narrative to comment: "A very few white people, but many Asiatics, can throw themselves into amazement as it were by repeating their own names over and over again to themselves, letting the mind go free upon speculation as to what is called personal identity. When one grows older, the power, usually, departs, but while it lasts it may descend upon a man at any moment."[46]

Perhaps no one has stated the puzzle of personal identity better than Alice as she awaked in Wonderland: "Dear, dear! How queer everything is today! And yesterday things went on just as usual. I wonder if I've changed in the night? Let me think: was I the same when I got up this morning? I almost think I can remember feeling a little different. But if I'm not the same, the next question is 'Who in the world am I? Ah, that's the great puzzle.'"[47]

Primitive people viewed the self as double. One self hunted and fought during the day; the other self occasionally hunted and fought in the world of dreams. The other self was a shadowy, ghostly counterpart of the body. A man, observed by his companions lying peacefully all night by the fire, upon awakening might report a successful hunt in which he had slain a bear. But since he could not produce the bear and could not be dissuaded from his belief, the conclusion was reached that there is a waking world in which body selves hunt body bears and another world, just as real but different, in which spirit selves hunt spirit bears. The world of primitive man was a world of doubles. The beasts of the field, his companions, his enemies, the rocks and the trees, and even himself were duplicated in the spirit world.

Mark Twain said that he had been born one of twins, but his twin brother had died in infancy. Twain added that this was not quite correct, since it was he who had died in infancy and it was his twin who survived!

Each of us is indeed a matrix of selves. Imagine, for example, that you are standing with your back to an open fireplace while carrying on an interesting conversation with a friend. Suddenly you jump away from the fire exclaiming, "I was not aware I was getting so warm." For some time you had been experiencing heat without being aware of the sensation, but finally the heat sensation had become so intense that you became aware of it. You might have explained to your friend, "Whereas a few moments ago my self was sensing heat without my self being aware of the sensation, now my self is aware that my self is sensing heat." Next day you might tell another friend, "My self now recalls the situation of my self telling another that my self had become aware that my self had been sensing heat without my self being aware of the sensation." Self-awareness appears to be the self-transcending of an infinity of selves! The problem of self-knowing is illustrated in a limerick:

> There was a young man who said, "Though
> It seems that I know that I know,
>   What I would like to see
>   Is the 'I' that knows 'me'
> When I know that I know that I know."

Immanuel Kant put the problem in another manner. There are three factors in a knowing relationship: subject, act, and object. In the case of self-knowing the subject and the object appear to be identical. The ego knows the ego. But this, said Kant, is impossible; for whenever the knower tries to know the knower it thereby turns the knower into the known. The knower knows the known, but not the knower. Or to express this in another fashion—the "I" cannot know the "I," it can only know the "me." And the "me" and the "I" are not identical. The "I," the self as knower, said Kant, cannot be an object of knowledge; it is transcendental to knowing. Kant appears to have made sure that the "I" could never be known by christening it "the original transcendental synthetic unity of apperception!"

Plato, recognizing that the knowing relationship requires both similarity and separation of subject and object, attempted to solve the paradox by claiming that the rational soul in a previous existence was identified with the Ideas, that is, the objects of knowledge, and in this life is separated from the Ideas. Knowing is recalling. The end of knowing is to restore the lost unity. But the Platonic resolution may have created as many problems as it solved, especially when applied to self-knowing. What can it mean to affirm that the "I" and the "me" were once closer than they are now? Did Plato believe that mortals have two souls, or did Plato anticipate the split-brain phenomenon by contending that the self is split into two parts, one rational and one appellative? He referred to both "things" and "parts": "Then we shall claim not unreasonably that these are two separate things and different from each other, calling the part of the soul with which it reasons the 'reasoning' part, and that by which it loves and hungers and thirsts, and is all aflutter about the other desires, the 'unreasoning' and 'desiring' part, a comrade of repletions and pleasures."[48] Plato was not satisfied with the dual or split self, since in a later dialogue he added a third soul, which arbitrates between the other two.[49]

Psychologists have usually stayed out of the metaphysical problems of selfhood by confining their attentions to activities and processes, thus avoiding questions as to the nature of the entity that acts and has processes. The faculty psychologists were concerned with the "faculties" of reasoning, willing, feeling, and the like, but philosophers, theologians, and laymen have persisted in asking questions about an entity that lies behind the concrete, visible acts. The layman might soliloquize in this fashion, "I have a pencil. It can be lost without any effect upon me. I have a fingernail, which I might lose by hitting it with a hammer, and that would have some effect upon me. I have a hand. The loss of a hand would have a great effect upon me. I have a body. The loss of the body would be—to put it mildly—a personal tragedy. But what is this 'I' that has a pencil, a fingernail, a hand, a body, and perhaps even a mind? What is myself?"

William James answered this puzzling question as follows: "In its widest possible sense . . . a man's Self is the sum total of all that he can call his, not only his body and his psychic powers, but his clothes and his house, his wife and children, his ancestors and friends, his reputation and works, his lands and horses, and yacht and bank-account."[50] The world, said James, can be divided into a half that one can call "me" and another half that can be called "not-me." The world of the me can be called the empirical or phenomenal self. This empirical self admits of three divisions: (1) the material self, (2) the social self, and (3) the spiritual self. The empirical self may be thought of as the bearer of subjective experiences, and the experiences can be classified into the material, the social, and the spiritual. William James concluded that there are four selves: (1) the material self, (2) the social self, (3) the spiritual self, and (4) the pure ego.

The material self is the body and the five organs of sense. They are the channels through which the body experiences the "not-me." They are part of this self. One's immediate family is also a part of one's self. Even one's clothes and one's home becomes a part of self. The creative work of one's hands is an extension of the material self. When Thomas Carlyle discovered that his maid had carelessly tossed into the fire his manuscript of *The French Revolution,* he must have felt a great loss of self.

The social self is the recognition that one receives from others. Honor, fame, reputation, and perhaps that which we denote by the word *character* constitute a very real self. According to James, "No more fiendish punishment could be devised, were such a thing physically possible, than that one should be turned loose in society and remain absolutely unnoticed by all the members thereof."[51] This would mean nothing less than the destruction of the social self. As Shakespeare wrote,

> Good name in man, and woman, dear my lord,
> Is the immediate jewel of their souls:
> Who steals my purse steals trash; 'tis something, nothing;
> 'Twas mine, 'tis his, and has been slave to thousands;
> But he that filches from me my good name
> Robs me of that which not enriches him
> And makes me poor indeed.[52]

James did not use the term *person,* but that may be a proper designation. The statement "I was not myself when I did that" expresses what James had in mind. "I was the same self ontologically, but that act was contrary to my self as a person. I acted in a contra-personal manner." The term *person* brings out more of the moral character of this self than does the term social self. George H. Mead wrote that "a self is a composite or interaction of these two parts of our natures—the fundamental impulses which make us co-operating neighbors and friends, lovers and parents and children, and rivals, competitors, and enemies; on the other side the evocation of this self which we achieve when we address ourselves in the language which is the common speech of those about us."[53] Part of the social self is the self in one's children. In India a son is sometimes called a father's "second self." Many parents, often unconsciously, expect their children to accomplish what they had hoped to achieve in their own lives. The social self is a reminder that the human self is never synonymous with the simple individual. Much of the being of a person is in what others think one is.

The spiritual self was described by James as "the psychic faculties taken concretely," "one's inner and subjective being," "the active element in consciousness," and "the source of effort and attention." This self is an inner being with which we have direct sensible acquaintance. This direct sensible acquaintance takes on the form of feelings of attending, checking, assenting, negating, and so on. James tried to give it a physiological status when he wrote ". . . the 'Self of selves,' when carefully examined, is found to consist mainly of the collection of these peculiar motions in the head or between the head and throat."[54]

The material self, social self, and spiritual self considered as a unit are the empirical self. There is still another self: the self as the unity of experience, the personal focus of life and thought, the identity that persists through changes. A new problem in self-identity arose in 1952 when the first sexual transplant was performed. After a series of operations and hormone injections had changed him from a male to female, George Jorgensen, now Christine Jorgensen, wrote the following to his/her parents, "I am still the same old Brud, but, my dears, nature made a mistake, which I have had corrected, and now I am your daughter."[55] This continuity of an individual James called "the pure ego," "the pure principle of personal identity," and "consciousness of personal sameness." Even though the body of each person goes through many changes during a lifetime, and even though the cells are renewed every seven years, there is a self-identity which persists. Each human being is like the ship of Theseus, which the Athenians constantly repaired. At the core of the material self, the social self, and the spiritual self is "the pure ego," the self that does not change, the self that neither waxes nor wanes. The self of selves is that which makes all experiences self-disclosure.

William James led Western minds to the temple of the pure ego, but he was not able to enter. We must go elsewhere to understand what he was talking about. We must go to the East, and specifically to Buddhism. D. T. Suzuki is one of the best guides. He reminded us that one "of the most fundamental differences between East and West as far as their way of thinking is concerned is that the Western mind emphasises the dualistic aspect of reality while the Eastern mind basically tends to be advaitist. Advaitism is not the same as monism; it simply asserts that reality is non-dualistic. . . . The West lives in a world separated into two terms: subject and object, self and not-self, yes and no, good and evil, right and wrong, true and false. . . . The Western mind abhors paradoxes, contradictions, absurdities, obscurantism, emptiness, in short, anything that is not clear, well-defined, and capable of determination."[56] James was blocked, because as a Western man he had come upon "a something which is neither subjective or objective, and further . . . a something . . . not to be subsumed under any category born of the dualistic concept of subject and object."[57] Suzuki wrote that he provisionally called this "mysterious something the First Person, 'I.' "[58] "It cannot be logically determined, temporally chronicled, spatially located. . . . Naturally, it cannot be clear and definable as far as our intellection is concerned. It is 'O taste and see.' The tasting-and-seeing is not intellectual; it is perceptual and personal and cannot be brought out to the open market of conceptualization."[59] This "First Person" is not a subject standing in relation to an object, nor a "self" opposing the "nonself." It is not an object of knowledge, nor does the term *intuition* seem adequate. Suzuki used the term *feeling*, with the caution that he meant feeling "in the most primary sense, somewhat in the way the eye sees and the ear hears."[60] Primary feeling-experience differs from sense-perception in that the latter has a sense-subject and a sense-object, but in the former subject and object are not differentiated—subject is object, and object is subject, for there is no particularizable substance to be known. Even the word *something*, which Suzuki used to denote the First Person, is inadequate and misleading: "What I state, though only tentatively, in this 'primary' experience is that, when I hear or see, it is my whole being wherein hearing is seeing and seeing is hearing, because in the totality of my being there are no such sense-differentiations as one observes in one's sense-perception."[61] Suzuki quoted in support a poem by Daitō Kokushi:

> When the ear sees,
> And when the eye hears,
> One cherishes no doubts:
> How naturally the rain drips
> From the eaves![62]

The First Person is known as Emptiness (*śunyatā* in Sanskrit; *k'ung* in Chinese; *kū* in Japanese). Emptiness, however, is not the notion of sheer nothingness but the notion of infinite possibilities—"a nothing filled with fullness of things, in which 'nothing is lost and nothing is added.' "[63] To go beyond this in designation or definition is to misconstrue. This is what the *Tao Teh Ching* means when it says that when one begins to define Tao, Tao ceases to be Tao.

A similar fourfold classification of selves is found in *Chāndogya Upaniṣad*, (8:7–12). The body self is the self seen when one looks into a pan of water and says, "I see myself reflected in the water." This is the self that can be ornamented and dressed. The empirical self is the self that persists unchanged even though the body becomes blind or lame. In the language of the *Upaniṣad* it is the dreaming self. The third self is the self that persists in sound sleep, and therefore it is the dreamless self. It is the "I" of the statement "I slept soundly. I had no dreams." The fourth self is the *Ātman* or Absolute Self. It is the Universal Self which is bodiless and deathless. It is not only the principle of cosmic identity but also the Supreme Person *(uttama purusa)*. It has ideal attributes beyond those of transcendental unification.

The classic example of the difficulty of self-knowing in Western philosophy is found in David Hume's *A Treatise of Human Nature*. He began by expressing amazement at the confidence other philosophers have in the reality of an entity called "the self," which gives them the experience of personal identity: "There are some philosophers who image we are every moment intimately conscious of what we call *our self;* that we feel its existence and its continuance in existence; and are certain, beyond the evidence of a demonstration, both of its perfect identity and simplicity. The strongest sensation, the most violent passion, say they, instead of distracting us from this view, only fix it the more intensely, and make us consider their influence on *self* either by their pain or pleasure. To attempt a further proof of this were to weaken its evidence; since no proof can be derived from any fact of which we are so intimately conscious; nor is there anything of which we can be certain if we doubt of this."[64] Hume set himself to the task of discovering this self that other philosophers claimed they know, assuming within his empirical epistemology that all ideas are faint images of vivid perceptions that he called "impressions," and assuming within his ontology that there may or may not be a world outside our experience, but that no one can produce any evidence to justify that belief. So if an impression of self were discovered, that would not establish the reality of a self. Those who have an idea of self must identify the impression on which the idea is based, but even if they can find an impression, that will not establish the reality of a self. However, there is no impression that gives rise to the idea of self. The self is not an impression, but "that to which our several impressions and ideas are supposed to have a reference."[65] The self is not that which can be seen, heard, tasted, smelled, felt, believed, thought, known, and so on; rather the self is that which sees, hears, tastes, feels, believes, thinks, knows, et cetera. There is no impression from which the idea of self can be derived, and hence there is no idea of self. "For my part," continued Hume, "when I enter most intimately into what I call *myself,* I always stumble on some particular perception or other, of heat or cold, light or shade, love or hatred, pain or pleasure. I never can catch *myself* at any time without a perception, and never can observe anything but the perception. When my perceptions are removed for any time, as by sound sleep, so long am I insensible of *myself,* and may trully be said not to exist. And were all my perceptions removed by death, and could I neither think, nor feel, nor see, nor love, nor hate, after the dissolution of my body, I should be entirely annihilated, nor do I conceive what is further requisite to make me a perfect nonentity. If any one, upon serious and unprejudiced reflection, thinks he has a different notion of *himself,* I must confess I can no longer reason with him. All I can allow him is, that he may be in the right as well as I, and that we are essentially different in this particular. He may, perhaps, perceive something simple and continued, which he calls *himself;* though I am certain there is no such principle in me."[66] Hume examined his manuscript carefully before sending it to the printer. "There is nothing I would more willingly lay hold of than an opportunity of confessing my errors," he wrote.[67] He added, "I have not yet been so fortunate as to discover any very considerable mistakes in the reasonings delivered in the preceding volumes, except on one article." That "one article" was his refutation of the idea of a self: "I had entertained some hopes, that however deficient our theory of the intellectual world might be, it would be free from those contradictions and absurdities which seem to attend every explication that human reason can give of the material world. But upon a more strict review of the section concerning *personal identity,* I find myself involved in such a labyrinth that, I must confess, I neither know how to correct my former opinions, nor how to render them consistent." We talk of self, Hume mused, so we must have an idea annexed to the word. Every idea is derived from an impression. But we have no impression of self. So we ought to have no idea of self. He added that we have no idea of self "in that sense." This was a frightful admission, for, according to Hume, there is no other sense in which we have ideas: all ideas are rooted in impressions. "I am sensible that my account is very defective," he admitted. Is the self a composition of reflections, or a substance, or a felt connection, or a reflected thought? Hume was humbled by his discovery of the one great mistake in his philosophy—a philosophy which otherwise was so promising. "But all my hopes vanish when I come to explain the principles that unite our successive perceptions in our thought or consciousness. I cannot discover any theory which gives me satisfaction on this head. . . . For my part, I must plead the privilege of a sceptic, and confess that this difficulty is too hard for my understanding."

What was Hume's problem? How could a man of his intellectual caliber arrive at such a bottleneck? One clue might be to examine carefully the paragraph quoted from the body of the book in which he argued that there is no principle of identity in himself, that is, *A Treatise of Human Nature,* (bk. 1, pt. 4, sec. 6, para. 3). The word *self* appears five times in the paragraph, and is stressed by being placed in italics. But the word *I* appears thirteen times, and is not placed in italics. Hume was trying to find personal identity in the objective *me* rather than in the subjective *I*. In the language of Kant, he was looking for "the original transcendental synthetic unity of apperception" in the phenomenal world. In the terminology of James, he did not differentiate pure ego from natural self, social self, and spiritual self. Plotinus observed that "the man who knows himself is double: there is the one who knows the nature of discursive reasoning . . . and there is the other who transcends the first one."[68]

The admonition "Know thyself" can be obeyed only if the self-as-knower gives up the immediate relationship to the self-as-known. Hume discovered that the "I myself" cannot be known. The "I" can know the self-as-man but not the self-as-self. The knowing-I becomes the known-I in the knowing relationship. The subject-I can know the object-I, but not the subject-I. The pure ego can know the empirical ego, but not the pure ego. I can know me; I cannot know I. Gilbert Ryle called this "the systematic elusiveness of 'I.'" He wrote, "To concern oneself about oneself in any way, theoretical or practical, is to perform a higher order act, just as it is to concern oneself about anybody else. To try, for example, to describe what one has just done, or is now doing, is to comment upon a step which is not itself, save *per accidens,* one of the commenting. But the operation which is the commenting is not, and cannot be, the step on which that commentary is being made."[69] Every hunt for the self fails, added Ryle, because the quarry is the hunter.

Modern psychologists respond differently to "Know thyself." "None of us really want to observe or know ourselves. Such observation is not natural to us, and it hurts and hinders far more than it helps us," wrote Otto Rank.[70] Psychology is thought to be divided into "purely subjective psychology," which seeks to develop "a doctrine of self-awareness," and "applied objective psychology," which is "a technique for understanding and controlling others."[71] But, if psychology is an effort to understand man scientifically—as it ought to be—the object of its observation and research cannot also be its subject. The soul had better be left to the philosophers! "The objective psychology which began as magic became the pedagogue's, the social worker's and the therapist's means of understanding, influencing, and controlling other persons."[72] Knowledge of self is not necessary to the understanding of others. It is a by-product that is tolerated, and then welcomed."[73] "Our psychological heritage from the race is the soul, the spiritual belief, the ancient psychology in which we all unconsciously believe, but which modern psychology helps us consciously to deny."[74] The modern psychoanalyst, according to rank, has an interesting problem: he knows that despite "all scientific attempts to prove its existence, the soul has evaporated just like the noble metals in the alchemist's retort," yet his "psychology without a soul" works in therapy "only as long as it can sustain man's ancient illusory belief in the soul, and only when it can offer him a soul without psychology."[75]

Rollo May agrees with Rank and with Hume that the self cannot be established, yet he recognizes with James, Kant, and the *Upaniṣads* that a discussion of the self presumes a self that discusses: "The experience of our own identity is the basic conviction that we all start with as psychological beings. It can never be proven in a logical sense, for consciousness of one's self is the presupposition of any discussion about it. There will always be an element of mystery in one's awareness of one's own being—mystery here meaning a problem the data of which encroach on the problem. For such awareness is a presupposition of inquiry into one's self. That is to say, even to meditate on one's own identity as a self means that one is already engaging in self-consciousness."[76] "I am most certain that I am," claimed Augustine. "For if I am deceived, I am. For he who is not, cannot be deceived; and if I am deceived, by this token I am. And since I am if I am deceived, how am I deceived in believing that I am? For it is certain that I am if I am deceived."[77]

3. *The Importance of Self-Knowledge*

I have already noted that according to Alexis Carrel "the knowledge of ourselves," which he also calls "the science of man," is both "the most difficult of all sciences" and "the most necessary of all sciences."[78] The difficulty and importance of knowing one's self is a common theme in Western literature. Shakespeare's *King Lear* is patently a study of the king's misjudgment of the character of his daughters, but it is also a study of the king's misjudgment of himself. This is indicated when Regan says of her father after his unwise rejection of Cordelia, "He hath ever but slenderly known himself."[79] Self-knowing is dominant in modern Western literature, according to Charles I. Glicksberg: "Who am I? This condition—the self deprived of any controlling sense of unity—has been portrayed with hallucinatory vividness in the literature of our time from Strindberg to Ionesco."[80] Four examples may suffice in support of this claim. Marlow in Joseph Conrad's *Lord Jim* says that "no man ever understands quite his own artful dodges to escape from the grim shadow of self-knowledge." Biff, at the close of Arthur Miller's "Death of a Salesman," says of his father, Willy Loman, "He had the wrong dreams. All, all, wrong. . . . He never knew who he was." The unidentified guest in T. S. Eliot's "The Cocktail Party" says to Edward Chamberlayne,

> Most of the time we take ourselves for granted,
> As we have to, and live on a little knowledge
> About ourselves as we were. Who are you now?
> You don't know any more than I do,
> But rather less. You are nothing but a
> Set of obsolete responses.

And in Ionesco's play "The Bald Soprano" two married couples—the Smiths and the Martins—engage in noncommunicative small talk: "Cockatoos, cockatoos, cockatoos. . . . Such caca, such caca, such caca. . . . Such cascades of cacas, such cascades of cacas, such cascades of cacas. . . ." When the Martins fall into bored slumer, the maid speaks to the audience, "Elizabeth is not Elizabeth, Donald is not Donald. . . . It is in vain that he thinks he is Donald, it is in vain that she thinks she is Elizabeth. . . . But who is the true Donald? Who is the true Elizabeth? Who has any interest in prolonging the confusion?" The self that is depicted as difficult to know, or even unknowable, in modern literature is usually the axiological self rather than the epistemological or ontological selves.

If the self is so difficult to know, why should an effort be made by man to know it? Why is self-knowing important? Nietzsche felt that self-knowledge is a duty: "Our duty is and remains first and all, not to get into confusion about ourselves."[81] A recurring theme in Christian theology is that through knowing self one will gain a knowledge of God. *The Gospel of Thomas* declares, "If you will know yourselves, then you will be known and you will know that you are the sons of the Living Father."[82] Meister Eckhart said self-knowledge is impossible: "Thus the soul knows about everything but itself.... Thus it knows about everything else but has no self-knowledge, for ideas always enter through the senses and therefore the soul cannot get an idea of itself."[83] Yet it is through knowledge of self, according to Eckhart, that one attains knowledge of God: "To get at the core of God at his greatest, one must first get into the core of himself at his least, for no one can know God who has not first known himself."[84] John Calvin claimed that knowledge of man and knowledge of God are reciprocal: "The knowledge of ourselves, therefore, is not only an incitement to seek after God, but likewise a considerable assistance towards finding him. On the other hand, it is plain that no man can arrive at the true knowledge of himself, without having first contemplated the divine character, and then descended to the consideration of his own."[85]

By what route does knowledge of the self lead to knowledge of God? The answer offered in Judaism and Christianity seems to be either the optimistic answer that if one searches diligently, the stamp of the Divine Creator can be found on one's person, or the pessimistic answer that when one discovers one's finite, weak, and sinful nature one will be impelled to search for that which is infinite, omnipotent, and pure. Hinduism has a long tradition that Brahman the Absolute is "hidden in the cave of the heart."[86] Śaṅkara, in his comments on this passage, said that the Self is manifested most in human beings. Knowing is the act that reveals the Self or *Ātman*. According to the *Kaṭha Upaniṣad*

> The Inner Soul of all things, the One Controller,
> Who makes his one form manifold—
> The wise who perceive Him as standing in oneself,
> They, and no others, have eternal happiness![87]

Aurobindo was the Indian philosopher of the twentieth century who stayed closest to the Upaniṣadic teaching of the self and self-knowledge. He appealed to *Kaṭha Upaniṣad* 5. 12 in support of his view of self-knowledge: "What appears here as man is an individual being of the Divine; the Divine extended in multiplicity is the Self of all individual existences. Moreover, it is through the knowledge of self and the world that man arrives at the knowledge of God and he cannot attain to it otherwise."[88] Aurobindo lamented, "The malady of the world is that the individual cannot find his real soul, and the root-cause of this malady is again that he cannot meet in his embrace of things outward the real soul of the world in which he lives. He seeks to find there the essence of being, the essence of power, the essence of conscious-existence, the essence of delight, but receives instead a crowd of contradictory touches and impressions. If he could find that essence, he would find also the one universal being, power, conscious existence and delight even in this throng of touches and impressions; the contradictions of what seems would be reconciled in the unity and harmony of the Truth that reaches out to us in these contacts. At the same time he would find his own true soul and through it his self, because the true soul is his self's delegate and his soul and the self of the world are one."[89] According to the *Upaniṣads* the self's discovery of the Cosmic Self proceeds in four stages: (1) the waking-self stage, which is the support of all physical experience; (2) the dream-self stage, which supports subjective experiences that have no objective referent; (3) the dreamless-self stage, which Aurobindo described as "a massed consciousness which is the origin of cosmic existence;"[90] and (4) the pure-self stage, which is "a state of superconscience absorbed in its self-existence, in a self-silence or a self-ecstasy."[91] Aurobindo described the path of self-knowledge leading to God in categories more palatable to modern minds when he said that the first step is for a person "to know that this life is not all," the second step is for a person "to learn that his surface waking state is only a small part of his being," and the third step is "to find out that there is something in him other than his instrumental mind, life and body, not only an immortal ever-developing individual soul that supports his nature but an eternal immutable self and spirit, and to learn what are the categories of his spiritual being, until he discovers that all in him is an expression of the spirit and distinguishes the link between his lower and his higher existence; thus he sets out to remove his constitutional self-ignorance. Discovering self and spirit he discovers God."[92]

A second argument for the importance of self-knowing is its relation to other forms of knowing. Aristotle began his work on the soul lauding self-knowledge as the highest form of knowing and as contributing to the understanding of the external world: "Holding as we do that, while knowledge of any kind is a thing to be honoured and prized, one kind of it may, either by reason of its greater exactness or of a higher dignity and greater wonderfulness in its objects, be more honourable and precious than another, on both accounts we should naturally be led to place in the front rank the study of the soul. The knowledge of the soul admittedly contributes greatly to the advance of truth in general, and, above all, to our understanding of

Nature."[93] "One must know one's self before knowing anything else," said Sören Kierkegaard.[94] "All distinctively philosophical problems have their ultimate solution in the self. Whatever the question asked of reality, its final answer must await upon the principle of selfhood," writes G. A. Wilson, a modern Western philosopher whose approach has an Eastern flavor.[95] Paul Deussen, a great German scholar, said the same thing; but whether he came to this conclusion before or after his study of the *Upaniṣads* is a debatable question: "If ever a general solution is reached of the great riddle, which presents itself to the philosopher in the nature of things all the more clearly the further our knowledge extends, the key can only be found where alone the secret of nature lies open to us from within, that is to say, in our innermost self."[96]

A third motivation for self-knowing—and the most important—is that the human being to be human must know itself. The question "When does a fetus become a living soul?" ought to be altered to "When does the infant first reveal its humanity?" A newborn infant is perhaps best described as a candidate for humanity. The proud and anxious parents are pleased if they discover that the baby performs well as an organism—breathes air, digests food, eliminates waste material, moves the body, responds to pain, and so on—but they must wait three or four years before being assured that they have brought forth a *human* being. A child becomes human when it recognizes itself as subject. At first the child will see itself and describe itself in the third person. It is one of the objects in the external world. Then with dramatic suddenness the child becomes self-aware. When Mary ceases to say, "Mary wants a glass of milk" and says "*I* want a glass of milk," Mary has joined the human race.

Self-discovery is beautifully illustrated in the literature of Mahāyāna Buddhism in a story similar to the parable of the prodigal son in the Gospel of Luke.[97] In the Buddhist version a youth runs away from his home and dwells in another country for many years. In his great need he becomes a beggar roaming about in quest of food and clothing and working at menial tasks. Meanwhile, his father, having searched in vain for his lost son, settles in another city and amasses great riches. The prodigal in his wanderings arrives at his father's door begging alms. When he sees a man seated on a couch surrounded by great riches, he flees at once, muttering: "This must be a king, or some one of royal rank; it is no place for me to obtain anything for the hire of my labor. I had better go to some poor hamlet, where there is a place for letting out of labor, and food and clothing are easier to get!" Although the son does not recognize his father, the father recognizes his son. He dispatches attendants to pursue the beggar and to bring him back. He hires his son to do scavenging work. Over the years the son is given more significant work. The son works diligently, and the father is pleased. One day the father says, "I am old and advanced in years, but you are young and vigorous; all the time you have been working you have never been deceitful, lazy, angry, or grumbling. I have never seen you, like the other laborers, with such vices as these. From this time forth you shall be as my own begotten son." The young man continues to grow in character, and finally, just before his death, the father assembles all his friends and relatives to announce that this is indeed his son, and that all his wealth belongs entirely to his son. The revelation of his personal identity was one for which the son was prepared after his growth in self-knowing. The parable concludes: "The very rich elder is the Tathāgata, and we are all as the Buddha's sons. . . . From of old we are really sons of Buddha . . . yet now the Great Treasure of the King of the Law has of itself come to us, and such things as Buddha-sons should obtain, we have all obtained." Sonship is both discovery and creation. All are Buddhas. All become Buddhas.

The human is the self-knowing animal, the only animal that is there for himself. It is the fate of all other animals and of all plants and rocks to be there without participating in their thereness. This is not to state that the human may or may not know itself. Rather self-knowing is the *sine qua non* of the human. Self-knowing makes us human. We are not born human. We become human. "Man becomes what he is. His is-ness is his becoming. He is a becoming, not a Being. His 'being' is becoming-ness. His is-ness is in process such that he never is with the finality of beast or god. He creatively discovers what he is, and he discovers creatively what he can become. The self is always infinitely more than it would be if it were only what it is."[98] Man's evolution is different from that of any other form of life, as Julian Huxley and Teilhard de Chardin have pointed out. All other living forms evolve into species—for example, 6,000 species of reptiles, 9,000 species of birds, and 800,000 species of insects. But there is only one species of man. Teilhard wrote in 1947, "Until the coming of man the pattern of the Tree of Life was always that of a fan, a spread of morphological radiations diverging more and more, each radiation culminating in a new 'knot' and breaking into a fan of its own. But at the human level a radical change, seemingly due to the spiritual phenomenon of Reflection, overtook this law of development. It is generally accepted that what distinguishes man psychologically from other living creatures is the power acquired by his consciousness of turning in upon itself. The animal knows, it has been said; but only man, among animals, knows that he knows."[99] Teilhard wrote elsewhere that "when the first spark of thought appeared upon earth, life found it had brought into the world a power capable of criticising it and judging it."[100] "Man is not the centre of the universe as once we thought in our simplicity, but something much more wonderful—the arrow pointing the way to the final unification of the world in terms of life."[101] "Man is unquestionably situated on the topmost point; and it is he, by his emergence and existence, who finally proves the reality and defines the trajectory—'the dot on the i.'"[102] Both Huxley and Teilhard described man as "evolution become conscious of itself."[103] Man is evolution in a state of self-awareness, self-knowledge, self-realization, and self-fulfillment. Man-as-self is both process and product. The self is man's finest creation. Man makes himself. In the words of Leon Eisenberg, "Man is his own chief product. The infant who discovers that he can control the movements of his own fingers transforms himself from observer into actor. The child who masters reading unlocks the treasury of the world's heritage. The adolescent who insists upon a critical reexamination of conventional wisdom is making himself into an adult. And the adult whose concerns extend beyond family and beyond nation to mankind has become fully human."[104]

"Who am I?" may be interpreted as "Who am I as an individual?" or "Who am I as a being?" The former is basic to one's self-development; the latter is basic to one's nature. Mere animals, locked in their animality, cannot raise the question; infinite beings—if there are such—need not raise the question; but man, the finite being with infinite aspirations, must raise the question. Sometimes bad answers have been given. The answer was bad when it diminished some human beings to the level of personal property, as in slavery. It was bad when women were treated as inferior to men. It was bad when in Nazi Germany it resulted in the mass murder of six million Jews. But the worth of the question must not be judged by the worth of the answer. Not to raise the question would be worse than to arrive at a bad answer. The jeremiad that the human being is "the unknown" must be tempered by the reminder that the human being continues to ask "Who am I?"

5
The Theories of the Self

Despite the problems of self-knowing we try, as we must in order to be human, to know ourselves both as beings and as individual beings, for "he who lives with *It* alone is not a man."[1] One of the first Western quests for knowledge of the self took the form "Where am I?" The question was a search for the bodily location of the center of vitality and consciousness, usually called "the soul." The ancient Egyptians said the soul was in the heart, belly, and breath. In other words, there are three souls. They were known as *ba*, *ka*, and *akh*. The *ba* was the personal self. It was represented in the tombs by a little bird with human head and arms. The *ka* was an impersonal detached self, a guardian spirit that the body joined in the afterlife. The *akh* was transfigured spirit that had no relation to the body. The Hebrews located the soul in the blood, and from this belief the Jews developed the custom of eating only kosher meat, that is meat from which the blood has been drained. The early Greeks referred to the self as *psychḗ* (the vital principle that was linked with the blood), *pneúma* (the breath of life), *daímōn* (the character of a person), *kḗr* (the ghost of the dead person), and *erinýs* (an angry and avenging ghost of a dead person).

The question "What is the self?" is a more philosophical and less loaded question than "Where is the self?" Three answers have been offered to this question: (1) the self is an independent substance, (2) the self is a dependent substance, (3) the self is a relationship.

1. Independent Substance Theories

According to the independent substance theories, the self is an entity having reality, attributes, and activities of its own. The self as independent substance has been conceived as either corporeal or incorporeal.

The ancient Greek philosopher Democritus is an excellent example of one who held the soul to be a material independent substance. He did not exclude the soul from his atomic metaphysics. The soul is "a sort of fire or hot substance."[2] Democritus compared soul atoms to dust particles seen in the air in shafts of light. Their spherical shape is designed to make them able to permeate everything everywhere, and their constant motion sets all other atoms in motion. Democritus, like many ancient Greek thinkers, held that soul and mind are identical. Aristotle had a low opinion of Democritean speculations, contending that the notion of soul as a kind of body creates the absurdity of "two bodies in the same place."[3] Hippo said the soul is water, Diogenes thought it was air, Heraclitus guessed it was warm air, and Empedocles declared it was formed out of all the elements, namely, earth, water, air, fire, love, and hate. The early Pythagoreans said souls are motes in the air. The later Pythagoreans thought of the soul as the harmony of ten complementary opposites: limit and unlimited, odd and even, individuality and plurality, right and left, male and female, resting and moving, straight and curved, light and darkness, good and bad, square and oblong. Aristotle, to whom we are indebted for information about early Greek views of the soul, wrote that they are absurd because "they all join the soul to a body, or place it in a body."[4] He criticized Plato's theories of the soul, pointing out that in the *Timeus* Plato fashions the soul out of the elements, in *On Philosophy* he speaks of the soul as "Animal-itself," and elsewhere he says the soul is a "number . . . formed out of the elements."[5]

A curious instance of the corporeal conceptions of the soul is found in medieval Christian art. The soul is often portrayed as a small human figure housed within the body. For example, Masolino da Panicale (1383–1447), in his fresco of the Crucifixion in St. Catherine's Chapel of St. Clemente in Rome, painted the soul as a tiny man coming out of the mouth of one of the dying thieves.[6] In the Art Institute of Chicago there is a small stained glass window from France dated about 1520 that portrays the soul of the dying Judas issuing from his stomach and being eagerly seized by the Devil. A mosaic, "The Death of the Virgin," in the Mascoli Chapel, St. Marco, Venice, which is accepted as having been made in 1443 from the design of Andrea del Castagno, is described as follows by Frederick Hartt: "The colossal Christ holds stiffly in his extended fingers a taut cloth, on which kneels weightlessly the Lilliputian soul of His mother."[7]

While the view of the self as a little figure hidden in the body seems quaint, even primitive, we must not forget that often we refer to the body as "I." Expressions like "I am here," "I'll meet you at three o'clock," and "I shall return" leave no doubt that the self denoted is the body. Physical self, social self, and creative self become identified with the pure ego in the conduct of daily life. Francis of Assisi referred to his body as "brother ass," and was accustomed to apologize for bringing the body with him on his travels.

The self as incorporeal substance can be traced back to the Homeric legends, where it is either the *psychē* (the principle of life) or the *pneuma* (the breath). The self in the *Iliad* and the *Odyssey* is a shadowy counterpart of the body, which at bodily death flies to Hades to remain forever in a condition worse than that of the meanest earthly servant. The only respite is an occasional short visit to the earth when offered draughts of fresh blood.

In the religious cults associated with the worship of Orpheus the soul is the most honored part of the human being. This view of the soul was imported from the East into the Greek world. According to the Orphics, the soul is unhappily imprisoned in the body, "the tomb of the soul." After many incarnations and many purgations the soul attains sufficient perfection to be reabsorbed into the divine.

a. The Platonic Theory of the Self

Plato in the *Phaedo* presented the Socratic view of the soul—a view that has remained dominant in the West. There are two kinds of existing things, says Socrates, one visible and one invisible. The visible changes, but the invisible remains constant. The body of man changes; but the other part, the part invisible to man, is presumed to be unchanging. "When soul and body are together, our nature assigns the body to be slave and to be ruled, and the soul to be ruler and master."[8] But the body is a reluctant slave, and the result is that the soul is often "dragged by the body towards what is always changing, and the soul goes astray and is confused and staggers about like one drunken."[9] The soul is "most like the divine and immortal and intellectual and simple and indissoluble and self-changeable, but on the contrary, the body is most like the human and mortal and manifold and unintellectual and dissoluble and ever-changing."[10] Socrates adds that when one dies, the body dissolves and finally disappears, but the soul "goes to another place noble and pure and unseen like itself, a true unseen Hades, to the presence of the good and wise God."[11]

The most important single influence in the shaping of the dominant Western conception of the self is the Platonic. The soul is indeed described by Plato as the most divine part of the human organism, but "divine" for Plato had the connotation of intellectual rather than spiritual. In Plato the Greek term *psychē* is more suitably translated "mind" than "soul." The Platonic influence has been so dominant in Western philosophical thought that even a careful author like David Hume used the terms *self* and *mind* interchangeably in his essay "Of Personal Identity." According to Plato self, soul, or mind is that part of the human being by which the Forms—the ideal and eternal epistemological/ontological objects—are known. Plato was too keen an observer of human nature to limit his conception of self to the intellect. He found three psychological tendencies. These three might be described as the passionate element in the person, which bids one to enjoy sensual experiences; the reasoning element in the person, which forbids one to enjoy sensual experiences; and the feeling element in the person, which inclines toward reason but sees the justice of the demands of passion. One of the first passages in the dialogues of Plato that reveal his struggle to develop a tripartite conception of the self is in *The Republic* 439. A man named Leontius on his way to Athens happens to come upon a gruesome sight: a number of corpses of recently executed prisoners. One self wants to see the sight; the second self is disgusted with the self that desires to see; the third self compromises, and, turning back, the man pulls his eyelids open with his fingers, shouting, "There, confound you! Stare your fill at the beautiful sight."[12] The fullest development of Plato's conception of the self appears in the *Phaedrus*. The analogy this time is a charioteer and his two horses. The passionate element of the soul is a black horse that is "crooked of frame, a massive jumble of a creature, with thick short neck, snub nose, black skin, and gray eyes; hot-blooded, consorting with wantonness and vainglory; shaggy of ear, deaf, and hard to control with whip and goad."[13] The feeling element of the soul is a white horse that is "upright and clean-limbed, carrying his neck high, with something of a hooked nose; in color he is white, with black eyes; a lover of glory, but with temperance and modesty; one that consorts with genuine renown, and needs no whip, being driven by the word of command alone."[14] The rational element of the soul is the charioteer. Whereas in the story of Leontius the struggle involves the fascination of the terrible, in the *Phaedrus* myth the struggle concerns sexual desires. "Now when the driver beholds the person of the beloved, and causes a sensation of warmth to suffuse the whole soul, he begins to experience a tickling or pricking of desire, and the obedient steed, constrained now as always by modesty, refrains from leaping upon the beloved. But his fellow, heeding no more the driver's goad or whip, leaps and dashes on, sorely troubling his companion and his driver, and forcing them to approach the loved one and remind him of the delights of love's commerce. For a while they struggle, indignant that he should force them to a monstrous and forbidden act, but at last, finding no end to their evil plight, they yield and agree to do his bidding . . . . And so it happens time and again, until the evil steed casts off his wantonness; humbled in the end, he obeys the counsel of his driver, and when he sees the fair beloved he is like to die of fear. Wherefore at last the soul of the lover follows after the beloved with reverence and awe."[15]

b. Gnostic Theories of the Self

The impact of Plato on the West is expressed in the memorable sentence of A. N. Whitehead: "The safest general characterization of the European philosophical tradition is that it consists of a series of footnotes to Plato."[16] Plato also affected the development of religion in the West, and especially in his theory of the self. His influence on the Christian view of the self entered to a large extent through Gnosticism, a term designating a variety of mystery religions that contended that salvation is attained through esoteric knowledge. After several centuries of conflict these mystery religions were crushed by the victorious anti-gnostic forces within the Christian church, but not before they had made an indelible impression on the orthodox view of the soul. Christianity began as a Jewish cult, whose leaders hoped to contain it as a small community waiting for the end of the world. They wished to keep it an undogmatic religion, that is, a religion without a doctrine. But these hopes became unrealistic because of the conflict with the Gnostic religions, and also because many of the converts coming from Gentile communities needed instruction in the tenets of the faith. Paul's letters to followers in Colossae, Ephesus, Galatia, Philippi, Thessalonica, Corinth, and Rome, which are preserved in the New Testament, reveal the distressing problems the new religion faced in Graeco-Roman culture. The chief intellectual problem was how to relate Christian insights and Greek philosophy. Was Hellenism to be absorbed into Christianity, or was Christianity to be absorbed into Hellenism? An enormos variety of cults known collectively as Gnosticism advocated a Christian Hellenism. A mere listing of the cults suggests the intellectual ferment of the first Christian centuries: Valentinians, Manichaeans, Mandaeans, Simonians, Marcionites, Nicolaitans, Barbelo-Gnostics, Ophites, Stratiotics, Encratites, Borborites, Dasitheans, Phibionites, Sethians, Cainites, Samothracians, Archiontics, Marcosians, Nassenes, Hermetics, Magharians, Basilidians, Carpocratians, and Priscillianists. The simple eschatological community became a hotbed of intellectual controversy. The conflicts were vicious. When debate failed, persecution, banishment, exile, and murder were utilized as methods of settling theological arguments. Out of these conflicts arose an orthodox position that avoided the absence of doctrine of the first generation of Christians and the declared heterodoxy of the Gnostics. The discovery of two Gnostic libraries—the Nag-Hammadi in Upper Egypt in 1945 and the Qumram on the west shore of the Dead Sea in 1947—has presented historians new information about the methods by which Christian doctrine was formed, and has confronted New Testament scholars with the necesssity of rethinking the uniqueness of Christianity. The Gnostic movements were efforts to develop a religion and a philosophy harmonious with Greek and Oriental philosophies. While not all the Gnostic systems can be said to be rooted in Plato, many of the ideas, especially regarding the self, were Platonic. The gnosis they sought was self-knowledge. Irenaeus, a second-century Christian leader who despised Gnosticism, wrote scathingly that "they affirm that the inner and spiritual man is redeemed by means of knowledge, and that they, having acquired the knowledge of all things, stand thenceforth in need of nothing else."[17] His use of the expression "the inner and spiritual man" was a reference to the Gnostic threefold division of mankind: (1) "the material," who are destined for corruption, (2) "the animal," who have a possibility of salvation, and (3) "the spiritual," who "shall be given as brides to the angels of the Saviour."[18] Irenaeus found the Gnostic claim to saving knowledge very distasteful: "But if anyone do yield himself up to them like a little sheep, and follows out their practice, and their 'redemption,' such an one is puffed up to such an extent, that he thinks he is neither in heaven nor on earth, but that he has passed within the Pleroma; and having already embraced his angel, he walks with a strutting gait and a supercilious countenance, possessing all the pompous air of a cock."[19] Clement of Alexandria, who was sympathetic to the Gnostics, described them as those who know "who we were and what we have become; where we were or where we had been made to fall; whither we are hastening, whence we are being redeemed; what birth is and what rebirth is."[20] The passionate subjectivity of Gnosticism is seen in a statement assigned to the Gnostic Monoimus by Hippolytus: "Abandon the search for God and the creation and other matters of a similar sort. Look for him by taking *yourself* as your starting point. Look who it is *within you* makes everything his own and says, '*My* god, *my* mind, *my* thought, *my* soul, *my* body.'"[21]

A story repeated in the writings of the various Gnostic schools tells that the Demiurge, upon completing the creation of the world, proclaimed, "I am God and there is none other than I." At once a voice from on high rebuked, "You are mistaken! Above you is Primal Man." Each human being is an image of Primal Man set in a physical body to preserve the spirit and to redeem the world. Man is constructed in a pattern opposed to the pattern of the cosmos. At the center of the cosmos is the earth, an inner material dungeon, and around it the cosmic spheres are arranged like enclosing shells. The regions of the heavens, that is, the spiritual spheres, are outermost. One Gnostic counted 365 heavens! Man's nature counters the cosmos in that in him "heaven," that is, spirit, *pneuma,* or spark, is within, and matter is without. The cosmos becomes more real and more valuable in moving *from* its center; man becomes more real and valuable in moving *to* his center. Man is the key to Gnostic salvation, that is, the release of spirit from the bonds of matter. Man is the only being able to know about the transmundane God and about himself. By reason of the attainment of this gnosis or divine knowledge his ascent assists in the restoration of the wholeness that the deity lost in the act of creating a physical universe. Man, now relieved of the material component, becomes his true Self; God ceases creating the physical universe; Primal Man is restored to His pristine purity and simplicity; and cosmic history comes to an end.

According to the Gnostics the human self is a spirit temorarily enclosed in a physical body. Human birth is a fall from a pure state. As *The Gospel of Philip* states, "No one will hide a great and precious object in a great vessel. But many times has someone put countless myriads into a vessel worth a farthing. So it is with the soul. It is a precious thing (and) got into a despised body."[22] Even the creation of the world is an undesirable event, since it also consists in placing spirit in matter. The human is the one being who has the capability of putting things right. Only the human being can regain the lost paradise of a spiritual self in a matterless world. Jesus, the ideal man, could not have been in an incarnate state during his years on earth. Gnostics proclaimed that Jesus lived a docetic life, that is, a life in which the body had only seeming reality. The real self of Jesus—the spirit—was housed in an unreal body. According to some Gnostics the body of Christ was so immaterial that a finger could be thrust through the entire body without encountering resistance, which may have some relation to the account in John 20:27, where the resurrected Jesus challenges the doubting Thomas to put his finger in his side. *The Gospel of Philip* affirms that "he did not reveal himself as he [really] was, but he revealed himself as they would be able to see him. To [all creatures] he revealed himself. He revealed himself to the great as great. He revealed himself to the small as small. He [revealed himself] [to the] angels as angel and to men as man."[23] The Gnostics contended that Jesus did not hunger, thirst, or die. In one Gnostic work—*The Acts of John*—the real Jesus is described as appearing to John on the Mount of Olives while the phenomenal Jesus was dying on a cross on the other side of the valley. Words and phrases such as *conceived, born, suffered under Pontius Pilate, crucified, dead,* and *buried* entered the Christian creeds to refute Gnosticism. But the Church was unable to remove from the Bible such Gnostic positions as Paul's opposition to marriage,[24] his many warnings about the sinfulness of the flesh, and his curious statement that he knew one man who was "caught up as far as the third heaven"[25] and at another time was "caught up into paradise."[26] The Fourth Gospel refers to Satan as "the ruler of this world"[27] and the father of the Jews.[28] Even the conservative *Hastings Encyclopedia of Religion and Ethics* admits, "It is the peculiarity of the Fourth Gospel that its underlying polemic against the Gnostic teachings is combined with a certain sympathy."[29] The issue of Gnosticism in Christianity has not ended, nor has the assessment of its importance; for example, on one hand one twentieth-century Christian authority (W. F. Albright) accused three other Christian authorities—Albert Schweitzer, Paul Tillich, and Arnold Toynbee—of being Gnostic[30] and on the other hand another Christian authority (Thomas A. Schafer) warned "let us neither forget nor despise the Gnostics. They and even more their foes, the early fathers, have a message for us today."[31] Still another Christian scholar has noted, "One of the most important issues facing New Testament scholarship today is the issue of Gnosticism."[32]

c. The Self in Chinese Thought

From ancient times the Chinese have honored their forebears both as a way to preserve the memory of ancestors and as a way to insure favorable treatment from the spirits of the dead. The soul *(p'o)* was not believed to be a special creation of God but the natural product of *yang* and *yin*. At the death of a human being the *yin* element was believed to return to the earth, and the *yang* to heaven. But the return was not immediate. During a variously specified period of time the *yin* component could appear as a *kuei* (ghost or demon) and bring harm. The *yang* component, on the other hand, could appear as a *shen* (benevolent spirit) and bless the bereaved. Much depended upon proper burial and upon the performance of sacrifices in honor of the dead. Confucius recommended that, in addition to ancestor worship, the ways of one's father should not be altered for three years after his death.[33]

The early philosophers of China for the most part accepted the view that the human self is an independent incorporeal substance. Their interests were more moralistic than metaphysical. Mencius, the greatest philosopher of the early Confucian tradition, said service to one's parents is the paramount duty. One should preserve one's self, not for the sake of the self, but for the sake of the ancestors. Rather than speculating as to the nature of the self, Chinese philosophers speculated largely as to the essential goodness or badness of the self. Confucius held that all people are born upright, meaning that they have the potentiality to become good through practice. This was drilled into the minds of children in the classical Chinese education, for example, the first sentence the child learned to write was "Men are alike in nature, but through practice they become different." Evil for Confucius was something to be overcome, not something to be explained. His emphasis was on human adaptability. But later philosophers felt compelled to make moral pronouncements regarding human nature. Mencius (fourth century B.C.) contended that all human beings are good by nature: "It can be said that all men have a capacity for compassions because, even today, if one chances to see a toddler about to fall into a well, one becomes apprehensive and sympathetic. This is not because one knows the child's parents; it is not out of desire for the praise of neighbors and friends; and it is not out of dislike for the bad reputation that would ensue if one did not go to the rescue. In the light of all this we can conclude that without compassion one would not be a human being."[34] Hsün Tzu (fourth century B.C.) held the opposite view: "The nature of man is evil; his goodness is acquired. His nature being what it is, man is born, first, with a desire for gain. If this desire is followed, strife will result and courtesy will disappear. Second, man is born with envy and hate. If these tendencies are followed, injury and cruelty will abound and loyalty and faithfulness will disappear. Third, man is born with passions of the ear and eye as well as the love of sound and beauty. If these passions are followed, excesses and disorderliness will spring up and decorum and righteousness will disappear. Hence, to give rein to man's original nature and to yield to man's emotions will assuredly lead to strife and disorderliness, and he will revert to a state of barbarism."[35] Kao Tzu (fourth century B.C.) believed human nature is morally neutral; it is disposed neither to good nor to evil, just as water is disposed to flow neither to the east nor to the west. Tung Chung-shu (second century B.C.) said man's nature is essentially good, but contains some evil elements; Yang Hsuing (first century A.D.) thought human nature is a mixture of good and evil; and Wong Ch'ung (first century A.D.) compromised still more between Mencius and Hsün Tzu, holding that there are three kinds of human beings: some born good, some born evil, and some born mixed.

By the third century A.D. the native views of the soul were supplemented by Buddhist conceptions. The Buddhist view of nonego was not integrated into the Chinese views of the soul, but the concept of *karma* that Buddhism had taken from Hinduism was added. The result was "a purgatorial system organized along Confucian bureaucratic lines, with a well-organized program of karmic bookkeeping, trial in courts exactly like those of the magistrates in the Chinese empire, and punishment in various hells where the tortures meted out exactly fitted the crimes of the guilty souls."[36] Thus China faced the problem of harmonizing two theories of the soul: one based on the *yin/kuei* and *yang/shen* conception developed from native tradition, the other based on the imported Indian belief in *karma*. This presented no insurmountable problem for the Chinese, for reconciling opposites appears to be their forte.

d. The Self in Indian Thought

A distinguishing feature of Indian philosophy—with the notable exception of the Hindu heresy known as Buddhism—is a scholastic attitude toward its ancient traditional writings. These are chiefly the *Ṛg Veda,* a collection of more than one thousand poems and petitions designed to accompany sacrifices to divinities, and the *Upaniṣads,* more than one hundred prosaic metaphysical speculations. The schools *(darśanas)* of Indian philosophy—Nyāya, Vaiśeṣika, Sāṁkhya, Yoga, Mīmāṁsā, and Vedānta—are interpretive variations on the themes raised in the *śruti* writings. A consistent view of the orthodox Hindu philosophical literature is that the human self is an independent incorporeal substance. In *Chāndogya Upaniṣad* four selves are distinguished.[37] One is the bodily self, described as the self seen in a pan of water and as the self that perishes immediately when the body perishes. Another is the dream self. It does not suffer defects from the defects of the body, but is subject to pleasure and pain, and thus does not exhibit the continuity that one expects of the true self. The third is the self in dreamless sleep. This is the self referred to in "I slept soundly. I had no dreams." This conception is also rejected because a conscious subject that has no objects of consciousness is not a subject, and therefore not a self. The fundamental problem in identifying the self with bodily self, dream self, or dreamless self according to the Hindu perspective is that all three regard the relationship of body and self as internal, when it is in fact external. The seer observes that the soul is attached to a body as a horse is attached to a cart. The three views have metaphysically put the cart before the horse! The true self—the fourth self—is deathless, bodiless, free from pleasure and pain, an inward spectator not identified with the objects of sense, the ego-identity that uses sense organs and mind as instruments of perception. These passages inform the reader that the self at death of the body rises up and appears in its own form, that is, the Supreme Person, but no further information is given here as to the nature of the Supreme Person.

In the earliest recorded Hindu reflection on the nature of the self, a sage suggests that the self is like two birds roosting in the same tree. One eats the sweet fruits growing on the tree; the other watches the eater.[38] The sage was not describing a schizophrenic personality but the normal division of the self into an acting self and a witnessing self. This is the same division that we have already noted between the perceiver and the apperceiver, between being aware and being aware that one is aware, between knowing and knowing that one knows.[39] This division was adumbrated in Plato's myths of Leontius and of the charioteer and the two horses, in James's distinction between the pure ego and the empirical ego, in Hume's confusion between the I-self of personal identity and the me-self the I examines, and maybe even in the split-brain phenomenon of modern neurophysiology. The dual self, added the Vedic seer, is the product of heaven its father and earth its mother. But the seer confessed that his hypotheses were uncertain: "I distinguish not if I am this all; for I go perplexed, and bound in mind."[40]

The chariot analogy of the self, which we have already noted in the *Phaedrus* of Plato, appears in the *Katha Upaniṣad* 1. 3. 3–7: "Know the Self *(Ātman)* as the lord of the chariot and the body as . . . the chariot. Know the intellect *(buddhi)* as . . . the charioteer and the mind *(manas)* as . . . the reins. The senses *(indriya)* . . . are the horses; the objects of sense the paths they range over; the self associated with the body, the senses and the mind . . . is the enjoyer. He who has no understanding, whose mind is always unrestrained, his senses out of control, [is] as wicked horses are for a charioteer. He who has understanding, whose mind is always restrained, his senses under control, [is] as good horses are for a charioteer."[41] The chariot analogy in the *Upaniṣads* is far more complicated than Plato's analogy. Plato's black horse appears as the "wicked horses," that is, "senses out of control" of the charioteer, and his white horse appears as the "good horses," that is, "senses under control" of the charioteer. The Vedic bird that eats the sweet fruit of the tree is the "enjoyer," that is, the self identified with the body (chariot), the senses (the horses), and the mind (the reins). The Vedic bird that watches the eater is the charioteer—a Freudian superego checking the life of appetite, sensation, and intellect. The distinction between *buddhi* and *manas* is the distinction between wisdom (theoretical understanding) and prudence (practical judgment). A significant addition in the Upaniṣadic chariot analogy—one that is characteristically Hindu—is the *Ātman,* the Universal Self, symbolized by the lord or owner of the chariot.

The distinction between the individual self and the Universal Self is presented in the *Bṛhad-Āraṇyaka Upaniṣad* in the story of the semi-legendary philosopher Yājñavalkya and his two wives, Kātyāmanī and Maitreyī.[42] Yājñavalkya, having decided to desert the life of a householder, summons his two wives to make arrangements for their maintenance after his departure. Kātyāmanī is mollified, but Maitreyī demands instruction about the way to immortality: "If the whole earth with all its wealth were mine, would I thereby be immortal?" Yājñavalkya confirms her suspicion that there is no hope for immortality through wealth, and assures her that while she was dear to him, she is now dearer, having raised the fundamental issue of immortality. A husband, wife, sons, wealth, caste, worlds, and gods are good only insofar as they are instrumental to the intrinsic good of the Supreme Self. Yājñavalkya concludes, "Lo, verily, not for love of all is all dear, but for love of the Universal Self *(Ātman)* all is dear." *Ātman* is the totality without which the parts—beings, worlds, gods—are nothing. [So] ". . . these worlds, these gods, these beings, everything here is what this Soul is." He warns, "Everything deserts one who knows everything in anything else than the Universal Soul." That can be stated obversely by noting that nothing deserts one who knows that nothing has reality or value outside the *Ātman*. The *Ātman* is the integration that is reality in the same manner as the sea is the integration of all that is water, the skin the integration of touch, the tongue the integration of all tastes, the nostrils the integration of all odors, the eyes the integration of all sights, and so forth. The goal of life adds Yājñavalkya, is the attainment of a state in where there is no consciousness of anything. Maitreyī expresses bewilderment, that the state of unconsciousness should be a desirable post-mortem condition. But Yājñavalkya corrects her. It is a state of no consciousness *of,* not of unconsciousness. The consciousness within the mortal state is inherently dualistic. In this condition one sees as it were another, smells as it were another, hears as it were another, speaks as it were to another, thinks as it were of another, and understands as it were another. This duality, however, is premised on the assumption that the "other" is real, whereas the "other" is *iva* (as it were), that is, phenomenal; but in the immortal state, the state of liberation *(mokṣa),* there is no duality: "Where, verily, everything has become the Self, then by what and whom should one smell, then by what and whom should one see, then by what and whom should one hear, then by what and to whom should one speak, then by what and on whom should one think, then by what and whom should one understand? By what should one know that by which all this is known. By what, my dear, should one know the knower?"[43] In the liberated state, that is, in the immortal condition the Self that is consciousness exists, but it cannot be a consciousness *of* anything since the *Ātman* is Brahman, and Brahman is Totality.

This Upaniṣadic insight into the nature of the self is presented in many parts of the *Upaniṣads,* but perhaps most clearly in the instruction of Śvetaketu by Uddālaka as recorded in *Chāndogya Upaniṣad* 6. Śvetaketu, having spent twelve years with a Vedic teacher, returns to his parental home proud of his learning. His father, Uddālaka, knows that his son's pride is an indication that he is still only a *Brahma-bandhu,* that is, a Brahmin in name only. He has acquired the discursive knowledge, but has not made the existential discovery of his own reality. His learning has not yet included "that teaching whereby what has not been heard of becomes heard of, what has not been thought of becomes thought of, what has not been understood becomes understood." The son, despite his pride in his formal instruction, has sufficient humility to request that he be taught that to which his father refers, and, upon this slim and necessary foundation, the father begins. The father asks the son if his *gurus* (spiritual teachers) informed him that pots are merely verbal distinctions of clay, copper ornaments verbal distinctions of copper, and things made of iron verbal distinctions of iron. Śvetaketu replies, "... those honored men did not know this; for, if they had known it, why would they not have told me?" The father astutely avoids answering the question by replying, "So be it, my dear." The father knows that there is a wisdom that must be discovered and that cannot be taught. *Gurus* can prepare the way for self-insight; they cannot instill self-insight. Uddālaka begins the reeducation of Śvetaketu with the cosmogonic myth that the world began as one Being *(sat)*—"one only, without a second." For reasons that we do not know, the world became many. The first multiplicity was "heat, water, and food," that is, temperature-potency, liquid-potency, and matter-potency. Just as these three have their roots in Being, so do all manifold things have their roots in fire, water, and earth. Uddālaka reminds Śvetaketu that honey is a unity made from the nectars of many trees and that rivers are a many that become one sea. The human being is the being who can understand both the many-ing of the one and the one-ing of the many. Only the human being can know whence he has come and where he is going. The human being can understand that the individual self *(jīva)* is a fragmented phenomenon of the Supreme Self *(Ātman)*. As a conclusion of many analogies the father states, "That which is the subtle essence, this whole world has for its sake. That is the true. That is the Self. That you are *(tat tva asi).*" At the close of the teaching the narrator adds, "Then he understood. Yea, he understood." Śvetaketu understood that his essential nature as a human self is identical in essence with the Brahman, that is, Totality. The human being is not a stranger in the universe, nor an intruder, and, most certainly, not a cancerous growth. The human self is a self who must awaken to the realization that itself is indeed The Self. The human potentiality is the gnostic discovery that each human being is *saccidānanda* (Being-without-a-second, Consciousness-without-objects, and Bliss-without-alloy).

Each of the metaphysical systems of Indian philosophy interpreted the Upaniṣadic insights within its own categories. The dualistic Sāṁkhya philosophers gave the cosmic *Puruṣa* (spirit) a telic role in the evolutes from *Prakṛti* (Matter). The atomic Vaiśeṣika philosophers conceived of a plurality of nonmaterial nonatomic selves *(Jīvātman)* to parallel their infinite number of atoms and also of a Supreme Self *(Paramātman)*, arguing that the Upaniṣadic *tat tvam asi* establishes a relation of similarity rather than identity. The Advaita Vedāntists in their efforts to stay close to the *śruti* texts, claimed that the Supreme Self *(Ātman)* is absolute reality *(sat)* and the individual self *(jīva)* is an appearance *(māyā)* under the limits of space and time. Śaṅkara (ca. 788–ca. 820) regarded himself as the only accurate interpreter of the *Upaniṣads,* a claim disputed by many students of Indian philosophy.[44] The ground of this assessment is based on the fact that he was the only one of the classical commentators on Bādarāyana's *Vedānta Sūtras,* that is, the Upaniṣadic doctrine in capsule form, who did not interpret the individual self as an atom, an agent, and a part of God. The *reality* of the self is no problem, said Śaṅkara. The problem is the *nature* of the self. He would have converted the Cartesian "I think, therefore I am" to "I am, therefore I think." Man *is,* and therefore he seeks to discover *what* he is. The chief difficulty in seeking the nature of the self is the confusion of the body and the self. The self is not the body. It is embodied. In the embodied state the self is covered with five sheaths *(koṣas)*: (1) *annamaya,* (2) *prāṇamaya,* (3) *manomaya,* (4) *vijñānamaya,* and (5) *ānandamaya.* A *koṣa* might be thought of as the reification of an incarnating tendency. *Annamaya koṣa* is the sheath formed by food, that is, the physical, nonmigrating body. *Prāṇamaya koṣa* is the sheath of the motor functions, that is, the principle of vitality. *Manomaya koṣa* is the sheath of volition. It directs the self to the performance of egocentric acts, although it does not know which is the real ego. *Vijñānamaya koṣa* is the sheath that motivates the self to seek the discursive, that is, nonintuitional, form of knowledge. Śaṅkara always insisted that the Brahman, the physical world, and the self could be known from two points of view: (1) *aparā vidyā,* the lower knowledge in which subject-object dichotomy is preserved, and (2) *parā vidyā,* the higher knowledge that transcends the subject-object dichotomy. The *prāṇamaya koṣa, manomaya koṣa,* and *vijñānamaya koṣa* constitute the body which migrates, that is, they in the next incarnation take on a new *annamaya koṣa. Ānandamaya koṣa* is the sheath of bliss. It is the agent that carries the *karma* from incarnation to incarnation. Since this is the principle that determines that there will be another carnate life and what that life will be, it is called the causal body. It is the sheath of bliss—but not of true bliss, for it tempts the self to seek the happiness of bodily existence rather than liberation of the self from its sheaths. The five sheaths constitute the psychophysical organism.

But this self is not the true Self. The *jīva* suffers the illusion that its apparent individuality is a genuine individuality. Śaṅkara wrote that the "individual self is to be considered a mere appearance of the highest Self, like the reflection of the sun in the water; it is neither directly that (i.e., the highest Self), nor a different thing. Hence just as, when one reflected image of the sun trembles, another reflected image does not on that account tremble also; so, when one soul is connected with actions and results of actions, another soul is not on that account connected likewise."[45] The burden of Śaṅkara's argument, however, is that the difference between *jīva* and *Ātman* is an unreal difference, a difference apparent to the unliberated, who understand only from the point of view of *aparā vidyā*, whereas the liberated realize that the *jīva* is the *Ātman* seen with false qualities. "As therefore the individual self and the highest Self differ in name only, it being a settled matter that perfect knowledge has for its object the absolute oneness of the two; it is senseless to insist (as some do) on a plurality of Selfs, and to maintain that the individual soul is different from the highest Self, and the highest Self from the individual soul. For the Self is indeed called by many different names, but it is one only."[46]

e. Ryle's Criticism of the Substance Theory

Gilbert Ryle in *The Concept of Mind* attacked the substance theory of the self. The theory is so prevalent, he said, that it deserves to be described as "the official doctrine." This doctrine, according to Ryle, is the following: "With the doubtful exceptions of idiots and infants in arms every human being has both a body and a mind. Some would prefer to say that every human being is both a body and a mind. His body and his mind are ordinarily harnessed together, but after the death of the body his mind may continue to exist and function."[47] In many places in his book Ryle referred to the "official doctrine" as "the dogma of the Ghost in the Machine."[48] This dogma results in "a philosopher's myth," which Ryle called "the two-worlds story."[49] One world is that of the body in space, subject to the mechanical laws that govern all spatial bodies. The life of the body is a public affair. The other world is that of the mind, which is not in space and not subject to mechanical laws. The life of the mind is a private affair. Each person is hence considered to live two lives through two collateral histories; one consists of what happens in and to the body, the other of what happens in and to the mind. The events of the physical world are said to be external; the events of the mental world are said to be internal. This, said Ryle, cannot be the case, since the mind as nonspatial cannot literally be inside anything.

The "official doctrine," according to Ryle, is "entirely false, and false not in detail but in principle. It is not merely an assemblage of particular mistakes. It is one big mistake and a mistake of a special kind. It is, namely, a category-mistake. It represents the facts of mental life as if they belonged to one logical type or category (or range of types or categories), when they actually belong to another."[50] The error is like thinking that Oxford University is a member of the class of things like colleges, libraries, playing fields, museums, scientific departments, and administrative offices; or like thinking of a military division as a member of the class of things like battalions, batteries, and squadrons; or like thinking of team spirit as a member of the class of things such as bowlers, batsmen, fielders, umpires, and scorers. Ryle put part of the onus for the "official doctrine" on Descartes who, as a man of scientific genius, endorsed the claims of mechanics provided by Galileo, yet as a religious man could not accept the view that human nature differs from strictly mechanical nature only in being more complex.

A mind or self, according to Ryle, is a certain way in which the incidents of one's life are ordered. We do not say "My eyes see the bird in the tree," but rather "I see the bird in the tree." Likewise we ought not to say "My mind knows the Pythagorean theorem," but "I know the Pythagorean theorem."[51] Ryle's argument is more complicated than I have indicated, but this is sufficient to suggest his rejection of the substance theories of the self and his insistence that the pronoun "I" does not refer to a "ghost in the machine" nor "some sort of committee or team of persons, all laced together inside one skin."[52]

2. *Dependent Substance Theories*

The second general theory of the nature of the self is the theory of dependent substance. According to this theory the self is not a corporeal entity nor an incorporeal entity that exists, that is, whose reality is independent of the reality of anything else, but it is an entity that subsists, that is, whose reality is dependent on the reality of something else. If the reality upon which it is dependent for its own reality is corporeal, the self may be identified as an emergent from the materialistic order; if the reality upon which it is dependent for its own reality is incorporeal, the self may be identified as an emanation from the idealistic order.

The theories that define the self as an emergent from matter are evolutionary theories, and therefore they did not appear in the West before the theory of organic evolution was presented in Charles Darwin's *The Origin of Species* in 1859. Thomas Huxley accepted the theory of evolution soon after it was made public, and commented how stupid he was not to have thought of it. As a biologist he held that the bodies of animals, including the human animal, are best regarded as mechanical systems. In his paper "On the Hypothesis that Animals are Automata" written in 1874 he described states of consciousness as effects of bodily processes that arise when matter has developed a special form or organization. Elsewhere he described consciousness as a function of the brain. In a more exacting mood he referred to consciousness as an "epiphenomenon" of the body rather than an "effect" or a "function." This fitted better his view that no state of consciousness can cause change in an organism. While a description of animals as conscious automata does not seem completely satisfactory, Huxley was correct in his understanding of an epiphenomenon as a product that has no capacity to affect that which produces it. The self-aware mind stands related to the body as the sound of the bell of the clock is related to the works, he explained. A better analogy would have been to compare the tick of the clock to consciousness and the works of the clock to the physical body. When Huxley was asked to clarify his meaning, he replied "I do not know," thereby taking refuge in agnosticism, a term he had coined in 1869. Frederick Copleston comments, "As one might expect in the case of a naturalist who makes excursions into philosophy, Huxley's philosophical theories are not well worked out."[53]

Meanwhile, George Henry Lewes had used *resultant* to designate a phenomenon predictable and understandable in terms of antecedent factors, and *emergent* for a phenomenon that could not be so predicted and understood. An emergent possesses properties novel with respect to the entities from which it came into being. Lloyd Morgan, having been turned from a career in engineering to biological studies by Huxley, substituted Lewes's *emergent* for Huxley's *epiphenomenon*. In addition to the connotation Lewes gave to *emergent*, Morgan stressed that an emergent has its own empirical qualities that make it possible for it to interact with the phenomenon from which it has emerged—something an epiphenomenon cannot do.

a. Alexander's Theory of the Self

The fullest presentation of the theory that the self is a dependent substance that has emerged from matter is the theory presented by Samuel Alexander of the University of Manchester in the Gifford Lectures of 1916–18, which appeared in 1920 as *Space, Time, and Deity*. According to Alexander's metaphysical system a consideration of the nature of reality must begin with an examination of Space and Time. (Alexander used upper-case initial letters when referring to extension and duration in general or as wholes.) He wrote, "It is not, I believe, too much to say that all the vital problems of philosophy depend for their solution on the solution of the problem what Space and Time are and more particularly how they are related to each other."[54] Space and Time are entities or forms of existence in which bodies occupy places and events occur. These events may be either mental, in which case they occur in Time only, or external, in which case they occur in Space-Time. Alexander, taking a cue from the theory of the evolution of species that matter itself is a product of evolution, wrote, "If it is asked . . . by what steps it is that mere motion under the guiding hand of Time leads to the emergence of the material complexes of motion which we find in the world of things; how a specific motion like that of light is generated, with constant and maximal velocity, and how atoms come into existence as combinations of electrons with or without the distinctively material nucleus, with relatively constant constitutions; I can only reply that I do not know, and that it is not for the metaphysician to say, in the absence of indications from the physicist himself. Yet it is difficult to refrain from hazarding conjecture by way of asking a question. And so I dare to ask if there may not be in these ages of simple existence something corresponding to the method pursued by nature in its higher stages, of natural selection; however natural selection is to be interpreted whether as operating upon insensible variations or upon large mutations. Whether that is to say, nature or Space-Time did not try various complexes of simple motions and out of the chaos of motion preserve certain types."[55] Alexander regarded this as more than a conjecture. Matter is the most successful of Space-Time's actions, which correspond to what is known as natural selection in the higher stages of nature. In addition to materiated Space-Time, there is in Alexander's view of reality what he referred to as "nisus," an upward thrust that results in new levels of reality and new levels of quality. At the time of the Pre-Cambrian geological period there were three realities—matter, nisus, and Deity. *Deity* in Alexander's nomenclature denotes the level of reality yet to come. Before life appeared on this planet Deity was life-not-yet-emerged, and before mind appeared Deity was mind-not-yet-emerged. In the present state of evolution nisus is still operative. Mind is the highest emergent we know, but there might be an infinite number of further emergents. "Deity" is still the name used to denote the next emergent. "God," on the other hand, means "the whole universe tending towards deity."[56]

Alexander informed his readers that he used the term *emergent* after the example of Lloyd Morgan to mark the appearance of novelty, and that it was to be contrasted with G. H. Lewes's *resultant*.[57] He rejected the term *epiphenomenon,* especially for mind, since this term suggests that mind is an associate of the body, "an inert accompaniment of neural process, a kind of aura which surrounds that process but plays no effective part of its own: the doctrine that mind is an epiphenomenon of nervous process, which nervous process would continue to work equally well if mind were absent."[58] He thought that *epiphenomenalism* carries the notion of accident, and mind is not an accident. "Mind is, according to our interpretation of the facts, an 'emergent' from life, and life an emergent from a lower physico-chemical level of existence."[59]

Mind emerges because there is a constellation of vital conditions—a collocation of conditions that constitutes something new: "Mental process is therefore something new, a fresh creation, which, despite the possibility of resolving it into physiological terms, means the presence of so specific a physiological constitution as to separate it from simpler vital processes."[60]

Although the emergent at each level is a new thing, Alexander stressed the emerging of new qualities, rather than new entities: "Out of certain physiological conditions nature has framed *a new quality* mind, which is therefore not itself physiological though it lives and moves and has its being in physiological conditions."[61] And again he described Deity as "a next higher empirical quality."[62] The qualities at the level of matter are the primary qualities, that is, the qualities inseparable from a body, for example, solidarity, extension, figure, motion, and number. The qualities at the level of life are the secondary qualities, that is, the qualities produced in living organisms by reason of the operation of the primary qualities upon them, for example, colors, tastes, odors. In other words, secondary qualities depend for their reality upon their relation to living organisms. The level of mind is the level of "conscious awareness"[63]—the level of the self, in our terminology. Alexander said that "tertiary qualities" emerge at this level. By *tertiary qualities* he meant such qualities as truth, goodness, and beauty. This is the level of values, and values subsist in physical reality only in relation to minds. Just as secondary qualities are novel qualities with respect to matter, and tertiary qualities are novel qualities with respect to life, so there are novel qualities with respect to mind. These Alexander called "divine qualities." He said they cannot be specified until they emerge, but "sanctity" is suggested as a possible designation.[64]

b. Teilhard's Theory of the Self

Another instance of a Western conception of a self that is rooted in an evolution from matter is the hypothesis shared by the atheistic biologist Julian Huxley and the Jesuit paleontologist Pierre Teilhard de Chardin. They distinguished a physical and biological evolution culminating in the appearance of man and a human evolution in which man is director. The former is an evolution of divergence in which genera fan out into species, and the latter is an evolution of convergence. The former, according to Teilhard, results in levels or spheres of increasing complexity: barysphere (metal), lithosphere (stone), hydrosphere (water), atmosphere (air), stratosphere (ether), biosphere (life), and noosphere (thought). The final sphere, which Teilhard on rare occasions called the theosphere (God), will culminate in the Omega Point, a unity that he conceived scientifically as a state in which the human race will fold in upon itself "to lapse slowly back into the dwindling mass of primordial energy"[65] and religiously as the "Cosmic Christ," the superior psychobiological focus of the universe comparable to Alexander's Deity. Much of Teilhard's fascinating speculations are not relevant to our concerns here, but what is important is that he held that the human being, the only animal that knows that it knows,[66] has emerged from matter. Matter, wrote Teilhard, "is not just the weight that drags us down, the mire that sucks us in, the bramble that bars our way. In itself, and before we find ourselves where we are, and before we choose, it is simply the slope on which we can go up just as well as go down."[67] Teilhard referred to Christ as "hidden power stirring in the heart of matter,"[68] and even composed a prayer to matter: "Matter, you in whom I find both seduction and strength, you in whom I find blandishment and virility, you who can enrich and destroy, I surrender myself to your mighty layers, with faith in the heavenly influences which have sweetened and purified your waters. The virtue of Christ has passed into you. Let your attractions lead me forward, let your sap be the food that nourishes me; let your resistance give me toughness; let your robberies and inroads give me freedom. And finally, let your whole being lead me towards Godhead."[69]

Huxley's and Teilhard's thesis of a double evolution has received support recently in the writings of Ilya Prigogine, a Belgian chemist, who claims that there are "dissipative structures" or "flowing wholenesses" at work in the physical universe, which explain how it is that living things have been running uphill in a universe that is supposed to be running down.[70]

c. Aurobindo's Theory of the Self

A dependent substance theory of the self as an emergent from matter has been developed by a twentieth-century Hindu, Aurobindo Ghose. Sri Aurobindo was a fiery Bengali who narrowly escaped execution at the hands of the British for his part in a bombing incident in Calcutta in 1908. He moved to Pondicherry in South India in 1910, where he established an ashram and lived in semi-seclusion, writing philosophical essays in flowery English until his death in 1950. Although his writings indicate possible familiarity with the writings of the emergent evolutionists, he did not indicate any indebtedness, nor did he quote authors other than the Vedic seers. One of his aims was to demonstrate that the Advaita Vedāntins were wrong in their claims that the individual self is unreal. Whereas Śaṅkara disparaged the physical world as illusory and knowledge of the physical world as a lower and inferior form of knowledge, Aurobindo valued the physical world as the locus of the progressive self-manifestation of the Brahman and knowledge of the physical world as an important part of man's way of liberation. Śaṅkara was unable to give a satisfactory reason for the existence of the material universe, finding it falling from reality and value into irreality and disvalue. But Aurobindo argued that the Brahman in creation realizes possibilities: "An infinite, indivisible existence all-blissful in its pure self-consciousness moves out of its fundamental purity into the varied play of Force that is consciousness, into the movement of Prakriti which is the play of *Māyā*."[71] *Māyā* as illusion "cuts the knot of the world problem, it does not disentangle it; it is an escape, not a solution."[72] The physical world, according to Aurobindo, is the masked form of the Absolute. It is the magical play of Brahman's infinite variability, the eternal manifested in time, the spaceless in space, the formless in form, the invisible in the seen, the inaudible in sounds, and so on. The world is the progressive self-manifestation of Brahman. The existence of the physical is not a falling from the spiritual but an expression of a delight in the variable realization of all possibilities. Value is inherent in mutable becoming, not in immutable being. The cosmos is the working out of the being of Brahman, and without this evolutionary movement the Brahman would not be the All. Hence the world process is not a regrettable fate, nor a material necessity, nor a moral retribution, nor a tragic experiment, but a joyous expression and fulfillment of Totality. The essence of Being is becoming. Hence the world process is a double or cyclical movement: an involution or devolution from Brahman to Matter and an evolution from Matter to Brahman. While Aurobindo referred to these movements as descent and ascent, the connotation of falling or rising in value must be avoided. The West's "bankruptcy of Spirit" and India's "bankruptcy of Life" must be healed by each learning from the other.[73]

Matter is "the involution of the conscious delight of existence in self-oblivious force and in a self-dividing, infinitesimally disaggregated form of substance."[74] Matter is the "extreme fragmentation of the Infinite,"[75] a "product" of Brahman,[76] a "mode" of Brahman,[77] and Brahman itself: "Brahman is not only the cause and supporting power and indwelling principle of the universe, he is also its material and its sole material. Matter also is Brahman and is nothing other than or different from Brahman."[78] Thus Matter is the involution of Brahman, and Brahman is the evolution of Matter. The gradations of evolution and involution constitute a "sevenfold chord of being." Three principles constitute the nature of the divine being: (1) the principle of transcendent and infinite Existence *(Sat)*, (2) the principle of transcendent and infinite Consciousness *(Chit)*, and (3) the principle of transcendent and infinite Bliss *(Ānanda)*. These higher principles operate in three subordinate powers: (1) Matter, the form the three higher principles, known integratively as *saccidānanda,* assume when subjected to space and time; (2) Life, the form *saccidānanda* takes under the form of energy; (3) Mind, the form *saccidānanda* takes when under the limitations of finite knowing.[79] Between the three higher principles and the three lower principles is an intermediate principle, which Aurobindo called "Supermind." This is the locus of creative action. It is the integration of the One and the Many. "The creation depends on and moves between the biune principle of unity and multiplicity; it is a manifoldness of idea and force and form which is the expression of an original unity, and it is an eternal oneness which is the foundation and reality of the multiple worlds and makes their play possible. . . . While to its original self-awareness all things are one being, one consciousness, one will, one self-delight and the whole movement of things a movement one and indivisible, it proceeds in its action from the unity to the multiplicity and from multiplicity to unity, creating an ordered relation between them and an appearance but not a binding reality of division, a subtle unseparating division, or rather a demarcation and determination within the indivisble."[80] Matter is for Aurobindo not a falling from a divine status nor a darkening of the divine light as it was for the Western Gnostics, but "a form and body of that which we realise as Spirit."[81] It is the last principle in the descent; it is also the first principle in the ascent. The physical body—the most immediate form in which the principle of matter is presented to man—is to be neither neglected nor despised. Aurobindo warned that "if we reject the mental and physical in our attraction to the spiritual, we do not fulfil God integrally, nor satisfy the conditions of His self-manifestation. . . . However high we may climb, even though it be to the Non-Being itself, we climb ill if we forget our base."[82]

Matter is not dead. It contains all the powers of the "sevenfold chord of being." Out of matter evolves Life, Mind, Supermind, Absolute Existence, Absolute Consciousness, and Absolute Bliss. All that evolves evolves from Matter even as Matter involves from Brahman. The evolutes of Matter are emergents, not epiphenomena, since the cause-effect relation between Matter and its evolutes is reciprocal. Aurobindo wrote, "Evolution comes by the unceasing pressure of the supra-material planes on the material compelling it to deliver out of itself their principles and powers which might conceivably otherwise have slept imprisoned in the rigidity of the material formula."[83] At the level of Mind an evolutionary change takes place—a change that has already been noted in Huxley's and Teilhard's interpretation of evolution. Evolution before the appearance of man is an unconscious evolution tending chiefly to survival, but after the appearance of man evolution becomes a conscious perfecting. Man is the end of the evolution up to the level of self, that is, the level of self-consciousness, and man is the means of evolution beyond self-consciousness. Struggle is the mark of prehuman evolution; harmony is the mark of post-human evolution. The aim of the first evolution is to be: the aim of the second evolution is to become perfected. Man is neither an animal emerging out of matter nor a mind housed in a physical body, but "a spirit using the mind, life and body for an individual and a communal experience and self-manifestation in the universe."[84] Man is "the most discontented" animal.[85] "He is the first son of earth who becomes vaguely aware of God within him, of his immortality or of his need of immortality, and the knowledge is a whip that drives and a cross of crucifixion until he is able to turn it into a source of infinite light and joy and power."[86] Man's paradox is that he is to achieve the divine life in an animal body; he is "to become and to live as a universal being."[87] Man is the vehicle in which the universe emerges most completely. He gives to the world for the first time a development of consciousness by which a full self-discovery becomes possible. "The ascent to the divine Life is the human journey, the Work of works, the acceptable Sacrifice. This alone is man's real business in the world and the justification of his existence, without which he would be only an insect crawling among other ephemeral insects on a speck of surface mud and water which has managed to form itself amid the appalling immensities of the physical universe."[88] Man must enlarge himself without losing himself; he must become divine without ceasing to be human.

The great human tragedy, according to Aurobindo, is that though man has evolved as a conscious being, he directs his knowing largely to externals. Hence, he cannot find his real self nor the real Self of the world in which he lives. He limits his knowledge to his surface existence, "a hasty, incompetent and fragmentary translation of a little out of the much that we are."[89] This self-imposed circumscription of self-awareness results in the identification of self with the body, or the life, or the mind: "The Soul forgetting itself experiences only this single knot in Matter and says 'I am this body'.... The Soul, still forgetting itself, says 'I am this life'.... The Soul identifies itself with this mental dynamo or station and says 'I am this mind.'"[90] The self is thus identified with the limitations and exclusions of the ego. The self is thought to be something that has individualized itself and exists only as long as it is individualized. Aurobindo wrote, "The formation of a mental and vital ego tied to the body-sense was the first great labour of the cosmic Life in its progressive evolution; for this was the means it found for creating out of matter a conscious individual."[91] Until man turns his vision inward, he is separated from his own true being. He lives in a false relationship with his environment. He does not yet understand that the limited ego is only an intermediate phenomenon necessary as a link in the total evolutionary development. He has yet to discover that he must exceed the ego to become his true Self, and that the awareness of his real Being is the ultimate meaning of individual and terrestrial existence. But man does not *become* Brahman; he *is* Brahman. The self is "the Divine in the individual ascending back out of limited Nature to its own proper divinity."[92] The ego is but a trembling ray on the surface. But the self does not lie on the surface: "Our ego is only a face of the universal being and has no separate existence; our apparent separative individuality is only a surface movement and behind it our real individuality stretches out to unity with all things and upward to oneness with the transcendent Divine Infinity."[93] "In our depths we ourselves are that One."[94] Thus Aurobindo made peace with Śaṅkara—a peace conditional on the reality of the individual self.

Aurobindo is significant as an Eastern philosopher who acts as a bridge between the materialism associated with the West and the spiritualism associated with the East. In addition, for our purposes he is important in his assertion that the human self is dependent on its evolution from Matter and its involution from Spirit.[95]

d. Plotinus's Theory of the Self

The dependent substance theories of the nature of the self examined thus far picture the self as emerging from an evolutionary process beginning with matter. The movement may be compared to ascending a wooden ladder that rests firmly on the ground. We now turn to dependent substance theories of the idealistic order. The movement in this case may be compared to descending a rope ladder that is securely fastened at the top. If the former is evolution from matter, the latter is devolution from spirit. The fountainhead of this view of the self in the West is Plotinus, a fourth-century Greek-speaking Egyptian who founded a school in Rome in his fortieth year, made many friends and few enemies, and was consulted for advice by the highest Roman officers, including the Emperor Gallienus. His pupil, Porphyry, collected the sparse writings of his master, arranging them in six books, each containing nine chapters. In lieu of a descriptive title he called the collection *Enneads* (The Nines), and that remains the title to this day. Plotinus regarded his teachings and writings to be the correct interpretation of Plato. Although Plotinus admitted that Plato did not say everything that he (Plotinus) put in his system, he insisted that he was saying what Plato intended to say. Since the nineteenth century the thought of Plotinus has been called "Neo-platonism" rather than "Platonism." The system that Plotinus insisted was Plato's he located in the dialogues of Plato by selecting allegorical, mystical, and mythical passages, treating them out of context, and relating them to other passages with no regard to the development of thought within each dialogue. According to Frederick Copleston, "Neo-Platonism was really the intellectualist reply to the contemporary yearning for personal salvation, those spiritual aspirations of the individual, which are so marked a feature of the period."[96]

According to Plotinus a great evil has befallen human beings. This evil he called *tólma,* a term sometimes translated "self-will." But for Plotinus it had stronger connotations. For him *tólma* meant the audacity to venture on a bold and rash undertaking without consideration of all the consequences. The first reckless act was being born. Plotinus was particularly incensed by the human striving to be different from one's fellows. They who assert their individuality forget who they are and from whence they have come. "Once having tasted the pleasures of independence, they use their freedom to go in a direction that leads away from their origin. And when they have gone a great distance, they even forget that they came from it. Like children separated from their family since birth and educated away from home, they are ignorant now of their parentage and therefore of their identity."[97] Most people, he said, are like choral singers who have been distracted from following the conductor by gazing at the audience. Plotinus set himself to the task of helping people find the proper focus of their lives by rediscovering their origin, turning around, and ascending to the divinity from which they came.

The divinity from which all come is known as the One. The word *one (hen, monás)* had different meanings for the ancient Greek philosophers. According to Aristotle, Xenophanes as the first to postulate a unity; however, he "gave no clear statement . . . but with reference to the whole material universe he says the One is God."[98] For Parmenides it was Being—entire, immovable, and without end. For the Pythagoreans it was the point, that is, substance with position. For Democritus and Leucippus it was the atom, that is, the indivisible particle. For Aristotle it was that which "is not divisible in any dimension and is without position."[99] Plato distinguished the One and the Many, praising the study of the former as leading to the knowledge of true being,[100] and swore if he could find a teacher able to see the One and the Many in nature he would "walk in his footsteps as if he were a god."[101] Plotinus believed he was such a teacher. The One of Plotinus was not a numerical one, not the first in the numerical order, not the unity of all units, not even the Being constitutive of beings. In the words of William Inge, "We must be careful not to give 'the One' a merely numerical sense. In this, the numerical sense, unity and plurality are correlatives, so that we cannot have the former without the latter. . . . But for Plotinus the One is the source from which the differentiation of unity and plurality proceeds; it is the transcendence of separability rather than the negation of plurality."[102] The One, which Plotinus also termed "God," "the Good," "Father," and "Fatherland," is the first principle of all reality. Plotinus called it the *hypóstasis*. The Greek term *hypóstasis* means literally the sediment that settles to the bottom of a liquid mixture, hence the support, foundation, or basis of a substance. A *hypóstasis* is the groundwork of a thing. It is that which exists with respect to something that subsists. In Plotinus's metaphysics the primal *hypóstasis* is the One. The One is absolutely transcendent. It is beyond being, beyond thought, beyond will, beyond activity. Plotinus's reasons for these claims are that a being is a being only in a class of beings, thinking assumes a separation between thinker and object of thought, willing requires another upon which one can exert will, and acting is a relationship with other things. But there is no duality—ontological, epistemological, volitional, or active—in the One. The One is neither subject nor object. The One transcends all existence, thought, valuation, and action. The One cannot be self-aware, since self-awareness presupposes a dichotomy of self-as-subject and self-as-object, and thus the One would lose its essence as the principle of unity.

The One as the basic principle of reality is also the principle of totality or fullness that was known for centuries in the West as "the great chain of being." Plotinus was realistic enough to recognize the reality of sensed objects, but idealistic enough to believe that the sensed objects were not the fundamentally real objects. In Platonic language the cave may be "the prisonhouse of sensation," but it is still real in its cave-ness. The One in order to be totality must actualize all possibilities. How is it, asks Plotinus, that from the One there proceed many? "Why did the One not remain within itself, why did it emit that manifoldness that we find to characterize Being and which we seek to trace back to the One?"[103] His answer is that perfection requires production: "Everything that has arrived at its point of perfection becomes productive. That which is eternally perfect is eternally productive."[104] The necessary productivity of perfection requires quasi-oxymoronic terms: perfection requires imperfection, being requires becoming, knowledge requires opinion (if not ignorance), goodness requires the lesser goods, beauty requires all grades of beauty, and so on. Plotinus confessed that the idea was beyond speech. The Advaita Vedāntins face the same problem with respect to the Brahman. One of the best statements on the issue has been that of a Western student of Indian thought: "Nothing is external to absolute Reality; the world is therefore a kind of internal dimension of Brahman. But Brahman is without relativity; thus the world is a necessary aspect of the absolute necessity of Brahman. Put in another way, relativity is an aspect of the Absolute."[105]

Plotinus is more explicit in accounting for *how* it is that the One multiplies than in explaining *why* the One multiplies. The issue was so momentous and the way so precarious that Plotinus began the search with a prayer: "In approaching this problem let us first invoke the divinity. Let us do so not with words but with a lifting of our souls to it and thus to pray alone to the Alone."[106] His explanation for the production of the self and its worlds can best be understood as an effort to express systematically the Platonic principle that the lower is to be explained in terms of the higher. He uses the terms *flow (hreō)* and *overflow (aporreō)* to suggest the process by which lesser beings come from the One. The One brings into reality that which is less than the One, as the sun radiates light which is of the sun, and yet it is not the sun. Again a physical object causes itself to appear in a mirror, yet the reflection both is and is not the object reflected. In a less metaphorical manner Plotinus writes, "The One 'overflows' and its excess begets an other than itself; begotten turns back towards begetter and is filled and becomes its contemplator The Intelligence; its abiding with The One constitutes its Being; its contemplating The One constitutes its being Intelligence; because it abides with The One in order to see, it becomes—at one and the same time—Intelligence and Being."[107] This form of production is known as emanation, and it can be understood as emergence stood on its head, inasmuch as emergence of self, as already noted, is production of a higher level of reality from a lower, while emanation of self is production of a lower level of reality from a higher. Emanation is production by essence alone, a production without loss, a production involving neither consciousness nor effort. Although Plotinus claimed that the One in emanating does not lose unity, rank, or dignity, his description suggests otherwise. Divine Reason or Divine Intelligence *(Noûs)*, the first emanation and the second *hypóstasis,* is ontologically, epistemologically, and axiologically lower than the One, that is, Intelligence is less in the order of being than is the One, is understood in terms of the One, and is inferior in value to the One. The process of emanation, as noted in the above quotation, has two parts: (1) a going forth *(próödos)* of an overflow or effulgence, and (2) a turning back *(epistrophé)* to that from which it emanated. This is an indication of the conflict of the ideals of fullness and unity. Nothing can be extraneous to the One, yet the One cannot retain unity if the One emanates a not-One. The process might be described animistically as an expression of exuberance of being, and then a regret that the exuberance has created a dichotomy. However, since emanation from the One does not take place in time, this animistic interpretation is flawed. Going forth and returning are two ways of considering the same process. Perhaps Plotinus's claim that emanation is creation without loss might be saved by arguing that Intelligence, the second *hypóstasis,* is not a not-One but the One considered under the aegis of contemplation.

The Divine Reason, which is the first emanation of the One, "does not occupy the first rank. Above it there must be a principle the discovery of which is the ultimate object of all our previous discussion. The manifold must be posterior to unity. Intelligence is at once intelligence and the intelligible, and is therefore two things at once."[108] To assert that at the level of intelligence the One becomes contemplator of the One is to state that the One becomes a Self, since awareness of self, as has been noted again and again, is the essence of what it means to be a self. Moreover, the description of the Divine Reason's contemplation as the form in which it is "two things at once" restates what has been noted before about the unity-disunity of self-consciousness. In Plotinus's total system the Divine Reason as *hypóstasis* also overflows and returns, resulting in the emergence of the World Soul, and from the World Soul emerges the Physical Universe. But from the Physical Universe no further ontological principles emerge. The emergent energy of the One has been exhausted. The light has become dark. The good has become evil.

The descent of emergents from the One to the Physical Universe is not the only line of production. At the levels of the Divine Reason, the World Soul, and the Physical Universe there are also horizontal productions. Transcendental productivity is manifested not only in the vertical emergence as causation of lesser from greater, but also in horizontal creation as causation, in which the cause and effect are of the same ontological order. Individual human minds proceed from the Divine Reason, individual human lives (or souls) proceed from the World Soul, and individual human bodies proceed from the Physical Universe.

Man is the microcosm of the macrocosm. Hence to know one's self is to know the universe. "What subject of inquiry, analysis, or discussion could be preferable to this? . . . Desirous as we are to explore all things knowable . . . we should surely explore that which makes the exploration."[109] Man is the union of several elements or faculties: the One, the Divine Reason, the individual mind, the World Soul, the psychophysical mechanism of sensation, vegetable life, and matter. Although the body is a "chain" and a "tomb," and the sensations are a "cave" and a "grotto,"[110] and although man has suffered "loss of wings,"[111] the human being can consciously engage in the turning back *(epistrophē)* to the "Fatherland." The image of the One is not completely lost. The image remains in the self-aware animal. The human is the being who can reverse the direction from descent to ascent. "When the soul descends, she will by her nature never reach complete nothingness. She will fall into evil and, in this sense, into nothingness, but not into complete nothingness. In a similar way, when the soul reverses her direction, she does not arrive at something different, but at herself. But as she is in her self alone and not even in the world of Being, she is in the existence beyond."[112] But human efforts are not enough. There must be a vision. And that can come only from the One. Plotinus tried to describe the vision: "He who has the vision becomes, as it were, another being. He ceases to be himself, he retains nothing of himself. Absorbed in the beyond he is one with it, like a center that coincides with another center. While these centers coincide, they are one; but they become two when they separate. It is in this sense only that we can speak of the One as something separate. Hence it is very difficult to describe this vision."[113] The life of the mystic is as "the life of the divinity and of divine and blessed men: detachment from all things here below, scorn of all earthly pleasures, the flight of the lone to the Alone."[114]

e. Fichte's Theory of the Self

The most significant dependent substance theories of the idealistic order in the West following Plotinus are to be found among the eighteenth- and nineteenth-century German idealists who were responding to the legacy of Kant. According to Kant the human mind is forever cut off from the real world. We cannot know things as they are; we can know them only under the limiting conditions of our sensing and understanding. Appearances, not realities, are all we can know. Only insofar as things can take on spatiality and temporality can we experience them, and only insofar as things can conform to causality can we know them. But since everything—and all of anything—

fails to conform to these limits, we cannot know things as they are in themselves.

Many German philosophers—especially Fichte, Schelling, Hegel, and Schopenhauer—rebelled against the Kantian critical philosophy. Each in his own way attacked the notion of things-in-themselves, which according to Kant must exist to account for sensation, and which also, according to Kant, cannot be shown to exist since the forms of sensation, that is, space and time, and the categories of the mind, that is, cause and effect, cannot be used to give us knowledge of the real world, even knowledge of the existence of the real world.

I shall take the thoughts of Johann Gottlieb Fichte (1762–1814) as an example of German idealism. According to Fichte, the error Kant made was in thinking statically. Reality is dynamic process, not static being. In his classroom at the University of Jena Fichte asked his students to think of a manufactured object, then of the one who thought the object, then of the one who thought of the one who thought the object, and so on. The chain is endless, since there always remains an ego that transcends being an object of thought. An epistemological object stands in relation to an epistemological subject; and, since epistemological subjects become transmogrified into epistemological objects, there is infinite regression. The name given to this process is "Absolute Ego." But the name must not reify the process. The Absolute Ego is "a doing [*Thun*] and absolutely nothing else; one should not even call it an active thing [*ein Tätiges*]."[115] The Absolute Ego is the universe seeking to become fully self-aware; or to state this conversely, the universe is the Absolute Ego in the eternally unfinished process of self-consciousness. The goal of the process is a completely free activity engaged in for no purpose outside itself. This goal Fichte called "God." As might be expected, Fichte often had to defend himself against the charge of atheism. His God, like the Deity in Alexander's metaphysics, is an unrealized and unrealizable ideal.

The world results from the Absolute Ego's producing its own experience out of the self-consciousness that is its nature. The reasoning offered by Fichte for this conclusion is that the self-consciousness of the Absolute Ego, like the self-consciousness of which each of us is aware, requires both the epistemological subject and the epistemological object—the "I" that knows and the "me" that is known. If we begin with the assumption that there is an activity of knowing, then we must acknowledge that there is a self that knows. This is the subjective-thing-in-itself—and this Kant should have recognized. In the absence of a self there is no knowing; but there is knowledge, so there is a self. This syllogism holds not only for the finite knowing of humans but also for the infinite knowing of the Absolute Ego. However, added Fichte, the logic of the argument must not be pressed. The first principle of knowing—the reality of a self—must be felt and lived, rather than thought and proved. Frederick Copleston compares Fichte's view of the Absolute Ego with Hume's view of personal identity, and finds Fichte's preferable: "Fichte is, in the opinion of the present writer, perfectly justified in affirming the I-subject or transcendental ego. Hume, looking into his mind, so to speak, and finding only psychical phenomena, tried to reduce the self to the succession of these phenomena. And it is understandable that he acted in this way. For part of his programme was to apply to man the empirical method, as he conceived it, which had proved so successful in 'experimental philosophy' or natural science. But the direction of his attention to the objects or data of introspection led him to slur over the fact, all-important for the philosopher, that psychical phenomena became phenomena (appearing to a subject) only through the objectifying activity of a subject which transcends objectification in the same sense. Obviously, there is no question of reducing the human being to a transcendental or metaphysical ego. And the problem of the relation between the self as pure subject and other aspects of the self is one that cannot be evaded. But this does not alter the fact that a recognition of the transcendental ego is essential to an adequate phenomenology of consciousness. And in regard to this point Fichte shows a degree of insight which Hume lacked."[116]

The second principle of knowing is the object of knowing. Knowing requires both an ego and a nonego. This distinction between subject and object is within experience, and, in the case of the self-consciousness of the Absolute Ego, which is by nature a process of consciousness, requires a strife between the knower and the known. But the Absolute Ego is one. So in order to become a self-conscious process it must limit itself by polarization of empirical ego and empirical non-ego. For the Absolute Ego, to be is to be conscious and to be conscious is to strive, and that requires a limiting self and a non-self. Moreover, in accord with the principle of plenitude—which is more often assumed than stated—infinite profusion and variety is necessary for the self-consciousness of the Absolute Ego. Fichte traced the process of the Absolute Ego's self-knowledge in six movements or thrusts *(Anstösse)*, each of which marks a unique psychological-epistemological level. The first *Anstoss* creates unreflective sensation. The second creates perception, that is, the awareness that one is sensing. At the third *Anstoss* the perceptions are turned into objects, that is, the awareness of things. The fourth level is reached when things are classified. This is the level of general terms. At the fifth *Anstoss* the general ideas are arranged in logical relations to one another. The final *Anstoss* is marked by self-consciousness—a recognition that one is indeed the originator of the laws of thought and knows oneself as the founder of one's own knowledge. The finite ego, the self-conscious human animal, is the instrument through which the Absolute Ego eternally strives to become self-conscious.

f. Viśiṣṭādvaita Vedānta Theory of the Self

Unfortunately, those both in the West and in India who know only a little of Indian philosophy assume that Śaṅkara's Advaita Vedāntism with its view of the Brahman as *Sat* (Reality) and the physical world and the individual self as *māyā* (illusion) is Indian philosophy. A fairer assessment could be made if Rāmānuja's Viśiṣṭādvaita Vedāntism were also well known. A twentieth-century Indian philosopher has written, "In contemporary Indian philosophy, Vedānta is overweighted on the side of Advaita; and the balance will be restored only when the other systems of Vedānta, notably that of Rāmānuja, are widely known and appreciated in the west as well as in the east."[117] Another Indian philosopher has observed, "Considering the philosophy of Śaṅkara as typical of Indian thought, Western critics have accused Hinduism of illusionism, i.e., of regarding the world of experience, the world of life and activity, as unreal; and on this ground, they have urged that Hinduism can in the end provide no basis for the living of life in this world. Even if such a criticism be true of Śaṅkara's philosophy, it certainly cannot claim to be true of all Hindu philosophy. Rāmānuja, at any rate, repudiates at every turn the doctrine of the illusoriness of the material world and the finite self, and postulates that ultimate Reality is one in which the material world and the finite self find a necessary place."[118]

The difference between Advaita Vedānta and Viśiṣṭādvaita Vedānta can be understood by considering how Śaṅkara and Rāmānuja interpreted the Upaniṣadic aphorism, *tat tvam asi*. For Śaṅkara it was an analytic statement, that is, a statement in which the predicate term adds no information to that contained in the subject term. What one is in essence and what the universe is in its essence is identical. *Ātman* is Brahman, and Brahman is *Ātman*. But *Ātman* (Universal Self) is not *jīva* (individual self). It is the individual self in its essence as Self, not in its individuality, that is identical with the Brahman. For Rāmānuja *tat tvam asi* is a synthetic statement, that is, the predicate term adds information not contained in the subject term. His own words are: "In texts, again, such as 'Thou art that,' the co-ordination of the constituent parts is not meant to convey the idea of the absolute unity of a non-differenced substance: on the contrary, the words 'that' and 'thou' denote a Brahman distinguished by difference. The word 'that' refers to Brahman omniscient, etc., which had been introduced as the general topic of consideration in previous passages of the same section, such as 'It thought, may I be many'; the word 'thou,' which stands in co-ordination to 'that,' conveys the idea of Brahman in so far as having for its body the individual souls connected with non-intelligent matter."[119] For Rāmānuja *tat tvam asi* asserts the partial identity of the two manifestations of the same substance: Brahman in the causal state and Brahman in the effected state. The former is Totality pre-manifested; the latter is Totality manifested. In the former the physical world and individual selves exist potentially; in the latter they exist actually. *Tat* (Brahman creative) and *Tvam* (Brahman created) are both Brahman. *Nirguṇa* (Totality undifferentiated) is Brahman, and *Saguṇa* (Totality differentiated) is also Brahman.

The term *Advaita* (non-dual) means that the self in its essence and Totality in its essence are identical. The term *Viśiṣṭādvaita* means that the self in its essence and Totality in its essence are qualifiedly *(viśiṣṭ)* identical. The *jīva* is a fragment *(amśa)* of Brahman, an inseparable attribute *(viśeṣana)* of Brahman, a mode *(prakāra)* of Brahman, and an effect *(kārya)* of Brahman. The meaning, of course, is that the reality of the self is dependent on the reality of Brahman. According to Rāmānuja, "The individual soul is a part of the highest Self; as the light issuing from a luminous thing such as fire or the sun is a part of that body; or as the generic characteristics of a cow or horse, and the white or black colour of things so coloured, are attributes and hence parts of the things in which these attributes inhere; or as the body is a part of an embodied thing. For by a part we understand that which constitutes one place of some thing, and hence a distinguishing attribute is a part of the thing distinguished by that attribute."[120] When Rāmānuja refers to the individual self as an effect of Brahman, he does not mean that the *jīva* is a creation in the sense in which ether or water are creations. *Jīvas*, as well as the elements of the physical world, exist prior to their manifestation. There is the causal state, and there is the effected state. "By a thing being an effect we mean its being due to a substance passing over into some other state; and from this point of view the self is also an effect."[121] There is a difference, however, in referring to the *jīva* as an effect and also to the physical elements as an effect. "Effect" as "creation" may be appropriate with respect to the physical elements, but not with respect to the self. The change from the unmanifested state to the manifested state of physical elements involves a substantial change; the change from the unmanifested state to the manifested state of *jīvas* involves a qualitative change. In the words of Rāmānuja, "The 'otherness' on which the self depends consists in the contraction and expansion of intelligence; while the change on which the origination of ether and so on depends is a change of essential nature."[122]

Rāmānuja believed that in contending the *jīva* to be a part of the Brahman he avoided two errors: (1) the error of thinking that the self is cut off from the universe, and (2) the error of thinking that the self is identical with the universe. He saw both of these as errors because in either case no relations are possible between the self and the universe. His theory, he believed, preserved the individuality of the self and also preserved the integrity of the Whole.

3. Relationship Theories of the Self

Thus far we have considered the substance theories of the nature of the self. These theories regard the self as a thing, a being, or an existent having either an independent or a dependent status. Now we shall examine the theories of the self as a relationship. There are two types—associationism and functionalism.

a. Hume's Theory of the Self

The best example of associationism in the West is that of David Hume. We noted in the previous chapter the difficulty Hume had in knowing the self. Now we ask what was the nature of the self he found so difficult to know. The self, he said, is "nothing but a bundle or collection of different perceptions, which succeed each other with an inconceivable rapidity, and are in a perpetual flux and movement."[123] According to Hume there are two kinds of perceptions: (1) vivid perceptions, i.e., sensations, which Hume called "impressions," and (2) faint perceptions, i.e., ideas, which according to Hume are derived from impressions. Thus a self is a relationship among impressions and/or ideas. Whatever the self is, it is not a fixed entity or relationship, since according to Hume no "power of the soul . . . remains unalterably the same, perhaps for one moment."[124] "The mind is a kind of theatre, where several perceptions successively make their appearance; pass, repass, glide away, and mingle in an infinite variety of postures and situations."[125] Hume must have realized that the word *where* in the above sentence was ambiguous. His substance-minded readers would immediately think of the theater as the *place* where shows are performed. To head off this misunderstanding Hume added, "The comparison of the theatre must not mislead us. They are the successive perceptions only, that constitute the mind; nor have we the most distant notion of the place where these scenes are represented, or of the materials of which it is composed."[126] Hume was strangely loose in his terminology regarding the self. He used the words *self, soul, mind, identity, personal identity, identity of the person, substance,* and *subsistence* interchangeably. *Theatre* in Hume's analogy means spectacle, panorama, or passing scene rather than the building in which plays are performed.

Identity, said Hume, is the sameness which we note in the diversity of perceptions. He added that identity may refer to the sameness of plants and animals, probably because he had in mind John Locke's references to the identity of watches, oak trees, cats, and parrots.[127] Identity with respect to human beings, according to Hume, may be sameness in thoughts or sameness in emotions. He was concerned with the former only. But identity as such is never observed: "the understanding never observes any real connection among objects."[128] The succession that is identity consists of parts connected by resemblance, contiguity in time and space, and causation. Hume held, contrary to the received view, that the fundamental aspect of causation is the psychological feeling of necessary connection based on habitual or customary ways of thinking: ". . . even the union of cause and effect . . . resolves itself into a customary association of ideas."[129] Yet the self or personal identity does not in reality belong to these perceptions. The self is "merely a quality which we attribute to them, because of the union of their ideas in the imagination when we reflect upon them. . . . It is therefore on some of these three relations of resemblance, contiguity, and causation that identity depends."[130] Thus once again Hume placed himself in an embarrassing position: he denied that the self is a thing, and affirmed that it is a relationship. He wanted to argue that it is a relationship of "parts," but by insisting that the "parts" are "perceptions," and especially in his analysis of causation as psychological expectation based on custom, he came embarrassingly close to maintaining that the self is a construction of the mind. Since he used *mind* and *self* interchangeably, he found himself holding that the mind is a construction of the mind! No wonder he confessed in the appendix that he was not satisfied with his view of the self. His difficulty is exposed when he argued as follows: if we had no memory, we would have no notion of causation; and if we had no notion of causes and effects, we would have no self; so if we had no memory we would have no self. Again he must have had in mind a passage from Locke: "For, should the soul of a prince, carrying with it the consciousness of the prince's past life, enter and inform the body of a cobbler, as soon as deserted by his own soul, every one sees he would be the same person with the prince, accountable only for the prince's actions: but who would say it was the same man?"[131] Hume withdrew from the logical conclusions of his own position by stating categorically, if not convincingly, "Memory does not so much produce as discover personal identity."[132] Unfortunately, he could not have it both ways, that is, either memory creates the self, or memory discovers the self, but not both.[133]

b. The Self in Buddhist Thought

The chief association theory of the self in the East is to be found in Buddhism. According to the Buddhist tradition Siddhartha Gautama inaugurated his reformation movement with a speech given to a small audience in a park in Benares. In this Deer Park Sermon he stated four propositions that have been called The Four Noble Truths:

1. All life is suffering *(duḥkha)*.
2. All suffering is caused by craving *(tṛṣṇa)* and cleaving *(upādāna)*.
3. Anything that is caused can be eliminated *(nirodha)*.
4. The way of elimination *(duḥkha-nirodha-mārga)* has eight elements divided into three disciplines:
    a. Morality *(sila)*. Proper speech, proper action, proper vocation.
    b. Concentration *(samādhi)*. Proper effort, proper mindfulness, proper meditation.
    c. Intuition *(prajñā)*. Proper understanding, proper attitudes.

Proper understanding or intellectual insight consists of three basic metaphysical positions:

1. All things are impermanent *(anicca)*.
2. All things bring suffering *(duḥkha)*.
3. There is no permanent self *(anātman)*.

The doctrine of *anātman* struck at the heart of the Hindu doctrine of *Ātman*, thus insuring that the movement would be a revolt rather than a reformation. The *anātman* doctrine was in no sense an addendum, since it was fundamental to the other two doctrines; that is, because there is no real human self, there is no duration in human experience; and because there is no duration in human experience, there is no genuine happiness. T. R. V. Murti writes, "Buddha and Buddhism can be understood only as a revolt not merely against the cant and hollowness of ritualism ... but against the ātma-ideology, the metaphysics of the Substance-view."[134] Vidhushekhara Bhattacharyya in his monograph on *anātman,* entitled *The Basic Conception of Buddhism,* says that "the existence of a permanent Self or *ātman,* as accepted in other systems, was utterly denied by the Buddha."[135] According to T. I. Stcherbatsky, "When Buddha calls the doctrine of an eternal self 'a doctrine of fools' it is clear that he is fighting against an established doctrine. Whenever in his Sermons he comes to speak about Soullessness or Wrong Personalism *(satkāyadṛṣṭi)* a sense of opposition or even animosity is clearly felt in his words.... We may add that the whole of the history of Buddhist philosophy can be described as a series of attempts to penetrate more deeply into this original intuition of Buddha, what he himself believed to be his great discovery."[136] Edward Conze says, "The chief purpose of Buddhism is the extinction of separate individuality, which is brought about when we cease to identify anything with ourselves."[137] Christmas Humphreys adds an important caveat: "The Anatta doctrine is basic to Buddhism, and must, therefore be understood. It is, however, being at the very heart of the living man, a problem to be transcended rather than solved, a doctrine to be experienced rather than described. The difficulties in its understanding are inherent, for it is the Self which is striving to understand itself."[138]

In the sixth century B.C. the Upaniṣadic insight "*Ātman* is Brahman," which meant that the essential nature of mankind is identical with the essence of Totality, was slipping into "*ātman* is Brahman," that is, there is an immortal self or soul in each human being that is the real person separate and distinct from every other soul. The Buddhists, seeing this view as destructive of the unity of mankind and the unity of all life, called it the delusion of self-separateness *(satkāyadṛṣṭi)*.[139] The issue that Gautama the Buddha raised did not die—nor has it died. When Śaṅkara fifteen hundred years later said the individual soul *(jīva)* was *māyā,* he was accused of being a crypto-Buddhist.

Rāmānuja, in opposition to Saṅkara and inadvertently in opposition to Buddhism, gave the individual self full substantial permanent reality. The Buddha in his analysis of man discovered five aggregates, groups, or collections *(skandhas,* literally "heaps") of qualities or attributes: (1) The physical body *(rupa).* (2) Feelings and sense experiences *(vedana).* (3) Preceptions of sensing and thinking *(samna).* (4) Impulses and volitions *(sankhara).* (5) Acts of consciousness *(vijñāna).* "I have a headache" becomes according to this analysis "There is an awareness (5) of a head (1) accompanied by pain (2) which is perceived as unpleasant (3) and impels the seeking of relief (4)." No individual self is noted. *Vijñāna* is the most culpable of the *skandhas* inasmuch as it is the activity likely to produce the fiction of a permanent integral substratum. But the "I" is a sign whose referent changes every moment—a moment being measured in Buddhism as one-seventeenth of a second. The "I" of this moment has added novelty to the "I" of the preceding moment—another breath, another sensation, another emotion, another volition, another idea, and so forth. Each act adds to the flux. There is no stability to be designated *the self. Self* is a word symbolizing a stream of perishing physical and psychological phenomena. There is no *ātman* that is permanent and unchanging. The Buddhist doctrine of *anātman* is not the doctrine of self in constant change, but the doctrine of change such that no "thing" can be identified as the substratum of change. According to Buddhist psychology, elimination of the notion of a stable individual self sets one free. When I realize that I am not a self but a process of self-ing, then the future is open-ended. I am not a what; I am a no-thing. I am a process of I-making over countless reincarnations. According to Buddhist ontology being is a moment in becoming. A living being is just what the term connotes—a *living* being. "Strictly speaking, the duration of the life of a living being is exceedingly brief, lasting only while a thought lasts. Just as a chariot-wheel in rolling rolls only at one point of the tire, and in resting rests only at one point; in exactly the same way, the life of a living being lasts only for the period of one thought. As soon as that thought has ceased the being is said to have ceased."[140]

The reference to "Buddhist psychology" in the previous paragraph, which must be qualified as the Buddhist's doctrine of *anātman,* is the fruit of religious experience, not of psychological analysis. According to D. T. Suzuki, "We must remember that the Buddha's teaching of Anatman or Anatta is not the outcome of psychological analysis but is a statement of religious intuition in which no discursive reasoning whatever is employed.The Buddhist experience found out by immediate knowledge that when one's heart was cleansed of the defilements of the ordinary ego-centered impulses and desires, nothing was left there to claim itself as the ego-residium. It was Buddhist philosophy that formed the theory, but that which supplied it with facts to substantiate it was Buddhist experience."[141]

The Theories of the Self

The relationship of Buddhism to the Upaniṣadic concept of the *Atman* is debatable. There are some passages in Buddhist scriptures that can be interpreted to signify that the Buddha sought to eliminate the concept of *ātman*, but not of *Ātman*, for example, "I have taken refuge in the Self,"[142] and "Seek for the Self."[143] Perhaps it is enough to state that whereas the *Upaniṣads* sought to free individuals from ego-attachment by pointing out that the real self is the Universal Self rather than the individual self, the Buddha sought to free individuals from ego-attachment by pointing out that there is no individual self to which to become attached.

Buddhist literature contains many analogies intended to clarify the Buddhist theory of the self. A flame that burns all night is the same flame, yet the flame of the first watch is not the same as the flame of the middle watch, nor is it the same as the flame of the last watch. Milk that changes to sour cream, then to fresh butter, and finally to clarified butter may be said to be the same milk throughout. "In exactly the same way . . . do the elements of being join one another in serial succession: one element perishes, another arises, succeeding each other as it were instantaneously. Therefore neither as the same nor as a different person do you arrive at your latest aggregation of consciousness."[144] One of the most informative analogies appears in a reported conversation between King Milinda and the teacher Nāgasena. "What is your name?" asked the King. Nāgasena replied, "I am called Nāgasena. My fellow-priests address me as Nāgasena. It is nevertheless but a way of counting, a term, an appellation, a convenient designation, a mere name. For there is no ego here to be found." The King then runs through a long list of what "Nāgasena" might designate: hair, nails, teeth, skin, flesh, sinews, bones, kidneys, heart, liver, spleen, lungs, stomach, faeces, bile, blood, sweat, fat, form, sensation, perception, predispositions, consciousness, et cetera. (Note that the last five are the *skandhas*.) Milinda, upon discovering that none of these is Nāgasena, concludes "Nāgasena is a mere empty sound. There is no Nāgasena." Nāgasena counters by asking King Milinda, "What is a chariot? Is it the pole, axle, wheels, body, staff, yoke, reins, or goad?" When Milinda answers that it is none of these, Nāgasena responds, "The word 'chariot' is a mere empty sound. What chariot is there? You speak a falsehood. There is no chariot." But Milinda says, "I speak no lie. The word 'chariot' is but a way of counting, term, appellation, convenient designation, and name for pole, axle, wheel, etc." "In exactly the same way, your majesty," adds Nāgasena, "in respect of me 'Nāgasena' is but a way of counting, term, appellation, convenient designation, mere name for the hair of my head, brain, form, sensation, perception, the predispositions, and consciousness. But in the absolute sense there is no ego here to be found."[145] The chariot analogy appears also in *Visśddhi-Magga* (chap. xviii), with the important addition that the parts of the chariot and the aspects of the living human being are said to be "placed in a certain relation to each other"[146] but in the "absolute sense there is only name and form."[147] The Buddhist theory of the self is that the term *self* denotes a relationship of the parts teleologically organized to perform a function. For this reason the theory can be classified as both associationism and functionalism. "Self" is merely a conventional term applied to a series of impersonal processes. Sometimes it is described as a name for a series of *dharmas*, that is, consequences of acts. The moral implications of the doctrine of *anātman* are laudatory: "All men ought to deny their own selves and endeavor to help each other and to look for co-existence, because no man can ever be truly independent."[148] "Individuals" are so intimately related to one another that there are no individuals in the absolute sense. Such a condition might be described as a penetrating state of relationships that constitutes a whole. But the Buddhists, finding this view too similar to the *Ātman* syndrome, expressed their intuition as the denial of individuality altogether. Suzuki wrote, "Individuality is merely an aspect of existence; in thought we separate one individual from another and in reality too we all seem to be distinct and separable. But when we reflect on the question more closely we find that individuality is a fiction, for we cannot fix its limits, we cannot ascertain its extents and boundaries, they become mutually merged without leaving any indelible marks between the so-called individuals. A most penetrating state of interrelationship prevails here, and it seems to be more exact to say that individuals do not exist, they are merely so many points of reference, the meaning of which is not at all realizable when each of them is considered by itself and in itself apart from the rest."[149] Suzuki put the issue in typical Zen manner: "Individuals are recognizable only when they are thought of in relation to something not individual; though paradoxical, they are individuals so long as they are not individuals. For when an individual being is singled out as such, it at once ceases to be an individual."[150]

The Buddhist denial of the self has not been easy to hold. Such questions as "What is it that we seek to save?" and "What migrates from one incarnation to the next?" are not easily answered in the context of the *anātman* doctrine. The Japanese Buddhologist Hajime Nakamura states categorically that "the principle of anatta, non-ego, has been held throughout Buddhism";[151] yet two pages later he admits that "it remains difficult to assume rebirth without an abiding central substance. In order to solve this vulnerable problem, some Buddhists of later days assumed a sort of soul, calling it by different names."[152] Nakamura was referring to the Yogācāra school of Buddhism, which was developed in India about eight centuries ago and brought to China a century later. The Yogācārins introduced a transpersonal universal mind or self known as the *Ālaya-vijñāna* (Storehouse-consciousness), having characteristics reminiscent of the Upaniṣadic *Ātman*. Two other minds emerge from the activity of the *Ālaya-vijñāna*: the intuitive mind *(manas)* and the discriminating mind *(manovijñāna)*. In the words of the *Laṅkavatāra*: "The sense-minds and their centralised discriminating-mind are related to the external world which is a manifestation of itself and is given over to perceiving, discriminating, and grasping its maya-like appearances. Universal Mind (*Ālaya-vijñāna*) transcends all individuation and limits. Universal Mind is thoroughly pure in its essential nature, subsisting unchanged and free from faults of impermanence, undisturbed by egoism, unruffled by distinctions, desires and aversions. Universal Mind is like a great ocean, its surface ruffled by waves and surges but its depths remaining forever unmoved."[153] The Sāmmitīyas, a sub-sect of Yogācāra, introduced an individual soul that they called the *pudgala*. This was none other than the heresy of separateness (*satkāyadṛṣṭi*).

The Buddhist theory of the self is similar to Hume's. Conze writes, "Hume's denial of the existence of the ego, as an entity distinct from mental processes, comes very near the Anātta-doctrine. From the purely theoretical point of view Buddhism has in this respect little to teach that one cannot find as well, and probably in a more congenial form, in Hume and kindred thinkers, like William James. The difference between the Buddhist and the European and American philosophers lies in what they do with a philosophical proposition once they have arrived at it."[154] Conze adds that if a Western philosopher has proved there is no ego, he is apt to leave it at that, and to behave very much as if there were one! Conze might have gone further and pointed out that whereas Hume arrived at a relational view of the self that has stimulated hundreds of philosophy students to write dissertations analyzing the theory, the Buddha presented a similar theory that has shaped the lives of billions of people during the past 2,500 years.

c. The Aristotelian Theory of the Self

Although Hume's theory of the self is best identified as associationism, he also gave an excellent definition of functionalism: "a combination to some common end or purpose . . . a sympathy of parts to their common end."[155] Functional psychology regards the processes of sensation, emotion, volition, and thought as means the human biological organism uses for controlling and adapting itself to its environment. This type of psychology was developed in America by William James, G. T. Ladd, G. S. Hall, John Dewey, and J. R. Angell. They wrote in protest against the structural psychologists' view that the task of psychology is the analysis and description of consciousness. The job of psychology, said the functionalists, is to study what the organism does, not what it is. Functionalism is a characteristic of pragmatism, instrumentalism, and behaviorism. The roots of functionalism go far back into the ancient Greek period of philosophy, and, above all, into the works of Aristotle. His *De Anima (Concerning the Soul)* is regarded by modern students of Aristotle as "the linchpin of his whole philosophy"[156] and as one of the best introductions to the study of the Aristotelian opera.[157]

The first problem to be solved in the study of the soul, according to Aristotle, is that of the class to which the soul is to be assigned. Is it a primary substance like Socrates, or a secondary substance like mankind? Is it a quantity? A relation? A place? A time? A position? A state? An action? An affection? Secondary questions include: "Is it potential or actual?" "Does it have parts?" "Is it homogeneous?" "Is it found in beings other than human beings?" An important methodological question is whether one should first study the nature of the soul or the function of the soul.

Aristotle devoted the first book of *De Anima* to an examination of the studies of the soul made by his predecessors. He found that, while the majority observe correctly, "there seems to be no case in which the soul can act or be acted upon without involving the body."[158] His predecessors' views involve the "absurdity"[159] of regarding the soul as a thing that can be joined to a body or placed in a body.[160] Those who think of the soul in this fashion, and who wish to avoid locating where the soul is by saying it is throughout the entire body, commit the additional absurdity of putting two bodies in the same place.[161] Language that hypostatizes the soul ought to be avoided, since "to say that it is the soul which is angry is as inexact as it would be to say that it is the soul that weaves webs or builds houses. It is doubtless better to avoid saying that the soul pities or learns or thinks, and rather to say that it is the man who does this with his soul."[162] His predecessors defined the soul in three different ways: (1) as the first cause of motion; (2) as a subtle, yet corporeal, body; (3) as composed of the elements.[163] But all misconstrued the nature of the soul by thinking of it as a being rather than a principle. Aristotle anticipated his own view at the opening of *De Anima* by referring to the soul as "the principle of animal life."[164]

He began Book 2 with the observation that he had learned nothing positive from the review of other studies of the soul: "Let the foregoing suffice as our account of the views concerning the soul which have been handed on by our predecessors; let us now dismiss them and make as it were a completely fresh start."[165] He began his own analysis of soul by drawing a distinction between two grades of actuality: (1) first grade of actuality, which is the possession of a power, and (2) second grade of actuality, which is the exercise of a power. They may be termed "capacity" and "activity." Soul is actuality in the first sense. Soul, therefore, must be named in a definition of the essential whatness of a body. If an eye were a natural body, then sight would be its soul. The eye would not need to be seeing all the time in order to be an eye, but the capacity of seeing must be a reality, or the "eye" is not in fact an eye. The "eye" of a statue is an eye only metonymically. If an axe were a natural body, its soul would be the capacity to chop wood—and would still be an axe even when it was not chopping wood. The soul is "actuality in the sense corresponding to the power of sight and the power in the tool."[166] He concluded, "This must suffice as our sketch or outline determination of the nature of the soul."[167]

Aristotle had said at the opening of *De Anima,* as noticed in the previous chapter, that "knowledge about the soul is one of the most difficult things in the world."[168] His assessment is confirmed when he at this point said he must again make "a fresh starting-point."[169] This time he began by reminding his readers that the word translated *soul* is also the word for life, and that life involves four distinct activities: nutrition and reproduction, locomotion, perception, and thought. Hence, soul is the capacity to nourish the body, to move in space, to sense, and to think. The soul of plants is the power for nutrition and reproduction. This is the only psychic power they possess. The lowest animals have two psychic powers: the power of nutrition-reproduction and the power of locomotion. The soul—or perhaps soul-ing—in higher animals is the capacity of nutrition-reproduction, locomotion, and sensation. Man and the other higher animals share in five senses—sight, hearing, touch, taste, and smell. The five senses form a unity in man, a unity of which man is aware and for which there is not sufficient evidence to assign a similar unity to the other animals. This unity, which he called "common sense" *(koinē aisthēsis),* enables man to apprehend such sensibles as movement, magnitude, and number through more than one sense, since all sense stimuli are reported to the same common sense organ (which Aristotle curiously located in the heart), but in addition, and more important, makes possible the distinction between sensation and perception. According to Aristotle "it is through sense that we are aware that we are seeing or hearing."[170] Soul-ing as sensing at the human level involves not only seeing, hearing, touching, tasting, and smelling but also being aware that one is seeing, hearing, touching, tasting, and smelling. This is the basis for thinking, that is, the psychic function peculiar to man. Thinking, according to Aristotle is "akin to a form of perceiving."[171] Thinking is a second-order activity brought to bear upon a first-order activity. Thinking is the potentiality of receiving the form of the sensed object, as opposed to the matter of the sensed object. One does not need an elephant to think of an elephant—contrary to what the citizens of Laputa believed! Two aspects are involved in the activity of thinking: (1) the passive or receptive, which varies according to the experience of each thinker, and (2) the active or universal, which makes it possible for all minds to communicate.

The soul or self, according to Aristotle, is the functioning of the total organism in nutrition-reproduction, which humans share with plants; in nutrition-reproduction-locomotion, which humans share with the lowest animals; in nutrition-reproduction-locomotion-sensation, which humans share with the higher animals; and in nutrition-reproduction-locomotion-sensation-perception-thought, which humans share with no other creatures. Human beings in their capacity to be aware they are sensing and to reflect upon the general form as opposed to the specific matter of what is being sensed discover themselves as beings who nourish and reproduce themselves, as beings who sense, as beings who are aware that they sense, as beings who think, and as beings who are aware that they think. The self is the functioning of the total organism. The self is unique. Only a human being, that is, a self, has the capacity to be sometimes in that good state in which God always is,[172] that is, a state of "thinking on thinking" *(noēsis noēseos noēsis)*.[173]

d. Dewey's Theory of the Self

John Dewey (1859–1952) was one of the greatest functionalists of the modern Western world, yet he hated labels, and once said that the division of psychologists into structuralists and functionalists seemed about as reasonable "as a division of botanists into rootists and flowerists."[174] But one who put so much stress on the *stream* of consciousness and so little on the *states* of consciousness must be described as a functionalist. He disliked the word *self,* preferring instead *biological-cultural human being*. There is no *self, subject, mind,* or *knower* as "an original separate entity set over against objects and the world."[175] Dewey in an early paper analyzed the Kantian transcendental ego, arguing that Kant had taken "the activity of synthesis of sense through thought" and had hypostatized the activity into thinghood.[176] Four years later, in an article entitled "The Ego as Cause," he sharply rebuked William James for having reintroduced the notion of the Pure Ego. Such a notion, said Dewey, is not needed to explain either consciousness or freedom: "If the stream of thought can run itself in one case, the stream of conduct can administer itself in the other."[177] From 1894 on, Dewey would have nothing to do with "soul psychology." He rejected the notion of an active self as agent of knowing and an efficient self as agent in willing. To be aware of a "self" was merely to be part of a total social awareness. He rejected completely "our old assumption of the self as outside of things."[178] In a letter to Arthur F. Bentley dated 1 June 1942 he used the word *self* apologetically "to distinguish a *particular* social communicator from other communicators."[179]

Dewey warned against the notion of "a solitary self without objective ties and sustenance."[180] He even described such a view of the self as abnormal: "In abnormal cases, one thinks of himself not as part of the agencies of execution, but as a separate object."[181] Again he wrote, "The traditional psychology of the original separate soul, mind or consciousness is in truth a reflex of conditions which cut human nature off from its natural objective relations. It implies first the severance of man from nature and then of each man from his fellows."[182] The first severance is clearly indicated in the mind-body dualism that has been a part of many philosophies and religions. The body is obviously natural; and, if the mind is opposed to the body, then the mind is not natural. The mind becomes "a mysterious intruder or a mysterious parallel accompaniment."[183] The second severance is in "exaggeration of individuality,"[184] which is often "a compensatory reaction against the pressure of institutional rigidities."[185] To live is to live with others. To think is to think with others. To be is to be with others. Dewey, the great apostle of democracy, always thought of democracy as more than a form of government. Democracy for him was primarily a mode of associated living, and only in a democracy, so defined, could there be what Dewey meant by *self*.

The self is not only social but also unfixed: "The moment we recognize that the self is not something ready-made, but something in continuous formation through choice of action, the whole situation clears up. A man's interest in keeping at his work in spite of danger to life means that his self is found *in* that work; if he finally gave up, and preferred his personal safety or comfort, it would mean that he preferred to be *that* kind of a self."[186] *Self* and *interest* are two names for the same fact. Dewey's psychology was based upon habits and customs. A person is what he does. Dewey praised clinical psychology because it fixed attention upon "the objective conditions in which habits are formed and operate."[187] Clinical psychology is "a protest against the futility, as a tool of understanding and dealing with human nature in the concrete, of the psychology of conscious sensations, images and ideas."[188] Traditional psychology, which deals with an "original individual consciousness," is a "false psychology."[189] Artificial explanations such as the mystic collective mind, consciousness, and over-soul fail to deal with the facts of habit and custom. Dewey believed that the terminology of ordinary language has become loaded in the direction of the reification of the self. Therefore he suggested that a statement like "I think" might be altered to a truer psychological statement, "It thinks."[190] Perhaps Dewey would have made himself clearer if he had suggested something like "I am the thinking" or "The activity of thinking is what is meant by the word *I*."

One acts *as* self, not *for* self, said Dewey. Every act tends to the fulfillment or satisfaction of a habit that is an element in the self. Acting is self-ing, and self-ing is the only self there is. Dewey blamed the belief in the fixity and simplicity of the self on "the theologians with their dogma of the unity and ready-made completeness of the soul."[191] Selfhood is "in process of making."[192] The constituents of selfhood are relative fluidity and diversity. There is no self behind activities. The self is a doing, not a being. The functioning is the self.

e. Sartre's Theory of the Self

This is an excellent point at which to turn to the examination of the last theory of the nature of the self that we shall consider in this survey of three types of theories: independent substance, dependent substance, and relational. This theory can be placed under the rubric "existential." Existentialism, wherever and whenever it appears, is a protest of thinking human beings against all threats to their individuality, freedom, and existence. The existentialist knows that he is a being in the natural world, yet he rebels lest his objectivity mitigate his subjectivity. He insists that he as an object ex-ists (stands out) in a unique manner from the background of nature. Other beings are *in* the natural world; man is *of* the natural world. He is creature in rebellion against his creator. The more he suffers, feels insecure, and discovers his homelessness in the universe, the more he knows that he exists. Whereas the Buddhists say to be is to suffer, the existentialists say to suffer is to be. Man has no nature as the lower animals have a nature. Man's nature is to create himself. In the words of Jean-Paul Sartre, man is "a being-which-is-not-what-it-is and which-is-what-it-is-not" that chooses to become "being-what-it-is-not and not-being-what-it-is."[193] This quest is his passion. Sartre says that "all human existence is a passion."[194] But it is unsatisfied: "Every human reality is a passion in that it projects losing itself so as to found being and by the same stroke to constitute the In-itself which escapes contingency by being its own foundation, the *Ens causa sui,* which religions call God. Thus the passion of men is the reverse of that of Christ, for man loses himself as man in order that God may be born. But the idea of God is contradictory and we lose ourselves in vain. Man is a useless passion."[195] The existentialists might say to Dewey, "Why did you name your book *Human Nature and Conduct?* Would not *Human Conduct* be a better title, since what a man does is his nature? Each human being seeks through suffering and insecurity his own individuality and existence. The seeking is his nature. Man is his choices."

Sören Kierkegaard (1813–55), the father of modern Western existentialism, indicated the nature of existentialism in these words: "Each age has its own characteristic depravity. Ours is perhaps not pleasure or indulgence or sensuality, but rather a dissolute pantheistic contempt for the individual man."[196] He sought to be an individual in a world that reduced the individual to his social and political functions, for example, husband, taxpayer, voter, plumber, churchman, union member, and the like. Kierkegaard requested that the epitaph on his tomb be "That Individual." He was aware, as few were in the early nineteenth century, of the powerlessness of individuals to avoid being dragged along by political and social events. Can an independent human being preserve his freedom in the modern world? According to the existentialists, three anguishes shadow the life of man. They are the constituents of consciousness, and also the glory and the misery of man. One is the anguish of being. Being is contingent. Things are, but they do not have to be. Not being is just as possible as being. The second anguish is the anguish of the here and now. Man is here and now, but there is no reason why he is not there and then. The third anguish is the anguish of freedom. Man is free—he can choose; but more than this, he *must* choose, because not to choose is not to be man. Man is condemned to be free. Things other than man simply are what they are. They are determined. But man is not so determined. Man is aware of the contrast between himself and things, of his relations to other humans, and of his eventual death. He is aware of nothingness—and this awareness produces dread and despair. Some existentialists, like Kierkegaard, have held that meaning and reality may be discovered by a miraculous disclosure, that is, a "leap" which affronts the intellect. This "leap" may be a paradox or an absurdity much like the *satori* experience triggered by a Zen *koan*.

Existentialism is a serious effort to come to terms with the shadow side of human life. It recognizes that life is greater than that which can be captured in thought. Existentialism is the creation of man asserting himself against all patterns of thought and action that push the individual into the background. It is especially in the West a protest against the sciences and technologies that dehumanize and impersonalize life and have fostered a growing sense of worthlessness, meaninglessness, and futility. The human is the one being in whom existence comes into focus. For him to exist is to struggle, to choose, to make commitments, and above all, to make individual choices.

The reality of a stone and the reality of a man are quite different. A stone has reality in-itself, but a man has reality for himself. Man exists in the sense that he sets himself as a being distinct from other beings, both human and nonhuman. He can choose, and he knows that he chooses. His choosing is his self. His choices are free, but he is not free not to choose. Man as a conscious subject stands constantly before a future. His self is not fixed. Nothing is determined. According to many existentialists, God the limiter does not exist. Hence everything is possible. We can say in the language of S. Alexander that there is no *nisus* pushing, and in the language of Teilhard that there is no Omega Point pulling. Sartre writes that "my future is virgin; everything is allowed to me."[197] However, "bad faith," that is, "not-believing-what-one-believes,"[198] is possible. Sartre's example of "bad faith" is that of a specific waiter: "Let us consider this waiter in the café. His movement is quick and forward, a little too precise, a little too rapid. He comes toward the patrons with a step a little too quick. He bends forward a little too eagerly; his voice, his eyes express an interest a little too solicitous for the order of the customer. Finally there he returns, trying to imitate in his walk the inflexible stiffness of some kind of automaton while carrying his tray with the recklessness of a tight-rope-walker by putting it in a perpetually unstable, perpetually broken equilibrium which he perpetually reestablishes by a light movement of the arm and hand. All his behavior seems to us a game. He applies himself to chaining his movements as if they were mechanisms, the one regulating the other; his gestures and even his voice seem to be mechanisms; he gives himself the quickness and pitiless rapidity of things. He is playing, he is amusing himself. But what is he playing? We need not watch long before we can explain it: he is playing at being a waiter in a café."[199]

Sartre in commenting on the illustration has the waiter explain, "I am a waiter in the mode of being what I am not."[200] And this makes one ponder if Sartre smuggled in a self that the waiter in his "bad faith" had missed.

The conflicting theories of the self are a reason for rejoicing rather than despairing. They remind us that the human being is a becoming—an incomplete being. To be human is to reject oneself as given. To be human is to be always in the making. The making is the being. To be human is to be not yet.

6
The Self-Realization of Human Beings

The life of human beings, when well lived, is the examined life, but he who examines life merely for the sake of the examination suffers from a disease akin to that of the one morbidly concerned about health. Philosophy can become intellectual hypochondria, that is, thought for its own sake rather than for the sake of action. "Vain is the word of a philosopher which does not heal any suffering of man," warned Epicurus.[1] Aristotle criticized those who "take refuge in theory and think they are being philosophers and will become good in this way, behaving somewhat like patients who listen attentively to their doctors, but do none of the things they are ordered to do. As the latter will not be made well in body by such a course of treatment, the former will not be made well in soul by such a course of philosophy."[2] Those who merely think are like the merchant in Chaucer's tale who "seemed busier than he was." Human busyness—whether of the thinking without action variety or of the acting without thinking variety—either accomplishes very little or accomplishes the wrong things.

Self-realization—a term encompassing self-discovery, self-knowledge, and self-creation—as a model of philosophical activity raises the question of how much value one ought to place on one's self. Aristotle noted, "The question is also debated, whether a man should love himself most, or some one else."[3] There are two points of view, he said. Some criticize those who love themselves most, calling them self-lovers, which is "an epithet of disgrace."[4] They seem to do everything for their own sake, while a good man acts for honor's sake. Others say that one ought to love best one's best friends, that a best friend is one who wishes one well, that this is the attitude one takes toward one's self, so one ought to love one's self best. Aristotle said both views are plausible, since there are two kinds of self-love: (1) "living as passion dictates,"[5] that is, assigning to one's self the greater share of the wealth, honors, and bodily pleasures, and (2) "living according to a rational principle,"[6] that is, being anxious that one act justly, temperately, and honorably. If the former is what one means, then self-love is not to be approved; if the latter is what one means, then the good man should be a lover of self. Loving one's self in the second sense does not always connote self-preservation, for the good man "does many acts for the sake of his friends and his country, and if necessary dies for them; for he will throw away both wealth and honors and in general the goods that are objects of competition, gaining for himself nobility; since he would prefer a short period of intense pleasure to a long one of mild enjoyment, a twelvemonth of noble life to many years of humdrum existence, and one great and noble action to many trivial ones."[7]

Some human beings have looked longingly at the composed existence of the lower forms of life: "Behold the fowls of the air: for they sow not, neither do they reap, nor gather into barns. . . . Consider the lilies of the field, how they grow; they toil not, neither do they spin."[8] They are not philosophical—yet they achieve values. Giovanni Battista Gelli, in a typically Renaissance book called *The Circe,* presented a series of dialogues between Ulysses and the beasts on Circe's island in which each unfortunate creature is given the choice of reverting to manhood or staying as he is. The mole, a former plowman, refuses to return to the human state because he worked harder as a man; the snake, a former physician, wishes to stay as he is since the body of a snake is subject to fewer ills than the body of man. Ulysses finally induces the elephant, a former philosopher, to return to his previous human existence. His clinching argument is that man alone has the ability to establish his own life goals: "Man, by having his choice free, can attain an end more or less worthy as he thinks fit, by letting himself down to creatures much below him, or by emulating those as much above. . . . Who therefore can look with astonishment on man, not only as the most noble, and the sovereign among animals, but who has this peculiar privilege indulged him by Nature, that he can make himself what he will."[9] If man is the being who can make himself what he will, what are the possibilities? What goals are open to the human? The American Council on Education in 1942 appointed a Committee on the Cooperative Study in General Education to determine the goals of American college and university students. The committee concluded that there are twenty major goal possibilities, namely,

1. Serving God, doing God's will.
2. Becoming a real, genuine person.
3. Pleasures for the greatest number.
4. Fine relations with other persons.
5. Handling the specific problems of life.
6. Being able to "take it."
7. Doing my duty.
8. Serving the community of which I am a part.
9. Self-discipline.

10. Getting deep pleasures out of life.
11. Peace of mind, contentment, stillness of spirit.
12. Self-sacrifice for the sake of a better world.
13. Making a place for myself . . . getting ahead.
14. Finding my place in life and accepting it.
15. Security—protecting my way of life.
16. Doing the best I can for myself and those dear to me.
17. Achieving personal immortality in heaven.
18. Survival, continued existence.
19. Power, control over people and things.
20. Living for the pleasure of the moment.[10]

Three students once asked Edward Westermarck, the great teacher of ethics, "Why are we here?" Westermarck answered, "Such a question should not be asked: here we are, and cannot alter it; questions which cannot be answered should not be asked!" Arthur Keith comments, "Dr. Westermarck revealed that, although he mastered human morality, he remained ignorant of human nature."[11]

The facets of self-realization we shall consider in this chapter are maturity as an ideal, the attitudes toward death, the question of immortality, and the goals of self-realization.

1. Maturity

Plato began his magnum opus with a question about the meaning and value of old age: "Is it a difficult time of life?" asks Socrates. Cephalos replies, "I will tell you how I feel. We often meet, a few of much the same age, like to like as the old proverb says. Most of us when we meet are full of lamentations; we miss the pleasures of youth, we talk of our old love affairs, and drinking and feasting, and other such things; and we regret them as if we had been robbed of great things, as if that were real life, and we were hardly alive now. Some even complain of mud-spatterings of old age by their nearest and dearest, and so they chant forever what evils old age has brought on them. But I think the blame does not lie there, Socrates; for if that were the reason, I too should have suffered the same for my old age, as the others who have come to my time of life. But in fact I have met others who don't feel like that about it, Sophocles the poet, for instance. I was with him once, when somebody asked him, 'What about love now, Sophocles? Are you still able to serve a woman?' 'Hush, man,' he said, 'I've escaped from all that, thank goodness. I feel as if I had escaped from a mad, cruel slave driver.' I thought it was a good answer, and I think so still. Indeed there is great and perfect peace from such things in old age. When desires go slack and no longer tighten the strings, it is exactly what Sophocles said; perfect riddance of frantic slave drivers, a whole horde of them. No, Socrates, both here and in family life there is only one reason for what happens; not old age, but the man's character. For if they are decent even-tempered people, old age is only moderately troublesome; if not, then youth is no less difficult than age is for such people."[12] Although Cephalos does not state that he is making a distinction between old age and maturity, that is what he does. The numbering of years is no guarantee of maturing. According to Walter Lippmann, dean of American journalists in the mid-twentieth century, "The critical phase of human experience . . . is the passage from childhood to maturity; the critical question is whether childish habits and expectations are to persist or to be transformed. We grow older. But it is by no means certain that we shall grow up. The human character is a complicated thing, and its elements do not necessarily march in step. It is possible to be a sage in some things and a child in others, to be at once precocious and retarded, to be shrewd and foolish, serene and irritable. . . . The successful passage into maturity depends, therefore, on a breaking up and reconstruction of those habits which were appropriate only to our earliest experience. In a certain sense this is the essence of education. For unless a man has acquired the character of an adult, he is a lost soul no matter how good his technical equipment."[13]

Few would disagree with Lippmann. But what is maturity? At this point differences surface. Maturity, according to Lippmann, is "the acquiring of a different sense of life, a different kind of intuition about the nature of things,"[14] namely, (1) a man's feeling of "the vast indifference of the universe to his own fate,"[15] (2) the discovery of "the necessity that is in the nature of things,"[16] (3) the discovery "that there is evil which is as genuine as goodness, that there is ugliness and violence which are no less real than joy and love,"[17] and (4) the knowledge "that everything changes and that everything comes to an end."[18] Lippmann's definition of maturity is an expression of his own naturalistic humanistic philosophy. A more comprehensive description is offered by Luella Cole: (1) a person of intellectual maturity, for example, can make up his/her own mind, can take responsibility, can think objectively about self, can maintain an open mind, can make a workable compromise with life, can bear the indifference of the world to his own fate; (2) a person of emotional maturity, for example, can bear tension, is indifferent to the kinds of stimuli that move the child and the adolescent, has outgrown adolescent moodiness and sentimentality; (3) a person of social maturity, for example, has achieved independence from one's childhood home, has found security in friendships among agemates, has settled upon a stable sexual pattern, has made an adjustment to accepted customs and conventions, has found interesting work; (4) a person of moral maturity, for example, has a code of morals, has a philosophy of life, has a sense of duty, is tolerant to others.[19]

Arthur Schopenhauer, in an essay titled "The Ages of Life," argued, "A complete and adequate notion of life can never be attained by any one who does not reach old age."[20] Although he incorrectly assumes that the older person will necessarily be the mature person, his essay is a remarkably complete listing of the differences between youth and age, which can be indicated in two columns as follows:

Youth
1. Uses intellect more than will.
2. A time of happiness.
3. Generalizes. Every individual represents the whole class.
4. Views life from a distance.
5. "a never-satisfied longing after happiness."[21]
6. Bears misfortune better than age does.
7. Feels abandoned by the world.
8. Feels that time moves slowly.
9. Sees life, as it were from the top or right side of a piece of embroidery.
10. "Death is not visible."[23]
11. More passionate, less restful.
12. Life seems long.
13. Makes many plans.
14. Less love of possessions.
15. Very conscious of surroundings.
16. Engaged by outward aspect of things.
17. A time for poetry.
18. Great intellectual powers.
19. Adequate notion of life impossible.
20. Does not know self.

21. Time to amass knowledge.
22. "marked by a certain melancholy and sadness."[26]

Age
1. Uses will more than intellect.
2. A time of unhappiness.
3. Ceases to generalize. Sees there are too many things to classify.
4. Views life quite closely.
5. "dread of misfortune."[22]
6. Better able to prevent misfortune from happening.
7. Feels one has escaped the world.
8. Feels that time moves rapidly.
9. Sees life, as it were from the bottom or wrong side of a piece of embroidery.
10. "Death comes in."[24]
11. More restful, less passionate.
12. Life seems short.
13. Lives in memories.
14. More love of possessions.
15. Less conscious of surroundings.
16. Engaged by inward aspect of things.
17. A time for philosophy.
18. Intellectual powers decline.
19. Adequate notion of life possible.
20. "it is only towards the close of life that a man really recognizes and understands his own true self."[25]
21. Time to reflect on knowledge.
22. Time of "genial sentiments."[27]

23. A time of unrest.	23. A time of repose.
24. Strives for good things.	24. Knows all things are vanity.
25. "the young man fancies there is a vast amount of good things in the world."[28]	25. "disillusion is the chief characteristic of old age."[29]

One of the defects in many conceptions of maturity is that maturity is assumed to be a stable, fixed goal to be attained. H. A. Overstreet did not see maturity in that fashion. For him, "A mature person is not one who has come to a certain level of achievement and stopped there. He is rather a maturing person—one whose linkages with life are constantly becoming stronger and richer because his attitudes are such as to encourage their growth rather than their stoppage."[30] Confucius was a maturing person, as is indicated in the following passage from the *Analects:* "At fifteen I set my heart upon learning. At thirty, I had planted my feet firm upon the ground. At forty, I no longer suffered from perplexities. At fifty, I knew what were the biddings of Heaven. At sixty, I heard them with docile ear. At seventy, I could follow the dictates of my own heart; for what I desired no longer overstepped the boundaries of right."[31]

The possibility of continued learning at the adult level was confirmed by the studies of the American psychologist Edward L. Thorndike. He reported, "We showed that the ability to learn increased from early childhood to about age 25 and decreased gradually and slowly thereafter, about one percent per year. Childhood was found to be emphatically not the best age for learning in the sense of the age when the greatest returns per unit of time spent are received. The age for learning that is best in that sense is in the twenties, and any age before 45 is better than ages 10 to 14."[32] After Thorndike established that adults are able to learn, he studied the problem of motivation. He found that interest in learning and in new experiences is the clue to learning, that adults can be stimulated to learn, and that when stimulated they learn. He concluded "Adults may excuse themselves from learning because they are tired or sleepy or in need of entertainment rather than improvement, but not because they cannot, being old, be sufficiently interested."[33] The mature person is the one who sees himself "as a creature who lives by and through relationships: who becomes himself through linkages with the nonself."[34] Such a person is "a unity of psychic experience, both capable of lifelong growth and subject to arrest of growth at any point where he habitually makes immature efforts at problem-solving."[35]

2. Death

According to Spinoza "A free man, that is, one who lives according to the dictate of reason alone, is not led by the fear of death, but directly desires what is good, that is, to act, to live, and preserve his being on the basis of seeking what is useful to him. And therefore he thinks of nothing less than of death, but his wisdom is a meditation of life."[36] While this may be true for Spinoza's "free man," the average man thinks of death. According to Lewis Loeser, "Death and our attitudes toward it are, in reality, our number one preoccupation. We devote more time to thinking about, talking about and avoiding this subject than any other."[37] Death is a dark and inevitable fact against which we rebel in vain. Loeser adds, "It is time we face up to it realistically in our Western culture."[38] Death is a subject that surfaces even in the happiest children's literature; for example, in *Through the Looking-Glass,* when Alice is informed that a "Bread-and-butter fly" lives on weak tea laced with cream, she asks, "Supposing it couldn't find any?" "Then it would die, of course," replies the Gnat. "But that must happen very often," Alice muses. And the Gnat says, "It always happens."[39]

The certainty of death makes it a reality upon which everyone must have some opinions—therefore ought to have *considered* opinions. The Roman philosopher Marcus Aurelius Antoninus (121–180) wrote, "Tho thou shouldst be going to live three thousand years, and as many times ten thousand years, still remember that no man loses any other life than this which he now lives, nor lives any other than this which he now loses. The longest and shortest are thus brought to the same."[40] The following epitaph I found on a tombstone dated 1761 in the graveyard of Melrose Abbey in England:

> The earth goeth on the earth
>   glistring like gold.
> The earth goeth to the earth
>   sooner than it wold.
> The earth builds on the earth
>   castles and towers.
> The earth says to the earth
>   all shall be ours.

The human being has been described as the only animal that anticipates death. Some students of animal behavior may question this statement, arguing that the elephant is one animal that seems to have some anticipation of death. But the human being certainly has a greater awareness of his mortality than other beings. There are three aspects of this confrontation: (1) What is the nature of death? (2) What attitudes ought to be taken toward death? (3) What values can be located in death?

There are three possible views of the nature of death. One is that death is the terminus of life. Another is that death is an experience. This view of death carries with it the notion that, as an experience, it is something to be lived through. The third is that death is a state of being. This state may be either with or without an end. Among the ancient Hebrews as expressed in the book of Job, all humans are appointed after earthly life to dwell in the house of the dead[41] called *Sheol* (the pit, the grave, the nether-world), a place of rest and social equality,[42] "the land of gloom and deep darkness."[43] The post-mortem state, according to Job, has no terminus: ". . . he who goes down to Sheol does not come up; he returns no more to his house."[44] Later the Jews referred to the abode of the dead as *Gehenna* (a place of refuse) and as *Hell* or *Hades* (a place of punishment).[45] Christianity tempered the hopelessness of the state of the dead with the creedal affirmation that the Christ himself visited Hell—"He descended into Hell," and also with the doctrine of the resurrection of the righteous and with the concept of Purgatory as a temporary abode of the dead. In Homer's *Iliad* Achilles observes after the visit of the ghost of his slain comrade, Patroklos, "Oh, wonder! Even in the house of Hades there is left something, a soul and an image, but there is no real heart of life in it."[46] In the *Odyssey* the place of the dead is described as a "sad place"[47] and the "abode of darkness."[48] Odysseus tries to embrace the spirit of his mother when he calls her back from the place of the dead, but, as he reports, "Thrice I sprung towards her and tried to clasp her in my arms, but each time she flitted from my embrace as it were a dream or a phantom."[49] His mother informs him, "The sinews no longer hold the flesh and bones together; these perish in the fierceness of consuming fire as soon as life has left the body, and the soul flits away as though it were in a dream."[50] The ghost of Agamemnon says, "I would rather be a paid servant in a poor man's house and be above ground than king of kings among the dead."[51] The Greeks thought there was no end to existence in the "house of Hades," but the Upaniṣadic thinkers speculated that since the living state comes to an end, so does the nonliving state. Thus arose the notion of *purarmṛtyu* (the death of death); for example, "He goes from death to death, who sees in it, as it were diversity."[52] The doctrine of "redeath" produced the correlative doctrine of rebirth.

What are the possible attitudes toward death? An organization of British sociologists, known as Mass-Observation, sends out every month a questionnaire to two thousand individuals. In May 1942, during the height of the bombing of England, the questionnaire was the following: "What are your own personal feelings now about death and dying? Do you think about it much, occasionally, or hardly at all? Has the war had any effect on the extent to which you think about it, or your general feelings about it?" Five hundred and thirty replies were received. The expressions of attitudes led to an interesting conclusion: "To the same person, death can appear both pleasant and terrifying, abhorrent and desirable, tragic and triumphant, awesome and repellent."[53] Elisabeth Kubler-Ross reports from her study of two hundred terminally ill patients that a dying person goes through five stages in the dying experience: denial and isolation, anger, bargaining, depression, and acceptance.[54]

The attitudes we shall examine are fear, denial, defiance, acceptance, and adventure.

Fear is the oldest and most universal attitude. According to Epicurus it is a groundless fear: "So death, the most terrifying of ills, is nothing to us, since so long as we exist, death is not with us; but when death comes, then we do not exist."[55] According to Socrates it is fear founded on ignorance: "For to fear death . . . is to think you are wise when you are not; for it is to think you know what you don't know. No one knows whether death is really the greatest blessing a man can have, but they fear it is the greatest curse, as if they knew well. Surely this is the objectionable kind of ignorance, to think one knows what one does not know?"[56]

The denial of death takes many forms. The semantic is the simplest. William Randolph Hearst "would never allow anyone to use the word 'death' in his presence."[57] Another way is to use euphemisms, for example, "perish," "expire," "pass on," "pass over," "pass away," "depart," "leave this world," "come to one's end," "be heard of no more," "draw the last breath," "go the way of all flesh," "go to one's glory," "reap one's reward," "join the heavenly host," and "claimed by God." Less elegant euphemisms include "pay his debts," "join the last roundup," and "kick the bucket." Another way to deny death is to claim that God made all that is real, that God did not make death, and so death is not real; for example, "Do not invite death by the error of your life, nor bring on destruction by the works of your hands; because God did not make death, and he does not delight in the death of the living."[58] Mary Baker Eddy, the discoverer of the principles of Christian Science and founder of the church based on those principles, referred to death as "an error of mortal mind."

A third attitude toward death is defiance. Among the Greeks wine was praised as a means of defiance; for example, three of the refrains from Epicurean literature were "Drink, for once dead you never shall return," "Drink, before you put on this raiment of dust," and "Make the burial-urn drunk with wine ere thou lay it under earth, and write on it, 'Love's gift to death.'" Among the Norsemen an old song defied death by laughter:

> Come laugh ye gods, Ha! Ha! Ha! Ha!
> Ring wild through life your laughter.
> We'll laugh Ha! Ha! at the gates of death,
> And, maybe, we'll laugh after.

Sir Thomas More evidenced humor toward death when, upon stumbling as he climbed the scaffold, he extended a hand to his executioner, saying, "Help me to ascend. I will shift for myself coming down."

Another attitude taken toward death is acceptance. Socrates recommended this attitude to his judges: "You are wrong . . . if you think a man with a spark of decency in him ought to calculate life or death; the only thing he ought to consider, if he does anything, is whether he does right or wrong, whether it is what a good man does or a bad man. . . . But you also, judges of the court, must have good hopes towards death, and this one thing you must take as true—no evil can happen to a good man either living or dead."[59] Diogenes Laertius reported that Epicurus was on the point of death when he wrote the following in a letter to his friend Idomeneus: "On this truly happy day of my life, as I am at the point of death, I write this to you. The disease in my bladder and stomach are pursuing their course, lacking nothing of their natural severity: but against all this is the joy in my heart at the recollection of my conversations with you."[60]

Lucretius (95–52 B.C.) in *De Rerum Natura* took an attitude toward death that may be described as acceptance and indifference: "Again a tree cannot exist in the ether, nor clouds in the deep sea nor can fishes live in the fields nor blood exist in woods nor sap in stones. Where each thing can grow and abide is fixed and ordained. Thus the nature of the mind cannot come into being alone without the body or exist far away from the sinews and blood. . . . Therefore when the body has died, we must admit that the soul has perished, wrenched away throughout the body. To link forsooth a mortal thing with an everlasting and suppose that they can have sense in common and can be reciprocally acted upon, is sheer folly; for what can be conceived more incongruous, more discordant and inconsistent with itself, than a thing which is mortal, linked with an immortal and everlasting thing, trying in such union to weather furious storms? . . . Death therefore to us is nothing, concerns us not a jot. . . . And if time should gather up our matter after our death and put it once more into the position in which it now is, and the light of life be given to us again, this result even would concern us not at all, when the chain of our self-consciousness has been snapped asunder. So now we give ourselves no concern about any self which we have been before, nor do we feel any distress on the score of that self. . . . [Thus] you may be sure that we have nothing to fear after death, and that he who exists now, cannot become miserable, and that it matters not a whit whether he has been born into life at any other time, when immortal death has taken away his mortal life."[61]

David Hume also accepted death, but his acceptance contained a note of positive value. He wrote a short autobiography in the last few months of his life that contains the following lines: "In the spring, 1775, I was struck with a disorder in my bowels, which at first gave me no alarm, but has since, as I apprehend it, become mortal and incurable. I now reckon upon a speedy dissolution. I have suffered very little pain from my disorder; and what is more strange, have, notwithstanding the great decline of my person, never suffered a moment's abatement of my spirits; insomuch, that were I to name a period of my life which I should most choose to pass over again, I might be tempted to point to this later period."[62]

The Indian acceptance of death appears in the *Mahābhārata:* "Thou knowest that all men are sure to die; none should grieve for that which is inevitable."[63]

The Chinese acceptance of death is illustrated in the following selection from the work of the third century B.C. Taoist philosopher Chuang Tzu: "When Chuang Tzu's wife died, Hui Tzu went to condole. He found the widower sitting on the ground, singing, with his legs spread out at a right angle and beating time on a bowl. 'To live with your wife,' exclaimed Hui Tzu, 'and see your eldest son grow up to be a man, and then not to shed a tear over her corpse,—this would be bad enough. But to drum on a bowl, and sing; surely this is going too far.' 'Not at all,' replied Chuang Tzu. 'When she died, I could not help being affected by her death. Soon, however, I remembered that she had already existed in a previous state before birth, without form, or even substance; that while in that unconditioned condition, substance was added to spirit; that this substance then assumed form; and that the next stage was birth. And now, by virtue of a further change, she is dead, passing from one phase to another like the sequence of spring, summer, autumn, and winter. And while she is thus lying asleep in eternity, for me to go about weeping and wailing would be to proclaim myself ignorant of these natural laws. Therefore I refrain.' "[64]

The most positive attitude man can take toward death is adventure. This was the note upon which Socrates completed his defense of himself and his life: "And now it is time to go, I to die, and you to live; but which of us goes to a better thing is unknown to all but God."[65] One of the best-known examples of death as an adventure is the description offered by John Bunyan in *The Pilgrim's Progress*. Bunyan reports as Christian approached the River of Death, which separated him from the Gate to the City of the Redeemed: "Now I further saw that betwixt them and the Gate was a River, but there was no Bridge to go over; the River was very deep: at the sight therefore of this River the Pilgrims were much astounded; but the men that went with them said, You must go through, or you cannot come at the Gate. . . . The Pilgrims then, especially Christian, began to dispond in his mind, and looked this way and that, but no way could be found by them by which they might escape the River. Then they asked if the Waters were all of a depth? They said, No; yet they could not help them in that case, for said they, you shall find it deeper or shallower, as you believe in the King of the place. . . . Then said Hopeful, My Brother, you have quite forgot the Text, where it is said of the wicked, There is no band in their death, but their strength is firm, they are not troubled as other men, neither are they plagued like other men. These troubles and distresses that you go through in these Waters are no sign that God hath forsaken you, but are sent to try you, whether you will call to mind that which heretofore you have received of his goodness, and live upon him in your distresses. . . . Then they both took courage, and the Enemy was after that as still as a stone, until they were gone over."[66]

The second aspect of man's relation to death and dying is the axiological: What values are inherent in death?

One obvious value is that death is often a palliative. Natural death may come as a release from great pain, insanity, feebleness, helplessness, or the problems of senility. Unnatural death in the forms of suicide and euthanasia has been defended as a way to terminate a very painful physical or mental condition or impossible economic situation, or an extremely serious moral obligation. Self destruction may be a dodge rather than a solution; for example, suicide does not pay off one's monetary obligations. Unnatural death in the form of a fatal accident may end a life scarcely worth living.

A second value of death is its necessary relation to life. Settembrini says in Thomas Mann's *The Magic Mountain* that "the only sane, noble—and I will expressly add, the only religious way to think of death is as part and parcel of life; to regard it, with the understanding and with the emotions, as the inviolable condition of life. It is the very opposite of sane, noble, reasonable, or religious to divorce it in any way from life, or to play it off against it. . . . Severed from life, it becomes a spectre, a distortion, and worse."[67] A world of births without deaths would soon become a hideous world. The *Mahābhārata* contains a strange tale of a time when Death (Yama) took a holiday: "O child, in days of yore, there was a terrible time in the Krita Yuga when the eternal and primeval Deity assumed the duties of Yama. And . . . when the God of gods began to perform the functions of Yama, there died not a creature while the births were as usual. Then there began to multiply birds and beasts and kine, and sheep, and deer and all kinds of carnivorous animals. . . . then the human race also increased by thousands even like unto a current of water. And . . . the Earth oppressed with the excessive burden, sank down . . . the Earth in distress sought the protection of Narayana, the foremost of the gods. The Earth spake saying, 'It is by thy favour, O possessor of the six attributes, that I had been able to remain so long in my position. But I have been overcome with burden and now I cannot hold myself any longer. It behoveth thee, O adorable one, to relieve this load of mine. I have sought thy protection, O lord; and do thou, therefore, extend unto me thy favour.' "[68] The "favour" was to reestablish the balance between births and deaths.

A third value of death is that it is the ultimate reminder that human beings are equal. Death is the common lot of all the sons and daughters of man. it is the equalizer—the ultimate democritizing principle.

> Golden lads and girls all must
> as chimney-sweepers, come to dust.[69]

Augustine wrote in *The City of God* (bk. 1, chap. 11): "Now the end of life puts the longest life on a par with the shortest. For of two things which have alike ceased to be, the one is not better, the other worse—the one greater, the other less."[70]

A fourth value of death is that it prevents human beings from seeing the breakdown of their culture. Imagine a rational being who has lived in Europe since the first century A.D. A personal memory of the rise and fall of empires, civilizations, reformations, revolutions, wars, social reforms, educational innovations, scientific changes, modes of behavior, fashions, and tastes of the last two thousand years would probably reduce the person with the memory into unspeakable anguish and stimulate a great desire for release. This was what C. S. Peirce had in mind when he wrote, "If man were immortal he could be perfectly sure of seeing the day when everything in which he had trusted should betray his trust, and, in short, of coming eventually to hopeless misery. He would break down, at last, as every good fortune, as every dynasty, as every civilization does. In place of this we have death."[71] One might add that it is no wonder that immortal gods in every culture are depicted as heavy-hearted beings.

3. Immortality

Hope for immortality is a positive way of dealing with the anticipation of death. He who proclaims he has no interest in, nor desire for, immortality is probably not aware of the dimensions of the self—pure ego, self-in-the-natural-world, self-in-the-social-world, and self-in-the-creative-world—and he is also probably not aware of the many kinds of immortality. "The immortality of the soul is a matter which is of so great consequence to us, and which touches us so profoundly, that we must have lost all feeling to be indifferent as to knowing what it is," wrote Pascal.[72]

Immortality in the widest sense means the survival of something beyond the dying experience. The forms of immortality may be classified as immortality of the physical self, of the social self, of the creative self, and of the pure ego.

The physical self is immortal chemically—and may be immortal biologically. The chemical elements that compose a human body cannot be destroyed. Hydrogen, oxygen, carbon, sodium, and the like, which constitute a human body, do not cease to be chemical elements on the surface of the planet Earth upon the death of the body. This is the immortality celebrated in William Cullen Bryant's "Thanatopsis."

> Earth, that nourished thee, shall claim
> Thy growth, to be resolved to earth again,
> And, lost each human trace, surrendering up
> Thine individual being, shalt thou go

> To mix forever with the elements,
> To be a brother to the insensible rock
> And to the sluggish clod, which the rude swain
> Turns with his share, and treads upon.

Biological immortality is immortality in one's offspring. Specifically, it is immortality of the germ plasm. Plato and Aristotle were both aware of this form of immortality. Plato wrote, "Marvel not then at the love which all men have of their offspring; for that universal love and interest is for the sake of immortality."[73] Aristotle likewise wrote, "Since then no living thing is able to partake in what is eternal and divine by uninterrupted continuance (for nothing perishable can for ever remain one and the same), it tries to achieve that end in the only way possible to it, and success is possible in varying degrees; so it remains not indeed as the self-same individual but continues its existence in something like itself—not numerically but specifically one."[74]

Social immortality is the immortality of being remembered. Plato appears to have thought this a motivating force in all lives—at least he reported the wise Diotima as saying to Socrates, "I am persuaded that all men do all things, and the better they are the more they do them, in hope of the glorious fame of immortal virtue; for they desire the immortal."[75] According to Samuel Butler, "To die completely, a person must not only forget but be forgotten, and who is not forgotten is not dead."[76] But very few of the billions of human beings who have lived on the Earth have social immortality, that is, relatively few have their names listed in the biographical pages of an unabridged dictionary, in *The Reader's Guide to Periodical Literature* or *Who's Who,* or have statues erected to their memory in city parks. Socrates, Siddhartha Gautama, and Confucius have social immortality, but what about Mrs. Socrates, the father of Gautama, and the servants of Confucius?

Immortality is also attained in the creative works of one's hands. All whose names are found in the card catalogues of libraries, whose works of art are in museums, whose constructions are in cities and villages, whose musical compositions are played, and so on, are immortal. Those who write their names or messages on the walls of public toilets, on highway signs, on rocks along roadsides, and the like, may be trying to immortalize themselves. "Kilroy was here" is a kind of immortality. But much of creative immortality is impersonal. We shall probably never know who were the artists who painted the bison in the cave of Altamira (Spain) or the reindeer in the cave of Font de Gaume (France), who were the stonemasons who carved the living rock temples at Elephanta (India), or who were the American Indians who made the petroglyphs at Chaco Canyon (Arizona).

In addition to immortality through chemical elements, inheritance, social influences, and creative works there is an immortality of absorption. This has already been noted in Śaṅkara's interpretation of the *tat tvam asi* passages in the *Upaniṣads*. According to Śaṅkara the individual self *(jīva)* has only phenomenal reality *(māyā)*. Its true reality is as *Ātman*—the one, only, universal Totality. *Ātman* is Brahman. He, who through discovery-creation existentially identifies himself as *Ātman,* can say with the Upaniṣadic seer, "I, indeed, am below. I am above. I am to the west. I am to the east. I am to the south. I am to the north. I, indeed, am this whole world."[77] We might ask what meaning does the "I" have when it ceases to be personal. When the pure ego is not the center of my experience but the center of all experience, it is a center that is everywhere—or nowhere. The self ceases to be a point of reference when it becomes the Universal Self. There is no point of view that is the view from no point. Rāmānuja in the eleventh century noted that the immortality of absorption appeals to few: "No sensible person exerts himself under the influence of the idea that after he himself has perished there will remain some entity termed 'pure light.'"[78] Similarly, the nineteenth-century Bengali mystic Ramakrishna said he did not want to become sugar, but rather he wanted to taste sugar.

Despite the various meanings of *immortality,* when one says "I believe in immortality," one is generally understood to be referring to personal immortality, that is, to the survival of individual identity beyond the dying experience. The desire for preserving selfhood is manifold—for example, to stay united with those one loves, to have additional opportunities for fulfillment of aspirations, to continue happy experiences or to have a chance to find missed happiness, to redress life's injustices, to satisfy the craving to feel important, and so on. The desire may be an expression of a strain of self-centeredness, or of an unwarranted conception of the importance of individuality, or of a reasoned conviction that values are integral to individual life and personhood.

What philosophical arguments can be offered in support of the belief in and hope for personal immortality? The almost-universality of the belief and the support of authoritative religious scriptures should be mentioned, although they are not philosophical arguments. Another argument is that man's sense of justice demands there be a time and place in which the maladjustments of earthly rewards and punishments shall be righted. Still another is that values are related to persons; goodness, beauty, and truth are eternal; therefore persons must be eternal. But all these arguments are rooted in finding good reasons for believing in that which one would believe in the absence of good reasons.

The ontological argument, which was first presented by Plato in the *Phaedo,* is that the conception of a soul necessarily implies the conception of life, just as the conception of a circle necessarily implies the conception of 360 degrees. Although Western philosophers have spent much time and effort in the analysis of the ontological argument, the obvious and fatal flaw is that the argument is concerned with the conception of soul and the conception of immortality, whereas what is sought is the reality of immortality, not the conception of immortality.

The empircal evidences for continuation of selfhood beyond death are open to fraud and deception. In 1883 the Society for Psychical Research was established in England to examine visions, presences, and other empirical evidence for personal immortality. More recently J. B. Rhine at Duke University has collected and studied these matters. The following is an example from his collection: "One evening when I was a boy of four, before I knew anything of school or the alphabet, my mother was working at her desk in our hotel and I got hold of a call pad and was busy making marks on it. This kept up for three or four small sheets of paper when mother, noticing what I was playing with, told me to stop and play with something else. I put away my pencil, folded the papers I had written on and stuffed them in my mother's mailbox and went away, the incident forgotten. The next morning mother found the papers in her box and was about to throw them away when the day clerk, who had taken shorthand at night school, told her they looked like shorthand. Mother explained that they were just my scribblings, but the clerk insisted on taking the papers to a teacher for examination. They were shorthand. The entire scribblings made sense and there was not one mistake or extra mark on the papers. It was written in the old-fashioned square-type shorthand, something of which I had never heard, let alone having the slightest idea of how to write. It was a message to my mother. It started: 'Dearest Beloved,' and spoke of a letter that had not been posted. It was an urgent letter concerning my father's safety-deposit box in the East. My father had died two weeks before. He had died in New York while mother and I were in Oregon. His death had been sudden and mother had not known the location of that box. Moreover, my father had always called my mother 'Dearest Beloved,' and while he was a young man he had learned shorthand the old-fashioned method. Mother still has those pieces of paper and the message has been translated by other people and is actually there. It was years later, when I was old enough to understand, that Mother told me the story and showed me the papers."[79]

4. The Goals of Self-Realization

Perfectionism was unqualifiedly supported by Jesus the Christ in the Sermon on the Mount: "You, therefore, must be perfect, as your heavenly Father is perfect."[80] But the Christian Church had difficulty in implementing perfection. In the fourth century Donatus persuaded almost half of the bishops of North Africa to limit church membership to the morally upright and to affirm that the validity of the sacraments depended upon the moral character of the officiating priests. However, Donatism was condemned in the fifth century. The condemnation did not prevent the rise of other forms of puritanism in Christianity.

How seriously should the goals of life be regarded? Are they ideals to be attained? Or are they standards by which progress is to be measured? Betty Heinmann argued that the "ideal of the final goal of Perfection is a Western postulate," that the "West thinks on results, believes in facts which ultimately can be reached and fulfilled," and that the West "clings to a clear-cut and distinct *Summum*."[81] "The West" she continues "is afraid of the embarrassing complexity in which one may lose one's own clear direction and certain position. From this angle of voluntary limitation to one single path, the Western ideal rests in perfection, the fulfillment of a distinct aim which can be accomplished by limitation and selection only. The end, the ideal, is static and changeless in its perfected individuality. . . . The Indian mind, on the other hand, rejoices in dynamic changes and divergent possibilities as a congenial expression of divine productivity. . . . [T]he Indian is never satisfied with any static end. . . . The end of development is for all phenomena a final re-flow and in-flow into the general receptacle of the 'Ocean,' the Brahman, the universal reservoire out of which all forms sprang forth and into which all of them, in the end, are reabsorbed."[82] One of the best supports for Heinmann's contention is the invocation that opens the *Īśa Upaniṣad*, which is translated by S. Radhakrishnan: "That is full; this is full. The full comes out of the full. Taking the full from the full the full in itself remains." The word *full (pūrṇa)*, which appears seven times in the two lines, may be regarded as the Indian counterpart of the Western concept of perfection. *Pūrṇa* is not an ideal to be attained or a rigid standard against which progress is to be measured, but rather it denotes a plenishing and replenishing of the hiatus between the terminus a quo and the terminus ad quem. The model is not static perfection but dynamic perfecting. In the words of Vivekānanda, "Man is to become divine, realising the divine more and more from day to day in an endless progress."[83] The ideal life is not the life that is perfect, but the life that is full. Man's life as the eternal pilgrim was beautifully expressed by Rabindranath Tagore: "Man is not complete; he is yet to be. In what he *is* he is small, and if we could conceive him stopping there for eternity we should have an idea of the most awful hell that man can imagine. In his *to be* he is infinite, there is his heaven, his deliverance. His *is* is occupied every moment with what it can get and have done with; his *to be* is hungering for something which is more than can be got, which he never can lose because he never has possessed."[84]

Perfection is suspect in many non-Western cultures. Mircea Eliade reports that among the Toradja people of the Celebres a dog that is always lucky in hunting is declared to be *measa* (ill-starred, a bringer of evil). Eliade generalizes, "Perfection in any sphere is frightening, and this sacred or magic quality of perfection may provide an explanation for the fear that even the most civilized societies seem to feel when faced with a genius or a saint. Perfection is not of this world. It is something different, it comes from somewhere else."[85] Perhaps only in the United States of America—and then only prior to the tragic World Wars I and II—have human beings regarded perfection as a reasonable goal. Alfred North Whitehead accurately reflected the caution of Europeans when he wrote, "The foundation of all understanding of sociological theory—that is to say, of all understanding of human life—is that no static maintenance of perfection is possible. . . . Advance or Decadence are the only possible choices offered to mankind."[86] Perhaps still more sagacity is contained in the Zen aphorism that to travel well is better than to arrive.

One of the earliest and best philosophical studies of goals of life is that made by Aristotle. He began his *Nicomachean Ethics* with this observation: "Every art and every inquiry, and similarly every action and pursuit, is thought to aim at some good."[87] The good, said Aristotle, is "that at which all things aim,"[88] and if "there is some end of the things we do, which we desire for its own sake (everything else being desired for the sake of this) . . . this must be the good and the chief good."[89] This "chief good" is examined by "the most authoritative art," "the most truly master art," the art of "politics."[90] This—"the highest of all goods achievable by action"[91]—is "living well and doing well,"[92] and its name is "happiness."[93] "Happiness" is not fully apropos as a translation of the Greek term *eudaimonia*. The literal meaning of *eudaimonia* is having a good *daimōn*. A *daimōn* among the early Greeks was a "supernatural presence or entity, somewhere between a god *(theós)* and a hero."[94] But by the fourth century B.C. *daimōn* denoted that which is one's essential nature. *Eudaimonia* or happiness, therefore, meant keeping in good condition that part of one's nature which makes one a member of a class of beings. If man were essentially a nutritive being, then his *eudaimonia* would be to maintain a strong and healthy body. If man were essentially a sensitive being, then his *eudaimonia* would be to perfect his sense organs. But man, according to Aristotle, is essentially a rational being, and therefore his *eudaimonia* is the well functioning of his rational principle *(lógos)*. Aristotle must have had in mind the ancient Greek proverb "Think mortal thoughts" when he wrote, "But we must not follow those who advise us, being men, to think of human things, and, being mortal, of mortal things, but must, so far as we can, make ourselves immortal, and strain every nerve to live in accordance with the best thing in us; for even if it be small in bulk, much more does it in power and worth surpass everything."[95] "Perfect happiness," he wrote, "is a contemplative activity. . . . Therefore the activity of God, which surpasses all others in blessedness, [96] must be contemplative; and of human activities, therefore, that which is most akin to this must be most of the nature of happiness."[97]

Some people, added Aristotle, think happiness is "some plain and obvious thing, like pleasure, wealth, or honour."[98] Those who identify happiness and pleasure are "men of the most vulgar type."[99] A life of pleasure is "a life suitable to beasts."[100] Those who identify happiness and wealth confuse things "good in themselves" with "things useful,"[101] that is, they confuse ends and means, goals and agencies, intrinsic values and instrumental values. He says that "wealth is evidently not the good we are seeking; for it is merely useful and for the sake of something else."[102] But he was no admirer of penury. Well-being and well-doing require "the proper equipment."[103] "The liberal man will need money for the doing of his liberal deeds."[104] Those who identify happiness and honor are often "people of superior refinement."[105] Honor is indeed "the end of political life,"[106] but honor "seems too superficial to be what we are looking for, since it is thought to depend on those who bestow honour rather than on him who receives it, but the good we divine to be something proper to man and not easily taken from him."[107]

Thus Aristotle concluded that the paradigmatic life for man requires the proper equipment,[108] requires honor as a "prize,"[109] requires "power"[110] and "opportunity,"[111] requires "leisure,"[112] requires the sense of touch for living[113] and the other senses for "well-being,"[114] involves pleasure [115] since "the pleasures intensify the activities,"[116] and involves three kinds of friends, that is, those bound by "a mutual and recognized love," those bound by "some good which they get from each other," and those bound by "the sake of pleasure."[117] Perfect happiness is "a contemplative activity."[118] Reason "more than anything else is man,"[119] is "the best thing in us,"[120] and "the most divine element in us."[121] Therefore "he who exercises his reason and cultivates it seems to be both in the best state of mind and most dear to the gods. For if the gods have any care for human affairs, as they are thought to have, it would be reasonable both that they should delight in that which was best and most akin to them (i.e., reason) and that they should reward those who love and honour this most, as caring for the things that are dear to them and acting both rightly and nobly. And that all these attributes belong most of all to the philosopher is manifest. He, therefore, is the dearest to the gods. And he who is that will presumably be also the happiest; so that in this way too the philosopher will more than any other be happy."[122]

Western philosophers have correctly detected a dichotomy in the Aristotelian summation of the proper goals of human life. On the one hand, man is to seek personal well-being in development and fulfillment of his rational nature, and on the other hand, as a political animal he is to seek his well-being and promote the well-being of all in the social organizations of family, village, and state. The former goal was stressed by the Epicureans. "The beginning and the root of all good is the pleasure of the stomach," wrote Epicurus.[123] "I spit upon the beautiful and those who vainly admire it, when it does not produce any pleasure."[124] But he avoided the extreme pleasures: "I am thrilled with pleasure in the body, when I live on bread and water, and

I spit upon luxurious pleasures not for their own sake, but because of the inconveniences that follow them."[125] He warned that "the pleasures of love never profited a man and he is lucky if they do him no harm."[126] Happiness, for Epicurus, was primarily negative. Positive pleasures are too monentary and sporadic to be a proper goal of human life. The pleasurable condition is the condition of not being uncomfortable. *Ataraxia*—serenity of mind and body, or, more properly preserving the negativity of the Greek term, absence of passion—is the only proper goal. *Ataraxia* meant for Epicurus relief from three kinds of suffering: physical pain, fear of death, and religious hopes and anxieties. Physical pain, said Epicurus, can be endured because it "does not last continually in the flesh, but the acutest pain is there for a very short time, and even that which just exceeds the pleasure in the flesh does not continue for many days at once."[127] Death—"the draught swallowed by all of us at birth"[128]—"is nothing to us: for that which is dissolved is without sensation; and that which lacks sensation is nothing to us."[129] Religion disturbs *ataraxia* more than does physical pain or the fear of death. Epicurus wrote to Herodotus that "the principal disturbance in the minds of men arises because they think that these celestial bodies [sun, moon, and stars] are blessed and immortal, and yet have wills and actions and motives inconsistent with these attributes; and because they are always expecting or imagining some everlasting misery, such as is depicted in legends."[130] In the opinion of Epicurus there are gods: "For gods there are, since the knowledge of them is by clear vision. But they are not such as the many believe them to be."[131] The gods in his view were superhumans, very much like humans but they have no concern for the affairs of man. The egoistic hedonism of Epicureanism was best expressed in an image found in Lucretius's *De Rerum Natura:* "It is sweet, when on the great sea the winds trouble its waters, to behold from land another's deep distress; not that it is a pleasure and delight that any should be afflicted, but because it is sweet to see from what evils you are yourself exempt."[132] The dubious pleasure of witnessing another's suffering was later incorporated into the Christian conception of heaven by Thomas Aquinas, who claimed that the redeemed in heaven would have their happiness increased by being able to look into hell to witness the tortures of the damned.

Hedonism as a goal of life in the West has usually been qualified by classifying pleasures into some form of higher and lower pleasures; for example, John Stuart Mill distinguished between the pleasures of Socrates and of a fool—between those of a human and those of a pig: "It is better to be a human being dissatisifed than a pig satisfied; better to be Socrates dissatisfied than a fool satisfied. And if the fool, or the pig, are of a different opinion, it is because they only know their own side of the question. The other party to the comparison knows both sides."[133] Aquinas linked hedonism, contemplation, and religion in his view that "man's ultimate happiness consists in the contemplation of truth."[134]

The Epicureans emphasized the egoistic side of Aristotle's *eudaimonía:* the Stoics emphasized the social side. The Epicureans sought *ataraxía,* that is, peace of mind by noninvolvement in political life; the Stoics sought *apátheia,* that is, peace of mind by doing one's duty and accepting the consequences. The outstanding Stoics were the Roman ex-slave Epictetus (50–138) and the Roman Emperor Marcus Aurelius (121–180).

The thoughts of Epictetus have been preserved by his pupil Arrianus in two forms: a collection of lectures and a shorter work known as the *Encheiridion* (Manual). The heart of Epictetus's admonition is the distinction between that which is within man's power and that which is outside man's power: "Of all existing things, some are in our power, and others are not in our power. In our power are thought, impulse, will to get and will to avoid, and, in a word, everything which is not our own doing. Things not in our power include the body, property, reputation, office, and, in a word, everything which is not our own doing. Things in our power are by nature free, unhindered, untrammelled; things not in our power are weak, servile, subject to hindrance, dependent on others. Remember then that if you imagine that what is naturally slavish is free, and what is naturally another's is your own, you will be hampered, you will mourn, you will be put to confusion, you will blame gods and men; but if you think that only your own belongs to you, and that what is another's is indeed another's, no one will ever put compulsion or hindrance on you, you will blame none, you will accuse none, you will do nothing against your will, no one will harm you, and you will have no enemy, for no harm can touch you . . . . Make it your study then to confront every harsh impression with the words, 'You are but an impression, and not at all what you seem to be.' Then test it by those rules that you possess; and first by this—the chief test of all—'Is it concerned with what is in our power or with what is not in our power?' And if it is concerned with what is not in our power, be ready with the answer that is nothing to you."[135]

Marcus Aurelius, perhaps because of his position as Roman Emperor, stressed man's sociality: "Whether the universe is a concourse of atoms [as the Epicureans claimed], or nature is a system [as the Stoics claimed], let this first be established, that I am a part of the whole which is governed by nature; next, I am in a manner, intimately related to the parts which are of the same kind with myself. For remembering this, inasmuch as I am a part, I shall be discontented with none of the things which are assigned to me out of the whole; for nothing is injurious to the part, if it is for the advantage of the whole . . . . By remembering, then, that I am a part of such a whole, I shall be content with everything that happens."[136] "Men exist for the sake of one another."[137] Therefore, man cannot be angry with his fellowmen, nor hate them, "For we are made for co-operation, like feet, like hands, like eyelids, like the rows of the upper and lower teeth. To act against one another then is contrary to nature."[138] The chief goal of life is to do one's duty: "Let it make no difference to thee whether thou art cold or warm, if thou art doing thy duty; and whether thou art drowsy or satisfied with sleep; and whether ill-spoken of or praised; and whether dying or doing something else."[139] There is even a duty to die well: "For it is one of the acts of life, this act by which we die; it is sufficient then in this act also to do well what we have in hand."[140] Duty has two parts, according to Marcus Aurelius: (1) Equanimity, that is, "the voluntary acceptance of the things which are assigned to thee by the common nature"; and (2) Magnanimity, that is, "the elevation of the intelligent part above the pleasurable or painful sensations of the flesh, and above that poor thing called fame, and death, and all such things."[141] Each man should therefore "Live as on a mountain. For it makes no difference whether a man lives there or here, if he lives everywhere in the world as in a state (political community). Let men see, let them know a real man who lives according to nature. If they cannot endure him, let them kill him. For that is better than to live thus as men do."[142] Marcus Aurelius summarized his moral advice with an effort to restore the harmony of Aristotle's self-interest and moral obligation: "Remember . . . that thou art formed by nature to bear everything, with respect to which it depends on thy own opinion to make it endurable and tolerable, by thinking that it is either thy interest or thy duty to do this."[143]

Immanuel Kant was the Western philosopher who placed the highest value on the duty principle. He wrote, "Nothing in the world—indeed even beyond the world—can possibly be conceived which could be called good without qualification except a good will. Intelligence, wit, judgment, and the other talents of the mind, however, they may be named, or courage, resoluteness, and perseverance as qualities of temperament are doubtless in many respects good and desirable. But they can become extremely bad and harmful if the will, which is to make use of these gifts of nature and which in its special constitution is called character, is not good."[144] By *good will* Kant meant an act done from a sense of duty, not merely in accordance with duty. In further spelling out of his meaning, he also described such an act as one done with respect to the law, that the principle or the act be one that could be universalized, and that it be an act that treats other people as ends rather than means. But even Kant, despite his emphasis on duty, did not exclude the hedonic element, admitting that "to secure one's own happiness is at least indirectly a duty."[145]

The Chinese view of the highest good for man is a harmonious joining of what cannot be changed in the social world with rejoicing in the simple pleasures offered in the natural world. In a story contained in the *Analects* Confucius is reported to have asked four students what they would do if they were given full authority in a state. Tzu-lu replied, "Give me a country of a thousand war-chariots, hemmed in by powerful enemies, or even invaded by hostile armies, with drought and famine to boot; in the space of three years I could endow the people with courage and teach them in what direction right conduct lies." Jan Ch'iu, said, "Give me a domain of sixty to seventy or say fifty to sixty leagues, and in the space of three years I could bring it about that the common people should lack for nothing. But as to rites and music, I should have to leave them to a real gentleman." Kung-hsi Hua replied, "In ceremonies at the Ancestral Temple or at a conference or general gathering of the feudal princes I should like, clad in the Straight Gown and Emblematic Cap, to play the part of junior assistant." When it came Tseng Hsi's turn to reply, he hesitated, pleading that his choice seemed inferior to the other three—the militarist, the economist, and ritualist. Confucius encouraged him, saying, "What harm is there in that? All that matters is that each should name his desire." Thus encouraged, Tseng Hsi said, "At the end of spring, when the making of the Spring Clothes has been completed, to go with five times six newly-capped youths and six times seven uncapped boys, perform the lustration in the river I, take the air at the Rain Dance altars, and then go home singing." Confucius sighed and said, "I am with Tseng Hsi."[146]

Poetry has been a favored form of expressing life goals in China. Wang Chi (584–644) expressed the Chinese hedonic ideals in this fashion:

> "Tell me now, what should a man want
> But to sit alone, sipping his cup of wine?"
> I should like to have visitors come and discuss
>   philosophy
> And not to have the tax-collector coming to
>   collect taxes:
> My three sons married into good families
> And my five daughters wedded to steady husbands.
> Then I could jog through a happy five-score years
> And, at the end, need no Paradise.[147]

Po Chü-i (722–846) in his poem added the element of acceptance:

> Keep off your thoughts from things that are past and
>   done;
> For thinking of the past wakes regret and pain.
> Keep off your thoughts from thinking what will happen;
> To think of the future fills one with dismay.
> Better by day to sit like a sack in your chair;
> Better by night to lie a stone in your bed.
> When food comes, then open your mouth;
> When sleep comes, then close your eyes.[148]

The goal of all Buddhists is to attain the condition known as *nirvāṇa*. The term means blown out or extinguished, but it is very difficult to state what it is that is extinguished. Edward Conze has written, "This 'Nirvana' is surely a very strange entity which differs greatly from anything that we have ever met before, and has nothing in common with objects about which assertion is possible. In order to do justice to it, one must withdraw from everything by which, of which or with which anything can be asserted. As the final deliverance Nirvana is the *raison d'être* of Buddhism, and its ultimate justification. All the Buddha's words are said to have the taste of Nirvana and 'the religious life is plunged in Nirvana, its aim is Nirvana, its end and outcome is Nirvana.'"[149]

All conceptions of *nirvāṇa* are misconceptions, because a conception is a thought-denoting class and sharable by minds such that interpersonal communication is possible. But *nirvāṇa* is unthinkable, inconceivable, and unspeakable. It is an experience unique to each individual. There is no way of establishing that any two individuals have the same experience of *nirvāṇa*. Buddhism is a taste-and-see way of life, and he who tastes-and-sees cannot tell another what he has tasted and seen. A's *nirvāṇa* is unique to A, B's to B, and so on. Within this caveat, however, it is possible to describe *nirvāṇa* as the enlightenment experience that yields insight into the meaning of life for each individual. It is a goal that cannot be sought nor craved, that cannot be shared, that cannot be described, but that alters everything when experienced. It is the scent that sinks into the robes. *Nirvāṇa* is a feeling of deathlessness, peacefulness, and security. The terms used to denote the security of *nirvāṇa*—the "fingers pointing to the moon"—include the following: "The Harbor of Refuge," "The Cool Cave," "The Island Among the Floods," "The Place of Bliss," "Safety," "The Home of Ease," "The Abiding," "The Farther Shore," "The Bliss of Effort," "The Supreme Joy," "The Holy City," and "The State of Him Who is Worthy."

Buddhism split by reason of two divergent views of *nirvāṇa* comparable to the dichotomy between self-fullfillment and social obligations that we have noticed in Aristotle. According to Theravāda Buddhism, which is popularly known as Southern Buddhism, *nirvāṇa* is the blowing out of the flames of personal desire, the ending of all craving for individuality, and the eradicating of the conception of an ego. The one who attains this condition is known as an *arhat,* a Never-Returner. He is rid of the awareness of a substantial ego in his being and in the being of others. In his selfless life he "wanders like a rhinoceros." Mahāyāna Buddhism or Northern Buddhism regards Theravāda as "a quiet but stagnant backwater."[150] It "emancipates Buddhism from its comparatively drab terrestrial and historical context and transfers it to a celestial context of dazzling beauty and irresistible emotional appeal; it mounts the priceless jewel of the Dharma in a ring of gold."[151] The Mahāyāna supplants the ideal of the *arhat,* the lonely seeker, with the ideal of the *bodhisattva,* the compassionate being who postpones his full *nirvāṇa,* known as *parinirvāṇa,* in order that he may assist others in attaining the condition of enlightenment. *Nirvāṇa*, according to Mahāyāna, is not the selfish state of selflessness as it is for Theravāda, but the compassionate state of concern for the liberation of others who are ultimately *anātmans* but who in their state of ignorance think they are *ātmans*. Whereas for the Theravāda *nirvāṇa* is liberation from *saṁsāra*, for the Mahāyāna *nirvāṇa* is in *saṁsāra*—or, since according to the Mahāyāna *saṁsāra* is empty, *nirvāṇa* is *saṁsāra*. *Nirvāṇa* is the condition in which one while in *saṁsāra* sees the *śūnyatā* (emptiness of *saṁsāra*) and as a collection of *skandhas* seeks to relieve other collections of *skandhas* from the illusion that they are substantial egos. D. T. Suzuki writes, "According to the Mahāyānistic conception Nirvāna is not the annihilation of the world and the putting an end to life; but it is to live in the whirlpool of birth and death and yet to be above it. It is affirmation and fulfilment, and this is done not blindly and egoistically, for Nirvāṇa is enlightenment."[152] According to the *Mādhyamakakārikā*, "Nothing of Saṁsāra is different from Nirvāṇa; nothing of Nirvāṇa is different from Saṁsāra. The limit of Nirvāṇa is the limit of Saṁsāra; there is not even the subtlest something separating the two."[153] However, in the logic of Buddhism an absolute identity does not exclude an absolute difference. The difference is that the same realities of our human pilgrimage are seen imaginarily (cf. the Upsaniṣadic *iva*) as *saṁsāra* and absolutely (cf. the Upaniṣadic *sat*) as *nirvāṇa*.

Hinduism is the philosophy that excells all others in the clarity and comprehensiveness of the formulation of its goals of life. There are four goals that are known collectively as the *puruṣārtha*, the aim of human existence. These four are divided into three secondary goals, known as the *trivarga* (group of three), namely, (1) *artha*, the material compenent; (2) *kāma*, the hedonic component; and (3) *dharma*, the moral component, and one primary goal, which is *mokṣa*, liberation.

Artha means wealth or possessions. It denotes all that one may amass, share, enjoy, lose, and destroy. The notion that India has always been a poor country, and that Hinduism glorifies asceticism is far from the truth. The *Pañchatantra*, a collection of animal fables that assumed its present form from about A.D. 600, contains many humorous praises of wealth and ridicule of poverty, for example,

> The wealthy, though of meanest birth,
> Are much respected on the earth:
> The poor whose lineage is prized
> Like clearest moonlight, are despised.
> The wealthy are, however old,
> Rejuvenated by their gold:
> If money has departed, then
> The youngest lads are aged men.
> Since brother, son, and wife, and friend
> Desert when cash is at an end,

Returning when the cash rolls in,
'Tis cash that is our next of kin.[154]

The second goal of the *trivarga* is *kāma* (physical love). *Kāma* refers to the pleasures of food, drink, physical comfort, and sex. Spiritous liquors were such an important part of the life of the early Hindus that they elevated drink to a divine level—the god Soma. Dance, music, sculpture, painting, and games are goals of the good life that must not be missed.

The *Kāma Sūtra* of Vātsyāyana (fourth century A.D.) is a classical textbook for lovers with its sixty-four arts auxillary to the joys of love, twelve non-coital forms of embrace, ten kinds of kisses, eight kinds of love-scratching, eight types of bitings, and eighty-four coital positions.

Dharma (law or duty) is the principle of social restraint brought upon the pursuit of wealth and pleasure. It is a Hindu recognition that man is a social animal, that hedonic satisfactions become values only in the framework of duties inherent in one's membership in extended family, *jāti*, and *varṇa*. *Dharma* in its broadest sense is identical with *ṛta* (cosmic order). The Hindu notion is that natural law is paralleled by moral law. The notion is that he who violates the rules of proper social behavior is also in violation of world order, and he who preserves moral order will find harmony with the universe itself. *Dharma* in its human context implies "justice, virtue, morality, religious merit and righteousness, law, duty, the Good, the True, the Norm, the Ideal, the Way."[155] The manifold *dharmas* of Hindus have been preserved in detail in forty-seven collections of law codes known as the *Dharma Śāstras*.

Artha, *kāma*, and *dharma* are important goals in Hinduism, but the chief goal is *mokṣa* (spiritual freedom). *Mokṣa* fulfills and transcends the *trivarga*. While *mokṣa* does mean deliverance from the necessity of returning again in earthly form to work out *karma*, since all *karma* has been exhausted and no new *karma* has been created, the ideal life on Earth is *jivān-mukti*, which is spiritual freedom while alive, release while in the incarnate state, release while still an individual self. The *mukta* (freed individual) does not have to wait until his death to enjoy the *mokṣa* condition. The *mukta* is released while still living—he is a *jivān-mukta*. Hence this earthly existence need not be a vale of tears, a prisonhouse, a place of sound and fury signifying nothing. Hinduism does not agree with early Buddhism that to live is to suffer.

Inherent in *mokṣa* is a polarity of freedom—freedom *from* and freedom *for*, release and opportunity. This is expressed beautifully in a prayer used often in Hinduism as a self-benediction:

Asato mā sad gamaya.
Tamaso mā jyotir gamaya.
Mṛtyor mā mṛtam gamaya.

> Lead me from unreality to reality.
> Lead me from darkness to light.
> Lead me from death to immortality.

Freedom *from* in Hinduism means freedom from the fear of death, freedom from sorrow, suffering, misery, and frustration, and the feeling of insignificance, freedom from *karma,* retribution, law, fate, and even the gods themselves, freedom from passions and desires that stand in the way of one's self-realization, freedom from change and the impermanence of things, freedom from doubt, ignorance, and intellectual blindness, freedom from finitude, and freedom from evil *(pāpa)* or sin *(pāpman)*. Freedom *for* is the freedom to become what one is. The full realization of human nature is the goal of positive freedom. "*Mokṣa* is the capstone and summary of the Hindu guest. It is the freedom to be and to become, freedom from all that ensnares and entangles man in the confusions and conflicts of life, and freedom to love and enjoy life in all dimensions, here and hereafter. It is the freedom to be free. No limits can be set to this liberation. 'In all worlds they possess unlimited freedom.' The man of *mokṣa*, the man who has entered Brahman-*nirvāṇa*, is the human paradigm, the ideal of the Perfection of Man."[156]

The philosopher is man becoming self-aware. Philosophy is the primary, the best, and maybe the only effective way of self-realization. To sense that one senses, to experience that one experiences, to be aware that one is aware, to know that one knows is to philosophize. These forms of sensing, experiencing, being aware, and knowing we now believe to be acts of the right hemisphere of the brain on the left hemisphere. This is the functioning in which Eastern philosophers have specialized. This is why Western philosophy can no longer ignore Eastern philosophy. But Eastern philosophy cannot ignore Western philosophy. The East must learn to cultivate the rational and inductive approach to man and his worlds; the West must learn to cultivate more feeling for and appreciation of man and his worlds. Intellectualizing without emotionalizing is mere ratiocination; emotionalizing without intellectualizing is mere sentimentalism. Each self is a polarity of reason and feeling. A polarity is not an opposition nor a conflict but an internal difference that stimulates and assists in a common growth. Polarities have both affinity for and repulsion to each other. The art of the good life is the reconciliation of differences. Everett Shostrom of the Institute of Therapeutic Psychology at Santa Ana, California, writes, "I believe that most of our struggles come in inner conflicts with the polarities of strength-weakness and anger-love. For example, most of us are taught to 'Stand up and be counted,' and yet we are also told, 'Blessed are the meek.' We are admonished to 'Love our neighbor,' and yet we must not 'let the sun set on our wrath.'"[157]

When strength-weakness and anger-love are treated as destructive opposites rather than complementary polarities, four possible lines of behavior may develop: (1) If one follows the path of anger exclusively, one may move from anger to blaming and attacking others, to sadistic delight in bringing pain to others, to paranoic suspicion and distrust of others, and finally to murder. (2) If one follows the path of love exclusively, one may move from love to extreme efforts to please and placate others, to masochistic pleasure in being abused and dominated, to feelings of inadequacy, sadness, and depression, and finally to suicide. (3) If one follows the path of strength exclusively, one may move from strength to controlling and conniving to force one's will on others, to narcissistic delight in using one's strength, to psychopathetic conceit of self and suspicion of others, and finally to tyranny over others. (4) If one follows the path of weakness exclusively, one may move from weakness to withdrawing and avoiding contact with others, to acts of a schizoid person, to schizophrenic delusions and hallucinations, and finally to complete withdrawal as a hermit. These four lines of behavior are manipulative or missionary levels of interaction. Those who reconcile and integrate the basic polarities of strength-weakness and anger-love operate at the actualizing or expressive levels of behavior. This reconciliation of polarities is found in the *Gospel of Philip,* a gospel rejected by the early Christian Church: "Light and darkness, life and death, right and left are brothers one of another. They are inseparable. Because of this neither are the good good, nor the evil evil, nor is life life, nor death death. For this reason each one will dissolve into its original nature. But those who are exalted above the world are indissoluble, eternal."[158]

Aristotle closed his *Nicomachean Ethics* with a curious sentence—"Let us make a beginning of our discussion." In this spirit I terminate this philosophic adventure. The ending is also the beginning. To be human is to become. "To become is our life's significance."[159] Human nature is not established; if a human being were established, he or she would be a god or a beast. It is human nature—a beast aspiring to be a god—to be ever in process. The human being is "a transitional being, an unfinished experiment."[160] "The human being is a *saṁsārin,* a perpetual wanderer, a tramp on the road. His life is incessant metamorphosis."[161] The human being is a *mārgāyatin,* a wayfarer. To be human is to be Prometheus, the culture-maker. The human being is both *homo hominatus* (the human being as made by the human being) and *homo hominans* (the human being as maker of the human being).

Notes

Preface

1. Agehananda Bharati, *The Light at the Center* (Santa Barbara, Calif.: Ross-Erikson, 1976), p. 11.
2. Nirad C. Chaudhuri, *Hinduism* (Oxford: Oxford University Press, 1979), p. 211.
3. Louis Renou, *Indian Literature*, trans. Patrick Evans (New York: Walker, 1964), p. 136.
4. Arthur O. Lovejoy, *The Great Chain of Being* (Cambridge: Harvard University Press, 1936), p. 312.
5. Mohandas Gandhi, *Young India*, 1 June 1921. This is inscribed over the entrance to the Indian National Library in Calcutta.

Chapter 1. The Human Being as Philosopher

1. Luther J. Binkley, *Conflict of Ideals* (New York: Van Nostrand Reinhold, 1969), p. 146.
2. Plato, *Gorgias* 484 (trans. Jowett).
3. Daniel H. H. Ingalls, "Dharma and Moksa," *Philosophy East and West* 7 (April–June 1957): 48.
4. Frederick Copleston, *Philosophies and Cultures* (New York: Oxford University Press, 1980), p. vi.
5. T. V. Smith, *The Philosophic Way of Life* (New York: Crofts, 1945), p. vii.
6. William James, *Pragmatism* (New York: Longmans, Green, 1908), p. 12.
7. Fredrick Waismann, *How I See Philosophy* (London: Macmillan, 1968), pp. 1, 2.
8. Curt J. Ducasse et al., *Philosophy in American Education, Its Tasks and Opportunities* (New York: AMS Press, 1945), p. 21.
9. Cicero, *De Officiis* (On Duties), bk. 2, chap. 5, sec. 5.
10. Committee of the American Philosophical Society, *Philosophy. A Brief Guide for Undergraduates* (Philadelphia: American Philosophical Association, 1982), p. 1.
11. W. H. Werkmeister, "Scientism and the Problem of Man," in *Philosophy and Culture—East and West*, ed. Charles A. Moore (Honolulu: University of Hawaii Press, 1962), p. 154.
12. Bertrand Russell, *Our Knowledge of the External World* (London: George Allen and Unwin, 1922), pp. 40–41.
13. See C. J. Ducasse, "Philosophy, the Guide of Life," *The Key Reporter* (January 1958).
14. William S. Haas, *The Destiny of the Mind: East and West* (New York: Macmillan, 1956), p. 133.
15. Agehananda Bharati, *The Tantric Tradition* (London: Rider, 1965), p. 13.
16. Ibid., p. 15.

17. Mervyn Sprung, "The Problem of Being in Mādhyamika Buddhism," in *Developments in Buddhist Thought: Canadian Contributions to Buddhist Studies,* ed. Roy C. Amore (Waterloo, Canada; Wildred Laurier University Press, 1979), p. 9.

18. Thomas Whittaker, *The Neo-Platonists* (Cambridge: Cambridge University Press, 1918), p. 206.

19. Tu Wei-ming, "The 'moral universal' from the perspective of East Asian Thought," *Philosophy East and West,* 31, no. 3 (July 1981): 259.

20. Nāgārjuna, in *Mūlamadhyamakakārikās, (Emptiness. A Study in Religious Meaning),* trans. Frederick J. Streng (Nashville and New York: Abingdon, 1967), p. 183.

21. *Immanuel Kant's Critique of Pure Reason,* preface to 2d ed., trans. Norman Kemp Smith (London: Macmillan, 1950), p. 22.

22. See Ralph Barton Perry, "The Ego-centric Predicament," *Journal of Philosophy* 7, no. 1 (1910): 5–14.

23. Wing-tsit Chan, "The Spirit of Oriental Philosophy," in *Philosophy—East and West,* ed. Charles A. Moore. (Princeton: Princeton University Press, 1946), pp. 166–67.

24. Ibid., p. 167.

25. Ibid.

26. George Bosworth Burch, review of *Contemporary Indian Philosophy,* ed. S. Radhakrishnan and J. H. Muirfield, *Philosophy East and West,* 7 (April–July 1957): 56.

27. Kalidas Bhattacharyya, *Alternative Standpoints in Philosophy* (Calcutta: Das Gupta, 1953), p. 366. The Earl of Lytton, Chancellor of Calcutta University, in the opening address of the First Indian Philosophical Congress said, "In the West, which delights in definition, philosophy has been a study; in the East, which loves infinity, it is a practice." *Proceedings of the First Indian Philosophical Congress* (Calcutta: Calcutta Philosophical Society, 1927), p. 6.

28. Mircea Eliade, *Yoga: Immortality and Freedom* (New York: Pantheon, 1958), p. 4.

29. Frederick Copleston, *Contemporary Philosophy* (Paramus, N.J.: Newman, 1972), p. 137.

30. Agehananda Bharati, *The Tantric Tradition,* p.18.

31. Ibid.

32. Ibid. p. 26.

33. William Ernest Hocking, "Value of the Comparative Study of Philosophy," in *Philosophy—East and West,* ed. Charles A. Moore, p. 5.

34. Wing-tsit Chan, "The Spirit of Oriental Philosophy," in *Philosophy—East and West,* ed. Moore, pp. 150–53.

35. Junjira Takakusu, "Buddhism as Philosohy of 'Thusness,'" in *Philosophy—East and West,* ed. Moore, pp. 107, 108.

36. K. W. Sen, *Hinduism* (Baltimore: Penguin, 1961).

37. P. N. Srinivasachari, *The Philosophy of Bhēdābhēda* (Adyar: The Adyar Library, 1950), p. 97.

38. Nirad C. Chaudhuri, *An Autobiography of an Unknown Indian* (London: Macmillan and Co., 1951), pp. 212–13.

39. Nirad C. Chaudhuri, *The Continent of Circe* (London: Chatto and Windus, 1965), p. 91.

40. Kewal Motwani, *India: A Synthesis of Culture* (Bombay: Thacker, 1947), p. 132.

41. Michael Edwardes, *Everyday Life in Early India* (New York: G. P. Putnam's Sons, 1969), p. 1.

42. Richard Lannoy, *The Speaking Tree* (London: Oxford University Press, 1971), p. 339.

43. *Mahābhārata* 12:300.

44. A. Charkravarti, *Humanism and Indian Thought* (Madras: University of Madras, 1935), p. 27. (Do not misinterpret! The text means "Thanks that I am a human being!").

45. D. T. Suzuki, *A Brief History of Early Chinese Philosophy* (London: Probsthain, 1914), p. 11.

46. Wing-tsit Chan, *A Source Book in Chinese Philosophy,* ed. Wing-tsit Chan (Princeton: Princeton University Press, 1963), p. 783.

47. D. T. Suzuki, *A Brief History of Early Chinese Philosophy,* p. 47.

48. E. R. Hughes, *Chinese Philosophy in Classical Times* (London: J. M. Dent, 1942), p. xi.
49. See Fung Yu-lan, *Hsin Yüan Jen* (Chungking, 1943), chap. 3. See also E. R. Hughes's translation of Fung Yu-lan, *The Spirit of Chinese Philosophy* (Boston: Beacon Press, 1962), pp. xiii–xiv.
50. *Bhagavad Gītā* 18:63.
51. Ibid., 18:47.
52. W. H. Werkmeister, "Scientism and the Problem of Man," in *Philosophy and Culture—East and West,* ed. Charles A. Moore, p. 136.
53. Max Müller, *India, What Can It Teach Us?* (New York: Funk and Wagnalls, 1883), p. 6.
54. Quoted by Prosanto Kumar Sen, *Biography of a New Faith* (Calcutta: Thacker, Spink, 1950), 1:250.
55. See Troy Organ, *The Hindu Quest for the Perfection of Man* (Athens, Ohio: Ohio University Press, 1970, 1980), p. 334, n. 2.
56. Nobuo Haneda, "What is Lacking in American Buddhism," *The Pacific World,* n.s., no. 1 (Fall 1985), p. 14.
57. Wing-tsit Chan, *Source Book in Chinese Philosophy,* p. 3.
58. H. D. Bhattacharyya, "The Place of the Philosopher in Modern Society," *The Silver Jubilee Commemoration Volume of The Indian Philosophical Congress,* (1950), p. 83.
59. Frederick C. Copleston, *Philosophies and Cultures,* pp. 165, 170.
60. Robert Rossow, Jr., "Natural Man, Philosophy, and Behavior," in *Philosophy and Culture—East and West,* ed. Charles A. Moore, p. 119. The need for dialogue on philosophical anthropology determined the planners of the Fourth East-West Philosophers' Conference at the University of Hawaii in 1964 to set as its theme "The Status of the Individual in Reality, Thought, and Culture in the East and West." The report of the conference appears in *The Status of the Individual East and West,* ed. Moore (Honolulu: University of Hawaii Press, 1968). See also my evaluation of the theme and the results in Troy Organ, *Western Approaches to Eastern Philosophy* (Athens, Ohio: Ohio University Press), 1975. pp. 54–61. J. R. Kantor in a recent book, *Interpersonal Philosophy* (Chicago: Principia Press, 1981), contends that Western philosophy traditionally rests on two objectionable postulates, namely, that of cosmological and psychophysical dualism and that claiming that the business of philosophy is to deal with absolutes and infallible truths. In so doing he treats philosophy as the acme of human orientation and evaluation of things and events in nature and culture. The only unhappy feature of the book is that Kantor is a psychologist! Philosophers have been for too reluctant to clean their own house.
61. Augustine, *The Confessions* 4. 4. 9.
62. A. C. Mukerji, *Self, Thought and Reality* (Allahabad: Allahabad Indian Press, 1957), p. 36.
63. *The Great Learning,* tran. Wing-tsit Chan, in *A Source Book in Chinese Philosophy,* pp. 86–87.
64. Abraham Kaplan, *The New World of Philosophy* (New York: Random House, 1961), p. 11.
65. Sarvepalli Radhakrishnan, *A Source Book in Indian Philosophy,* ed. Sarvepalli Radhakrishnan and Charles A. Moore (Princeton: Princeton University Press, 1957), p. xxix.
66. René Guenon, *East and West* (London: Luzac, 1941), p. 45. For another point of view see Oliver Reiser, *World Philosophy. A Search for Synthesis* (Pittsburgh: University of Pittsburgh Press, 1948).
67. Raghavan Iyer, *The Glass Curtain Between Asia and Europe* (London: Oxford University Press, 1965), pp. 348, 349.
68. Charles Eliot, *Hinduism and Buddhism* (London: Edward Arnold, 1921), p. xcvi.
69. William Ralph Inge, *Mysticism in Religion* (London: Hutchinson's University Library, n.d.), p. 8.
70. Colossians 2:8 (King James Version).
71. Cicero, *De Divinatine* 2. lviii.

204   PHILOSOPHY AND THE SELF

72. John Calvin, *Institutes* 3. 160.
73. John Milton, *Paradise Lost* 2. 557–65.
74. George Boas, *Dominant Themes of Modern Philosophy* (New York: Ronald, 1957), p. 637.
75. Thomas Merton, *Mystics and Zen Masters* (New York: Dell, 1961), p. 65.

Chapter 2. The Human Being as Speaker

1. Edward T. Hall, *The Hidden Dimension* (Garden City, N.Y.: Doubleday, 1969), pp. 159–60. See also idem, *The Silent Language* (Garden City, N.Y.: Doubleday, 1959).
2. Janet L. Hopson, *Secret Signals. The Silent Language of Sex* (New York: William Morris, 1979).
3. George Schwidetzky, *Do You Speak Chimpanzee?* (New York: Dutton, 1933). See Derk Bickerton, *Roots of Language* (Ann Arbor, Mich.: Karoma, 1981). Bickerton argues that Creole languages are the missing linguistic fossils from which linguists can construct the evolution of language. Man's study of the sounds of lower animals is amazingly culturally conditioned, e.g., whereas an American hears the rooster morning call as "Cock-a-doodle-do," the Frenchman hears "Cocorico," the German "Kikerikee," and the Israeli "Kurkeriko." The cat's cry is "Miaoww" in America, "Ron, ron" in France, "Schnurr, schnurr" in Germany, and "Zaa, zaa" in Japan. The dog's bark is "Bow, wow" in America, "Gnaf, gnaf" in France, "Guau, guau" in Spain, "Wung, wung" in Japan, and "Kpie, kpie" in Africa. See Lawrence Les and Henry Margenau, *Einstein's Space and Van Gogh's Sky* (New York: Macmillan Co., 1982), p. 27. Even the sounds of inanimate objects are heard differently in different cultures, e.g., "The sound of a shot is rendered *bang* or *crack* in English and *pum* or *paf* in Spanish." (Stephen Ullmann, *Semantics* [Oxford: Blackwell, 1962], p. 86.)
4. Otto Jespersen, *Language: Its Nature, Development and Origin* (New York: Holt, 1922). p. 429.
5. Ibid., p. 436. A similar use of words as sounds is to be found in early Tantric Buddhism, e.g., one of the mantras was the following: *"iti miti kiti bhiksāṁti padāni svāha."* Shashibhusan Dasgupta, in commenting on the mantra, writes that "the follower through concentration should realise the truth that these Mantras can have no meaning at all,—this unmeaningness is their real meaning." (*Obscure Religious Cults,* rev. ed. [Calcutta: Mukhopadhyay, 1962], p. 21.) However, the meaning might be in the sound of the words.
6. Susanne Langer, *Philosophy in a New Key* (New York: New American Library of World Literature, 1948), pp. 95, 96, 98.
7. Ibid., p. 98.
8. Ibid., p. 94.
9. Ibid., p. 96.
10. Ibid., pp. 108–9.
11. Genesis 2:19 (RSV).
12. See Norman Moss, *What's the Difference? A British/American Dictionary* (New York: Harper and Row, 1973).
13. Confucius, *Analects* 13:3, trans. Wing-tsit Chan.
14. Wing-tsit Chan, *A Source Book in Chinese Philosophy,* p. 1.
15. E.g., *Bṛhad-Āraṇyaka Upaniṣad* 2. 4. 12, 14; 4. 3. 13; 4. 5. 15.
16. Ibid., 4. 3. 13 (trans. Robert Ernest Hume).
17. Paul Tillich, *Systematic Theology,* Vol. 2. (Chicago: University of Chicago Press, 1957), p. 9.

18. Paul Tillich, *Systematic Theology,* Vol. 1. (Chicago: University of Chicago Press, 1951), p. 238.
19. Paul Tillich, *Dynamics of Faith* (New York: Harper and Row, 1957), p. 42.
20. Langer, *Philosophy in a New Key,* p. 237.
21. Ernst Cassirer, *Language and Myth,* trans. Susanne K. Langer (New York: Harper, 1946), p. 7.
22. John Locke, *Essay Concerning Human Understanding,* bk. 3, chap. 10.
23. George Berkeley, *A Treatise Concerning the Principles of Human Knowledge,* 1st ed., preface, sec. 21.
24. See J. L. Austin, *How To Do Things with Words* (New York: Oxford University Press, 1962).
25. Hajime Nakamura, *Ways of Thinking of Eastern Peoples: India-China-Tibet-Japan* (Honolulu: East-West Center Press, 1964).
26. Jerrold J. Katz, *The Philosophy of Language* (New York: Harper and Row, 1966), p. 4. "Semanticists like Alfred Korzybski and Benjamin Whorf warned that Indo-European languages trap us in a fragmented model of life. They disregard relationship. By their subject-predicate structure, they mold our thought, forcing us to think of everything in terms of simple cause and effect. For this reason it is hard for us to talk about—or even think about—quantum physics, a fourth dimension, or any other notion without clearcut beginnings and endings, up and down, then and now. Events in nature have simultaneous multiple causes. Some languages, notably Hopi and Chinese, are structured differently and can express nonlinear ideas with less strain. They can, in effect, 'speak physics.' Like the ancient Greeks, whose philosophy strongly influenced the left-brained West, we say, 'The light flashed.' But the light and the flash were one. A Hopi would more accurately say, 'Reh-pi!'—'Flash.'" (Marilyn Ferguson, *The Aquarian Conspiracy,* [Los Angeles: J. P. Tarcher, 1976], p. 149.)
27. Aldous Huxley, "Education on the Nonverbal Level," *Daedalus* (Spring 1962), p. 282.
28. Henry A. Barnes, "The Language of Bureaucracy," in *Language in America,* ed. Neil Postman, Charles Weingartner, and Terence P. Moran (New York: Pegasus, 1969), p. 50.
29. Fritz Güttinger, *Zielsprache: Theorie und Technik des Übersetzens* (Zurich: Manesse Verlag, 1963).
30. William P. Alston, "Philosophy of Language," in *The Encyclopedia of Philosophy,* 4:387.
31. Ludwig Wittgenstein, *Philosophical Investigations,* 1:11. ed. G. Anscombe and R. Rhees, trans. G. Anscombe (Blackwell: Oxford, 1953).
32. Ibid., 1:38.
33. Ibid., 1:109.
34. Ibid., 1:119.
35. Ludwig Wittgenstein, *Tractatus Logico-Philosophicus* 4.0031, trans. C. K. Ogden (London: Routledge and Kegan Paul, 1922).
36. Ibid., 4.112.
37. *Alfred North Whitehead: Essays on his Philosophy,* ed. George L. Kline. (Englewood Cliffs, N.J.: Prentice-Hall, 1963), p. 15.
38. Ibid., p. 16.
39. See Desmond Morris, Peter Collett, Peter Marsh, and Marie O'Shaughnessy, *Gestures* (New York: Stein and Day, 1980).
40. Viktor E. Frankl, *Man's Search for Meaning* (New York: Washington Square Press, 1963), p. 127.
41. Diogenes Laërtius, *Lives of Famous Philosophers* 8. 15. Porphyrius observed that "silence with them was of no ordinary kind." (*Vita Pythagorae* 19.)
42. Euripides, *Hippolytus,* sc. 1, ll. 394–96.
43. James 3:6–8 (RSV).
44. Aristotle, *Metaphysics* 1010 a 12.
45. Plato, *Seventh Letter* 341 (trans. Glenn R. Morrow).
46. Lovejoy, *The Great Chain of Being,* pp. 11–12.

47. Robert H. March, *Physics for Poets* (New York: McGraw-Hill, 1970), p. 128.
48. Quoted in Huston Smith, *Forgotten Truth* (New York: Harper & Row, 1976), p. 107. *Flatland*, written by Edwin A. Abbott in 1884, is a delightful account of the difficulties denizens of a two-dimensional world would have in comprehending a third spatial dimension.
49. Josef Pieper, *The Silence of St. Thomas* (Chicago: Regnery, 1957), p. 39.
50. *Meister Eckhart*, trans. Raymond B. Blakney (New York: Harper, 1941), p. 99.
51. Ibid., p. 100.
52. Ibid., p. 127.
53. Ibid., p. 107.
54. P. N. Srinivasachari, *The Philosophy of Visishtadvaita* (Adyar, Madras: Theosophical Publishing House, 1946), p. xxxvii.
55. Gotama, *The Nyāya Sūtras*, bk. 5, chap. 2, v. 16.
56. *Tao Te Ching* (trans. Wing-tsit Chan), chap. 1.
57. Ibid., chap. 2.
58. Ibid., chap. 5.
59. Ibid., chap. 23.
60. Ibid., chap. 41.
61. Ibid., chap. 56.
62. Ibid., chap. 52.
63. *Avataṁsaka Sūtra*, Fascicle xxxi.
64. Saraha's Treasury of Songs, no. 88, *Buddhist Texts Through the Ages*, ed. Edward Conze (New York: Harper and Row, 1954), p. 236.
65. D. T. Suzuki, *Essays in Zen Buddhism*, 2d ser. (London: Luzac, 1933), pp. 8–9.
66. Ibid., p. 7.
67. *Laṅkāvatāra Sūtra*, chap. 6, in *A Buddhist Bible*, ed. Dwight Goddard (New York: Dutton, 1952), pp. 311–12.
68. Wittgenstein, *Tractatus Logico-Philosophicus* 7.
69. Wittgenstein, *Philosophical Investigations* 1:116.
70. *Zen Buddhism*, ed. William Barrett (New York: Doubleday, 1956), p. 61.
71. Sonaku Ogata, *Zen for the West* (New York: Dial, 1959), p. 18.
72. *Meister Eckhart*, trans. Raymond B. Blakney, pp. 82–83.
73. Paul Reps, *Zen Flesh, Zen Bones* (Garden City, N.Y.: Doubleday, 1961), p. 62.
74. *Santi Parva*, sec. 300, in *The Mahabharata of Krishna-Dwaipayana Vyasa* (trans. Pratap Chandra Roy) (Calcutta: Oriental Publishing Co., n.d.) 9:405. Cf. "A gleam in an Eskimo's eye tells you more than a half dozen of our sentences concerning desire, repugnance, or another emotion. Each Eskimo world is like that gleam: it suggests at once what has happened and what is to come, and it contains that touch of the unexpressed which makes this people so mysterious and attractive. Their shades of expression are infinite.... They are Asiatic; and perhaps for that reason imperceptible to us. We are so habituated to our simple yes and no that we ignore the existence of a scale of gradations between affirmation and negation." (Gontran de Poncins, *Kabloona* [Alexandria, Md.: Time-Life, 1941], pp. 234–35.)

Chapter 3. The Human Being as Knower

1. *Chuang Tzu*, chap. 2 (trans. Wing-tsit Chan), *A Source Book of Chinese Philosophy*, ed. Chan, p. 190.
2. René Descartes, *Discourse on Method*, pt. 4, in *Descartes, Philosophical Writings*, trans.

Elizabeth Anscombe and Peter Thomas Geach (New York: Library of Liberal Arts, 1971), p. 36.

3. David L. Costill, "A Racer's Edge?", *The Runner* (April 1982), p. 70.

4. See Troy Organ, "The Images of Aristotle," *Ohio University Review* 4 (1962): 35–48.

5. George Boas, "The New Authoritarianism," *American Association of University Professors Bulletin* (Autumn 1952), p. 398.

6. John Henry Cardinal Newman, *The Idea of a University* (New York: Longmans, Green, 1912), p. 10.

7. William G. McLoughlin, Jr., *Billy Sunday Was His Real Name* (Chicago: University of Chicago Press, 1955), p. 132.

8. D. T. Suzuki, *Buddhist Philosophy and its Effect on the Life and Thought of the Japanese People* (Tokyo: Kokusai Bunka Shinkokai, 1936), p. 27.

9. Pierre Teilhard de Chardin, *Writings in Time of War*, trans. René Hague (London: Collins, 1968), p. 77.

10. Robert Jastrow, in a lecture to the American Orthopsychiatric Association reported in *Saturday Review*, 1 May 1965, p. 55. See Washington Platt and Ross A. Baker," The Relation of the Scientific 'Hunch' to Research," *Journal of Chemical Education* 8 (October 1931): 1969–2002. See also Arthur I. Miller, "On the Limits of the IMAGination," *National Forum* (Winter 1983), pp. 26–28.

11. Huston Smith, *Forgotten Truth*, p. 126.

12. Stephen Pepper, *Aesthetic Quality* (New York: Scribner's, 1938), p. 10.

13. Immanuel Kant, *Critique of Pure Reason*, Transcendental Logic, Introduction. trans. Norman Kemp Smith (New York: Macmillan, 1919), p. 93.

14. Michael Polanyi, *Personal Knowledge*. (New York: Harper & Row, 1958), p. 3.

15. 1 Corinthians 7:25 (RSV).

16. See A. D. White, *A History of the Warfare of Science with Theology in Christendom*, 2 vols. (New York: Appleton, 1897), 2: 369.

17. R. C. Pandeya, *The Problem of Meaning in Indian Philosophy* (Delhi: Motilal Banarsidass, 1963), p. lv.

18. Ibid.

19. James, *Pragmatism*, pp. 43–45.

20. "Linguistics. The Labyrinth of Language." *Britannica Perspectives* (Chicago: Encyclopedia Britannica, 1968), 3: 45.

21. James, *Pragmatism*, p. 200.

22. A. J. Ayer, *Language, Truth, and Logic*, (New York: Dover, n.d.), p. 31. Originally published in 1964.

23. Ibid., p. 5.

24. Ibid., p. 11.

25. Ibid.

26. Galileo Galilei, *Opere* iii. 1. 395.

27. Herbert Feigl, "The Logical Character of the Principle of Induction," *Philosophy of Science*, 1, no. 1 (January 1934): p. 28.

28. Lin Yutang, *The Importance of Living* (New York: Day, 1937), p. 423.

29. Quoted by D. D. Kosambi, *Ancient India. A History of Its Culture and Civilization* (New York: Random House, 1965), p. 177.

30. Wing-tsit Chan, "The Spirit of Oriental Philosophy," in *Philosophy—East and West*, ed. Moore, p. 161.

31. Suzuki, *A Brief History of Early Chinese Philosophy*, p. 12.

32. Wing-tsit Chan, "The Spirit of Oriental Philosophy," in *Philosophy—East and West*, ed. Moore, p. 163.

33. See B. N. Seal, *The Positive Sciences of the Ancient Hindus* (Delhi: Motilal Banarsidass, 1958), p. 252.

34. John Stuart Mill, *A System of Logic*, bk. 3, chap. 8. All quotations from Mill in this section are from chap. 8.
35. Francis Bacon, *Novum Organum*, bk. 1, aphorism 61.
36. All references will be to the translation of S. C. Vidyabhutsana, *Sacred Books of the Hindus*, vol. 8 (Allahabad: Panini, 1930).
37. S. Radhakrishnan, *Indian Philosophy* (New York: Macmillan Co., 1927), 2: 134.
38. *Nyāya Sūtra* 1. 1. 4.
39. Surendranath Das Gupta, *A History of Indian Philosophy* (Cambridge: Cambridge University Press, 1957), 1:336.
40. For an account of such claims see Dom Denys Rutledge, *In Search of a Yogi* (London: Routledge and Kegan Paul, 1962).
41. *The Nyāya Sūtras of Gotama* 1. 1. 5. All the translations from *The Nyāya Sūtras of Gotama* are by S. C. Vidyabhusana. *Sacred Books of the Hindus*, vol. 3 (Allahabad: Panini, 1930). See also *A Source Book in Indian Philosophy*, pp. 356–85.
42. Ibid.
43. Ibid., 1. 1. 33.
44. Ibid., 1. 1. 34.
45. Ibid., 1. 1. 36.
46. Ibid., 1. 1. 38.
47. Ibid., 1. 1. 39.
48. Ibid., 1. 1. 6.
49. Ibid., 2. 1. 44–45.
50. Ibid., 1. 1. 7.
51. Ibid., 2. 1. 57.
52. Ibid., 2. 1. 58.
53. Ibid., 2. 1. 59.
54. Ibid., 2. 1. 60.
55. Ibid., 2. 1. 68.
56. See D. M. Datta, "Indian Epistemological Methods," *Essays in East-West Philosophy*, p. 83.
57. Agehananda Bharati, *A Functional Analysis of Indian Thought and Its Social Margins* (Varanasi: Chowkhamba Sanskrit Series Office, 1964), p. 37.
58. Ramakant A. Sinari, *The Structure of Indian Thought* (Springfield, Ill.: Charles C. Thomas, 1970), p. 61.
59. E. A. Burtt, "What Can Western Philosophy Learn from India?" *Philosophy East and West* 5 no. 3 (October 1955): 206.
60. Edward Conze, *Buddhism, Its Essence and Development* (New York: Harper, 1959), p. 15.
61. Edward Conze, *Buddhist Thought in India*, p. 28.
62. *The Diamond Sūtra*, trans. Wai-tao, in Dwight Goddard, ed., *A Buddhist Bible* (New York: E. P. Dutton, 1952), p. 106.
63. *The Śūrangama Sūtra*, trans. in ibid., p. 111.
64. Ibid., p. 112.
65. *Lankavatāra Sūtra*, trans. D. T. Suzuki and Dwight Goddard, in *A Buddhist Bible*, p. 306.
66. Ibid.
67. Walker, *Hindu World*, 2: 15.
68. *Lankavatāra Sūtra*, *A Buddhist Bible*, p. 307.
69. Suzuki, *Buddhist Philosophy and Its Effects on the Life and Thought of the Japanese People*, p. 33.
70. E. A. Burtt, "What Can Western Philosophy Learn from India?" *Philosophy East and West* 5 no. 3 (October 1955): 206.

71. Bhikshu Sangharakshita, *A Survey of Buddhism* (Bangalore: The Indian Institute of World Culture, 1957), pp. 192–93, 195.
72. *Avataṁsaka Sūtra,* Fascicle xxxii.
73. D. T. Suzuki, *Buddhist Philosophy and Its Effect on the Life and Thought of the Japanese People,* p. 22.
74. Ibid., p. 26.
75. Zen Buddhism is known to the West primarily through the works of D. T. Suzuki. For a presentation of the Chinese background see Chang Chen-Chi, *The Practice of Zen* (New York: Harper, 1959).
76. D. T. Suzuki, *Essays in Zen Buddhism,* 2nd ser. (London: Rider, 1950), p. 16.
77. Chang Chen-Chi, *The Practice of Zen,* p. 167.
78. Suzuki, "Reason and Intuition in Buddhist Philosophy," in *Essays in East-West Philosophy,* pp. 17–18.
79. Ibid., p. 17.
80. Ibid.
81. Ibid., p. 23.
82. Ibid., p. 17.
83. Ibid., p. 29.
84. Ibid., p. 25.
85. Ibid., p. 24.
86. Ibid., p. 23.
87. Ibid., p. 43.
88. Ibid., p. 33.
89. Aristotle, *Metaphysics* 1006 a 15. Quotations from Aristotle, unless otherwise stated, are from the W. D. Ross translation.
90. Ibid., 1006 a 19–22.
91. Ibid., 1006 b 20–25.
92. Suzuki, "Reason and Intuition in Buddhism," *Essays in East-West Philosophy,* p. 43.
93. Ibid., p. 17.
94. Ibid., p. 25.
95. Ibid.
96. Ibid., p. 43.
97. E. A. Burtt, "What Can Western Philosophy Learn from India?" *Philosophy East and West* 5, no. 3 (October 1955): 203.

Chapter 4. The Human Being as Self-Knower

1. G. S. Kirk and J. E. Raven, *The Presocratic Philosophers* (Cambridge: Cambridge University Press, 1960), p. 222.
2. Ibid., p. 207.
3. Euripides, "Hippolytus," sc. 1, ll. 1078–79. (trans. David Grene).
4. *Phaedo* 96 (trans. W. H. D. Rouse).
5. *Phaedrus* 230 (trans. R. Hackforth).
6. A. C. Mukerji, *The Nature of the Self* (Allahabad: The Indian Press, 1943), p. 4.
7. Max Müller, *India; What Can It Teach Us?* (New York: Funk and Wagnalls, 1883), p. 33.
8. Confucius, *Analects* 1. 4 (trans. James R. Ware).

9. Ibid., 4. 17.

10. *Tao Teh Ching* 33 (trans. Wing-tsit Chan). These two lines can be used to illustrate the problem of translating Chinese into English. Ch'u Ta-Kao happens to give the same translation as Wing-tsit Chan. But notice the following variations:

> He who knows others is learned;
> He who knows himself is wise.
> (Trans. Lin Yutang)
> It is wisdom to know others:
> It is enlightenment to know one's self.
> (Trans. R. B. Blakney)
> Knowledge studies others,
> Wisdom is self-known.
> (Trans. Witter Bynner)
> One who knows other men is discerning;
> But one who knows himself is enlightened.
> (Trans. Paul Carus)
> He who knows other men is discerning;
> He who knows himself is intelligent.
> (Trans. James Legge)

11. D. T. Suzuki, *Buddhist Philosophy and Its Effect on the Life and Thought of the Japanese People,* p. 22.

12. Aristotle, *De Anima* 402 a 5 (trans. J. A. Smith).

13. Kant, *Critique of Pure Reason,* trans. Norman Kemp Smith, preface to 1st ed. A xi.

14. Ernst Cassirer, *An Essay on Man* (New Haven: Yale University Press, 1944), p. 1.

15. Psalms 8:4 (King James Version).

16. René Descartes, *Meditations,* trans. Laurence L. Lafleur (New York: Liberal Arts, 1951), p. 24.

17. Ibid., p. 22.

18. Ibid., pp. 23–24.

19. Ibid., p. 24.

20. Ibid., p. 25.

21. Ibid., p. 26.

22. Ibid., p. 28. At this point Descartes drew an interesting moral: "A person who attempts to improve his understanding beyond the ordinary ought to be ashamed to go out of his way to criticize the forms of speech used by ordinary men."

23. Ibid., p. 30.

24. Ibid., p. 72.

25. Ibid., p. 75.

26. Ibid., p. 76.

27. Ibid., p. 77.

28. Ibid., p. 80.

29. Rollo May, *Man's Search for Himself* (New York: Norton, 1953), p. 7.

30. Erwin Schrödinger, *Science and Humanism* (Cambridge: Cambridge University Press, 1952), p. 5.

31. Moritz Schlick, "Meaning and Verification," *The Philosophical Review* 45 (1936): 369.

32. Jean-Paul Sartre, *The Transcendence of the Ego,* trans. Forrest Williams and Robert Kirkpatrick (New York: Noonday, 1957), p. 31.

33. Alexis Carrel, *Man, the Unknown* (New York: Penguin, 1935), p. 16.

34. Ibid., pp. 23, 39.

35. A. S. Eddington, *Space, Time and Gravitation* (Cambridge: Cambridge University Press, 1920), p. 201.
36. Émile Bréhier, *The Hellenic Age,* trans. Joseph Thomas (Chicago: University of Chicago Press, 1963), p. 8.
37. José Ortega y Gasset, *The Revolt of the Masses* (New York: Norton, 1932), p. 170.
38. *The Panchatantra,* trans. by Arthur W. Ryder (Bombay: Jaico, 1949), p. 127.
39. *Rg Veda,* 1. 164. 37 (trans. H. H. Wilson).
40. Aristotle, *De Anima* 402 a 4–6 (trans. J. A. Smith).
41. Ibid., 402 a 10.
42. Cassirer, *An Essay on Man,* pp. 1–2.
43. Martin Heidegger, *Kant and the Problem of Metaphysics,* trans. James S. Churchill (Bloomington: Indiana University Press, 1962), p. 216.
44. Max Scheler, *Die Stellung des Menschen im Kosmos* (Darmstadt: Reich, 1928), p. 134. (My translation.)
45. Carrel, *Man, the Unknown,* p. 17.
46. Rudyard Kipling, *Kim,* beginning of chap. 11.
47. Lewis Carroll (C. L. Dodgson), *Alice's Adventures in Wonderland,* chap. 2.
48. Plato, *The Republic* 439 (trans. by W. H. D. Rouse).
49. Plato, *Phaedrus* 253–55. See Troy Organ, "Paul Elmer More and Platonic Dualism," *The Visvabharati Quarterly* 33, nos. 1 & 2 (1967–68): 1–28.
50. William James, *The Principles of Psychology* (London: Macmillan, 1901), 1: 291.
51. Ibid., p. 293.
52. Iago in *Othello,* act 3, sc. 3.
53. George H. Mead, "National-Mindedness and International-Mindedness," *International Journal of Ethics* 39, no. 4 (July 1929): 395.
54. James, *The Principles of Psychology,* 1: 301.
55. *Time,* 15 December 1952, p. 58.
56. D. T. Suzuki, "Basic Thoughts Underlying Eastern Ethical and Social Practice," *Philosophy and Culture—East and West,* p. 429.
57. Ibid.
58. Ibid., p. 430.
59. Ibid.
60. Ibid., p. 431.
61. Ibid.
62. Ibid.
63. Ibid., p. 432.
64. David Hume, *A Treatise of Human Nature,* bk. 1, pt. 4, sec. 6.
65. Ibid.
66. Ibid.
67. Hume, *A Treatise of Human Nature,* appendix. The remaining quotations from Hume are from the appendix.
68. Plotinus, *Enneads* 5. 3. 4 (trans. A. H. Armstrong).
69. Gilbert Ryle, *The Concept of Mind* (London: Hutchinson's University Library, 1949), p. 195.
70. Otto Rank, *Psychology and the Soul,* trans. William D. Turner (New York: Barnes, 1950), p. 6.
71. Ibid., p. 2.
72. Ibid., p. 7.
73. Ibid.
74. Ibid., p. 12.
75. Ibid., p. 32.
76. Rollo May, *Man's Search for Himself,* p. 90.

77. Augustine, *The City of God*, bk. 11, chap. 26 (trans. M. Dods).
78. Carrel, *Man the Unknown*, pp. 23, 29.
79. Shakespeare, *King Lear*, act 1, sc. 1.
80. Charles I. Glicksberg, *The Self in Modern Literature* (University Park: Pennsylvania State University Press, 1963), p. 182.
81. Friedrich Nietzsche, *Joyful Wisdom*, trans. Thomas Common (New York: Frederick Ungar, 1964), p. 350.
82. *The Gospel of Thomas*, 80:26. trans. A. Guillaumont, H.-Ch. Puech, G. Quispel, W. Till, and Yassah 'Abd Al Manīh (New York: Harper & Brothers, 1959).
83. Raymond B. Blakney, *Meister Eckhart*, p. 47.
84. Ibid., p. 246.
85. *Institutes of the Christian Religion by John Calvin*, trans. John Allen (Philadelphia: Presbyterian Board of Christian Education, 1936), 1:48.
86. *Taittirīya Upaniṣad* 2. 1. 3 (trans. Nikhilananda).
87. *Katha Upaniṣad* 5. 12 (trans. Robert Ernest Hume).
88. Sri Aurobindo, *The Life Divine* (New York: Greystone, 1949), pp. 615–16.
89. Ibid., p. 204.
90. Ibid., p. 404.
91. Ibid.
92. Ibid., p. 621.
93. Aristotle, *De Anima* 402 a 1–5 (trans. by J. A. Smith).
94. Sören Kierkegaard, *Journal*, 1 August 1835. *The Journals of Kierkegaard*. tr. Alexander Dru. (New York: Harper & Row, 1958) p. 46.
95. G. A. Wilson, *The Self and Its World* (New York: MacMillan Co., 1926), p. 273.
96. Paul Deussen, *The Philosophy of the Upanishads*, trans. A. S. Geden (New York: Dover, 1966), p. 40.
97. From the *Lotus of the Wonderful Law. The Teachings of the Compassionate Buddha*, ed. E. A. Burtt (New York: New American Library, 1955), pp. 150–54.
98. Troy Organ, *The Hindu Quest for the Perfection of Man*, p. 69.
99. Pierre Teilhard de Chardin, *The Future of Man*, trans. Norman Denny (New York: Harper and Row, 1964), p. 158.
100. Pierre Teilhard de Chardin, *The Phenomenon of Man*, trans. Bernard Wall (New York: Harper and Row, 1975), p. 230.
101. Ibid., p. 224.
102. Teilhard, *The Future of Man*, p. 67.
103. Teilhard, *The Phenomenon of Man*, pp. 20, 221.
104. Leon Eisenberg, "The *Human* Nature of Human Nature," *Science*, 14 April 1972, p. 127.

Chapter 5. The Theories of the Self

1. Martin Buber, *I and Thou*, trans. Ronald Gregor Smith (Edinburgh: T. and T. Clark, 1958), p. 34.
2. Aristotle, *De Anima* 404 a 1 (trans. J. A. Smith).
3. Ibid., 409 b 2.
4. Ibid., 407 b 15.
5. Ibid., 404 b 16–29.

6. See Raimond Van Marle, *The Development of the Italian School of Painting*, Vol. 9 (The Hague: Martinus Nijhoff, 1927), p. 301.
7. Frederick Hartt, *History of Italian Renaissance Art* (Englewood Cliffs, N.J.: Prentice-Hall, 1969), p. 220.
8. Plato, *Phaedo* 80 (trans. W. H. D. Rouse).
9. Ibid., 79.
10. Ibid., 80.
11. Ibid. Plato's expression "a true unseen Hades" is an interesting play on words, since the word *unseen* (*haeidēs*) and the word "Hades" (*haidēs*) are similar.
12. Plato, *The Republic* 439 (trans. W. H. D. Rouse).
13. Plato, *Phaedrus* 253 (trans. R. Hackforth).
14. Ibid.
15. Ibid., 254.
16. Alfred North Whitehead, *Process and Reality* (New York: Macmillan Co, 1929), p. 63.
17. Irenaeus, *Against Heresies* 1. 21. 4, in *The Ante-Nicene Fathers,* ed. Alexander Roberts and James Donaldson (Buffalo, N.Y.: Christian Literature Publishing Co., 1886), 1:346.
18. Ibid., 1:326.
19. Ibid., 1:440.
20. Clement of Alexandria, *Excerpta ex Theodoto* 78. 2. See R. M. Grant, *Gnosticism and Early Christianity,* rev. ed. (New York: Harper and Row, 1966), p. 7.
21. Monoemus, according to Hippolytus in *Refutatio* 8. 15. 1. See Grant, *Gnosticism and Early Christianity,* p. 8.
22. Werner Foerster, *Gnosis* (Oxford: Clarendon, 1974), 2:81.
23. Ibid., 2:82.
24. 1 Corinthians 7.
25. 2 Corinthians 12:3 (New English Bible).
26. 2 Corinthians 12:4. (New English Bible).
27. John 12:31; 14:30; 16:11 (RSV).
28. John 8:44 (RSV).
29. *Hastings Encyclopedia of Religion and Ethics,* 6:240.
30. W. F. Albright, *History, Archaeology, and Christian Humanism* (London: Adam and Charles Black, 1965), pp. 254–55.
31. Thomas A. Schafer, "Gnosticism Then and Now," *McCormick Speaking* (May 1965), p. 2.
32. Edwin Yamauchi, *Pre-Christian Gnosticism* (London: Tyndale, 1973), p. 13.
33. Confucius, *Analects* 1:11; 4:20; 17:19.
34. Mencius, *The Sayings of Mencius,* trans. James R. Ware (New York: New American Library, 1960), pp. 68–69.
35. *Hsun Tzu,* chap. 23, in *Sources of Chinese Tradition,* ed. Wm. Theodore de Bary (New York: Columbia University Press, 1960), p. 118.
36. Laurence G. Thompson, *Chinese Religion: An Introduction* (Belmont, Calif.: Dickenson, 1969), p. 11.
37. *Chāndogya Upaniṣad* 8: 7–12.
38. *Ṛg Veda* 1. 164. 20.
39. The image of two birds in a tree is also found in *Śvetāśvatara Upaniṣad* 4.6 and *Muṇḍaka Upaniṣad* 3. 1. 1.
40. *Ṛg. Veda* 1. 164. 37 (trans. H. H. Wilson).
41. Adapted from the translation of S. Radhakrishnan. The chariot analogy is also found in *Maitrī Upaniṣad* 2. 3–6 and 4. 4–6.
42. There are two versions of this story: *Bṛhad-Āraṇyaka Upaniṣad* 2. 4. and 4. 5.
43. *Bṛhad-Āraṇyaka Upaniṣad* 2. 4. 14 (trans. S. Radhakrishnan).
44. Sures Chandra Chakravarti says of Śaṅkara, "As an exponent of the art of dialectics, he

may be looked upon as a great success, but as an interpreter of the *Upaniṣads,* he is a huge failure." (*Human Life and Beyond* [Calcutta: University of Calcutta Press, 1947], p. 52.)

45. *The Vedānta Sūtras with the Commentary of Śaṅkarākārya,* 2. 3. 50 (trans. George Thibaut). *The Sacred Books of the East,* Vol. 38. (Oxford: Clarendon, 1896), p. 68.

46. Ibid., 1. 4. 22. *The Sacred Books of the East,* vol. 34. (Oxford: The Clarendon Press, 1890), pp. 282–83. The claim that Hindus are unique in self-knowledge and self-development has been challenged by Sudhir Kakar, an Indian psychotherapist at Jawaharlal Nehru University in New Delhi. He contends that the Indian ego is "underdeveloped" because Hinduism encourages men and women to be members of groups rather than self-determining individuals. See V. S. Naipaul, *India: A Wounded Civilization* (New York: Penguin, 1979), pp. 102–3.

47. Ryle, *The Concept of Mind,* p. 11.

48. Ibid., pp. 15, 20, 22, 27, 32, 50, 60, 63, 83, 114, 155, 161, 224, 318.

49. Ibid., p. 329.

50. Ibid., p. 16.

51. In a Dennis the Menace cartoon, Joey, when asked if he liked fireworks, replied, "My eyes do, but sometimes my ears get scared!"

52. Ryle, *The Concept of Mind,* p. 190.

53. Frederick Copleston, *A History of Philosophy,* Vol. 8, Part 1 (Garden City, New York: Doubleday, 1967), p. 128.

54. Samuel Alexander, *Space, Time, and Deity,* (New York: Dover, 1966), 1:35. This is a republication of the second (1927) impression of the original work published in 1920.

55. Ibid., 2:54–55.

56. Ibid., 1:xxxix.

57. Ibid., 2:14, n. 2.

58. Ibid., 2:8.

59. Ibid., 2:14.

60. Ibid., 2:7.

61. Ibid., 2:8. Emphasis added.

62. Ibid., 2:345. Emphasis added.

63. Ibid., 1:xiv.

64. Ibid., 1:xix.

65. Teilhard, *The Future of Man,* p. 122.

66. Teilhard, *The Phenomenon of Man,* p. 165.

67. Teilhard de Chardin, *Le Milieu Divin* (London: Collins, 1957), p. 107.

68. Ibid., p. 26.

69. Ibid., pp. 110–11.

70. See Ilya Prigiogine's book *From Being to Becoming* (San Francisco, Calif.: Freeman, 1980).

71. Aurobindo Ghose, *The Life Divine,* p. 102.

72. Ibid., p. 419.

73. See Troy Organ, "Spirituality—Indian and American," *The Philosophical Quarterly* (Amalner, India) (1960), pp. 243–48.

74. Aurobindo Ghose, *The Synthesis of Yoga* (Pondicherry, India: Sri Aurobindo Ashram, 1957), p. 512.

75. Aurobindo Ghose, *The Life Divine,* p. 219.

76. Ibid., p. 687.

77. Ibid., p. 223.

78. Ibid., p. 222.

79. Aurobindo capitalizes Matter, Life, and Mind when they denote metaphysical principles.

80. Aurobindo Ghose, *The Life Divine,* pp. 241–42.

81. Ibid., p. 222.
82. Ibid., p. 37.
83. Ibid., 237, 238.
84. Aurobindo Ghose, *The Synthesis of Yoga*, p. 713.
85. Aurobindo Ghose, *The Life Divine*, p. 46.
86. Ibid., p. 227.
87. Ibid., p. 103.
88. Ibid., pp. 42–43.
89. Ibid., p. 205.
90. Aurobindo Ghose, *The Synthesis of Yoga*, pp. 383, 384, 385.
91. Ibid., p. 406.
92. Aurobindo Ghose, *The Life Divine*, p. 140.
93. Ibid., p. 362.
94. Ibid., p. 97.
95. For a fuller study of Aurobindo's theory of the self see Troy Organ, *The Self in Indian Philosophy,* chap. 8. See also Troy Organ, "The Status of the Self in Aurobindo's Metaphysics—and Some Questions." *Philosophy East and West* 12, no. 2 (July 1962): 135–51.
96. Frederick Copleston, *A History of Philosophy* Vol. 1, Part 2. (Garden City, N.Y.: Doubleday, 1962), p. 216. For an excellent study of the period see S. Angus, *The Mystery-Religions and Christianity* (New York: Scribners, 1925).
97. Plotinus, *Enneads* 5. 1. 1 (trans. Elmer O'Brien).
98. Aristotle, *Metaphysics* 986 b 24 (trans. W. D. Ross).
99. Ibid., 1016 b. 25.
100. Plato, *The Republic* 525.
101. Plato, *Phaedrus* 266 (trans. Benjamin Jowett).
102. William Inge, *The Philosophy of Plotinus* (New York: Longman's, 1929), 2:108.
103. Plotinus, *Enneads* 5. 1. 6 (trans. Joseph Katz).
104. Ibid.
105. Frithjof Schuon, *Language of the Self,* trans. Marco Pallis Macleod Matheson (Madras, India: Ganesh, 1959), pp. 22–23.
106. *Enneads* 5. 1. 6 (trans. Elmer O'Brien)
107. Ibid., 5. 2. 1.
108. Ibid., 3. 8. 9 (trans. Joseph Katz).
109. Ibid., 4. 3. 1 (trans. Elmer O'Brien).
110. Ibid., 4. 8. 3.
111. Ibid., 4. 8. 4.
112. Ibid., 6. 9. 11 (trans. Joseph Katz).
113. Ibid., 6. 9. 10.
114. Ibid., 6. 9. 11 (trans. Elmer O'Brien). A. H. Armstrong translates the last line ". . . escape in solitude to the Solitary."
115. Johann Gottlieb Fichte, *Werke* (Leipzig, 1908–12), 3:24.
116. Frederick Copleston, *A History of Philosophy* Vol. 7, Part 1 (Garden City, N. Y.: Doubleday, 1965), pp. 62–63.
117. P. N. Srinivasachari, *The Philosophy of Visishtadvaita*, pp. xlviii–xlix.
118. Bharatan Kumarappa, *The Hindu Conception of the Deity as Culminating in Rāmānuja* (London: Luzac, 1934), p. xiii.
119. *Vedānta Sūtras* 1.1.1, in *Sacred Books of the East,* 48:130.
120. Ibid., 2. 3. 45, in *Sacred Books of the East,* 48:563.
121. Ibid., 2. 3. 18, in *Sacred Books of the East,* 48:541.
122. Ibid.
123. Hume, *A Treatise of Human Nature,* vol. 1, pt. 4, sec. 6.

124. Ibid.
125. Ibid.
126. Ibid.
127. Locke, *Essay Concerning Human Understanding*, bk. 2, chap. 27, secs. 4, 5, 8.
128. Hume, *A Treatise of Human Nature*, vol. 1, pt. 4, sec. 6.
129. Ibid.
130. Ibid.
131. Locke, *Essay Concerning Human Understanding*, bk. 2, chap. 27, sec. 15.
132. Hume, *A Treatise of Human Nature*, vol. 1, pt. 4, sec. 6.
133. See Troy Organ, "The Self as Discovery and Creation in Western and Indian Philosophy," in *Western Approaches to Eastern Philosophy*, pp. 39–53 for another approach to this issue.
134. T. R. V. Murti, *The Central Philosophy of Buddhism* (London: George Allen and Unwin, 1960), pp. 16–17.
135. Vidhushekhara Bhattacharyya, *The Basic Conception of Buddhism* (Calcutta: University of Calcutta, 1932), p. 70.
136. "The Soul Theory of the Buddhists," *Adhadharmakoṣa*, appendix (trans. T. I. Stcherbatsky). Reprinted from the *Bulletin de l'Academie des Sciences de Russia*, 1920.
137. Edward Conze, *Buddhism: Its Essence and Development*, p. 106.
138. Christmas Humphreys, *Buddhism* (Harmondsworth: Penguin, 1954), p. 85.
139. Support for the Buddhist position has recently come from an unexpected source—modern zoology. J. S. Medawar in an article entitled "Revising the Facts of Life" in *Harpers*, February 1977, p. 59 writes, "In spite of all its frightening groans and rattles, the great world machine can still be made to work, but not unless it comes to be accepted that the long-term welfare of human beings cannot be secured by policies that promote the interests of some people at the expense of others or even the interests of mankind at the expense of other living beings. The unity of nature is not a slogan but a principle to the truth of which all natural processes bear witness. The lesson has been learned too late to save some living creatures, but there may just be time to save the rest of us."
140. *Visuddhi-Magga*, chap. viii. Henry Clarke Warren, *Buddhism in Translations* (New York: Atheneum, 1963), p. 150.
141. D. T. Suzuki, *Essays in Zen Buddhism*, 2d ser., p. 290.
142. *Digha Nikaya* ii. 120.
143. *Vinaya Pitaka* i. 23.
144. *Milindapañha* 40, in Warren, *Buddhism in Translations*, p. 149.
145. Adapted from *Milindapañha* 28, in Warren, *Buddhism in Translations*, pp. 129–33.
146. Warren, *Buddhism in Translations*, p. 133.
147. Ibid., p. 134.
148. Junjiro Takakusu, *The Essentials of Buddhist Philosophy* (Honolulu: University of Hawaii, 1947), p. 24.
149. Suzuki, *Essays in Zen Buddhism*, 2d ser., p. 258.
150. Ibid.
151. Hajime Nakamura, "Unity and Diversity in Buddhism," in *The Path of the Buddha*, ed. Kenneth W. Morgan (New York: Ronald, 1956), p. 377.
152. Ibid., p. 379.
153. *Laṅkāvatāra Sūtra*, chap. 5, trans. D. T. Suzuki and Dwight Goddard. *The Buddhist Bible*, p. 306.
154. Conze, *Buddhism: Its Essence and Development*, pp. 19–20.
155. Hume, *A Treatise of Human Nature*, bk. 1, pt. 4, sec. 6.
156. G. E. R. Lloyd, *Aristotle: The Growth and Structure of His Thought* (Cambridge: Cambridge University Press, 1968), p. 181.
157. F. J. E. Woodbridge, *Aristotle's Vision of Nature* (New York: Columbia University Press, 1965), p. 27.

158. Aristotle, *De Anima* 403 a 5. All the selections from *De Anima* are from the translation of J. A. Smith.

159. Aristotle in *De Anima* deserts his usual unemotional treatment of a subject matter and his usual appreciation of the work of his predecessors. In at least eight places—407 b 14, 23, 24; 408 a 2; 409 a 34; 410 a 24; 411 a 14; and 414 b 25—he characterizes their views of the soul as "absurd."

160. 407 b 15.
161. 409 b 1–3.
162. 408 b 12–15.
163. 409 b 19–23.
164. 402 a 6.
165. 412 a 1–4.
166. 413 a 1.
167. 413 a 10.
168. 402 a 10.
169. 413 a 20.
170. 425 b 11.
171. 427 a 19.
172. Aristotle, *Metaphysics* 1072 b 24.
173. Ibid., 1074 b 34 (trans. W. D. Ross). Richard Hope translated this "its intelligence is the intelligence of intellect."
174. John Dewey, "Psychology as Philosophic Method," *Berkeley University Chronicle* (1899).
175. John Dewey, *The Philosophy of John Dewey*, ed. Paul Arthur Schilpp (Evanston, Ill.: Northwestern University Press, 1939), p. 586.
176. John Dewey, "On Some Current Conceptions of the Term 'Self,'" *Mind* (January 1890), pp. 58–74.
177. John Dewey, "The Ego as Cause," *The Philosophical Review* 3, no. 3 (May 1894): 340–41.
178. John Dewey, *On Experience, Nature, and Freedom*, ed. Richard J. Bernstein (Indianapolis, Ind.: Bobbs-Merrill, 1960), p. 51.
179. *John Dewey and Arthur F. Bentley: A Philosophical Correspondence 1932–1951*, ed. Sidney Ratner and Jules Altman (New Brunswick, N.J.: Rutgers University Press, 1964), p. 107.
180. John Dewey, *Human Nature and Conduct* (New York: Holt, 1922), p. 55.
181. John Dewey, *Democracy and Education* (New York: Macmillan Co., 1916), p. 204.
182. Dewey, *Human Nature and Conduct*, p. 85.
183. Ibid.
184. Ibid.
185. Ibid., p. 86.
186. Dewey, *Democracy and Education*, p. 408.
187. Dewey, *Human Nature and Conduct*, p. 86.
188. Ibid.
189. Ibid., p. 87.
190. Ibid., p. 314.
191. Ibid., p. 137.
192. Ibid.
193. Jean-Paul Sartre, *Being and Nothingness*, trans. Hazel E. Barnes (New York: Philosophical Library, 1956), p. 627.
194. Ibid., p. 626.
195. Ibid., p. 615.
196. Sören Kierkegaard, *Concluding Unscientific Postscript*, trans. David F. Swenson (Princeton: Princeton University Press, 1964), p. 317.
197. Sartre, *Being and Nothingness*, p. 65.

198. Ibid., p. 70.
199. Ibid., p. 59.
200. Ibid., p. 60.

Chapter 6. The Self-Realization of Human Beings

1. Epicurus, in *The Stoic and Epicurean Philosophers,* ed. Whitney J. Oates. New York: Random House, 1940. p. 49.
2. Aristotle, *Nicomachean Ethics* 1105 b 13–18 (trans. W. D. Ross).
3. Ibid., 1168 a 28.
4. Ibid., 1168 a 30.
5. Ibid., 1169 a 5.
6. Ibid.
7. Ibid., 1169 a 19–25.
8. Matthew 6:26, 28 (King James Version).
9. Giovanni Battista Gelli, *The Circe,* trans. by H. Layng (London, 1744), p. 249.
10. Information about "The Inventory of Student's General Goals of Life" may be secured from the American Council on Education, 15 Amsterdam Avenue, New York, N.Y.
11. Arthur Keith, *Evolution and Ethics* (New York: Putnam, 1949), p. 16.
12. Plato, *The Republic* 329 (trans W. H. D. Rouse).
13. Walter Lippmann, *A Preface to Morals* (New York: Macmillan Co., 1929), pp. 183–84.
14. Ibid., pp. 186–87.
15. Ibid., p. 187.
16. Ibid.
17. Ibid., p. 188.
18. Ibid.
19. Luella Cole, *Attaining Maturity* (New York: Farrar and Rinehart, 1944), chaps. 3–6.
20. Arthur Schopenhauer, *Complete Essays of Schopenhauer,* trans. T. Bailey Saunders (New York: Willey, 1942), p. 135.
21. Ibid., p. 120.
22. Ibid.
23. Ibid., p. 124.
24. Ibid.
25. Ibid., p. 137.
26. Ibid., p. 139.
27. Ibid.
28. Ibid. p. 140.
29. Ibid., p. 141.
30. Harry Overstreet, *The Mature Mind* (New York: Norton, 1949), p. 43.
31. Confucius, *Analect* II. 4. (trans. Arthur Waley).
32. Edward L. Thorndike, *Adult Interests* (New York: Macmillan Co., 1935), p. 2.
33. Ibid., p. 15.
34. Overstreet, *The Mature Mind,* p. 71.
35. Ibid.
36. Benedict Spinoza, *Ethics,* pt. 4, prop. 67 (trans. A. Boyle).
37. Review of Lewis Loeser, *Death and Identity,* by Robert Fulton. *Mental Hygiene* 49, no. 3 (July 1965), p. 470.

38. Ibid. Euripides in a lost tragedy observed that life and death may be incorrectly designated:

> Who knows whether the life is not death
> And what we call death, in the underworld is called
>   life?

(*Polyidos*. Fragment 638. Eduard Zeller, *Outlines of the History of Greek Philosophy*. 13th ed., trans. L. R. Palmer [London: Kegan Paul, Trench, Trubner, 1931], p. 16.)

39. Lewis Carroll, *Through the Looking Glass*, chapter 3.
40. Marcus Aurelius Antoninus, *Meditations* II. 14 (trans. G. Long in *The Stoic and Epicurean Philosophers*, p. 500.
41. Job 30:23.
42. Job 3:17–19 (RSV).
43. Job 10:21 (RSV).
44. Job 7:9–10 (RSV).
45. See, e.g., the word *Gehenna* in Jeremiah 7:31–32 and Isaiah 66:24, and *Hades* in Luke 16:22–23.
46. Homer, *Iliad*, bk. 23, ll. 103–4. (trans. Richard Lattimore).
47. Homer, *Odyssey*, bk. 11, l. 93 (trans. Samuel Butler).
48. Ibid., l. 153.
49. Ibid., l. 205.
50. Ibid., ll. 219–21.
51. Ibid., ll. 489–91.
52. *Bṛhad-Āraṇyaka Upaniṣad* 4. 4. 19 (trans. S. Radhakrishnan).
53. Harold Orlans, "Some Attitudes Toward Death," *Diogenes*, no. 19 (Fall 1957), p. 78.
54. Elisabeth Kubler-Ross, *On Death and Dying* (New York: Macmillan, 1969).
55. Epicurus, *Letter to Menoeceus* (trans. C. Bailey). *The Stoic and Epicurean Philosophers*, p. 31.
56. Plato, *Apology* 29 (trans. W. H. D. Rouse).
57. Rollo May, *Man's Search for Himself*, p. 19.
58. The Wisdom of Solomon 1:12–13 (The Oxford Annotated Apocrypha).
59. Plato, *Apology* 28, 41 (trans. by W. H. D. Rouse).
60. Diogenes Laërtius, *Letter to Idomeneus*, trans. C. Bailey, in *The Stoic and Epicurean Philosophers*, p. 58.
61. Lucretius, *De Rerum Natura*, trans. H. A. J. Munro, in *The Stoic and Epicurean Philosophers*, pp. 130, 131.
62. David Hume, *An Enquiry Concerning Human Understanding and Selections from A Treatise of Human Nature* (Chicago: Open Court, 1935), p. xv.
63. *Mahābhārata, Adi Parva*, sec. 160 (Pratap Chandra Roy trans.) 1:370.
64. Chuang Tzu (trans. Herbert A. Giles), in *The Bible of the World*, ed. Robert O. Ballou (New York: Viking, 1939), p. 540.
65. Plato, *Apology* 42 (trans. W. H. D. Rouse).
66. John Bunyan, *The Pilgrim's Progress*, ed. William Vaughn Moody, (Boston: Houghton Mifflin, 1896), pp. 187, 188, 189.
67. Thomas Mann, *The Magic Mountain*, translated by H. T. Lowe-Porter. New York: Knopf, 1927, p. 256.
68. *Mahābhārata, Vana Parva*, sec. 141, pp. 302–3. (Pratap Chandra Roy trans.).
69. Shakespeare, *Cymbeline*, act 4, sc. 2, l. 262.
70. Augustine, *The City of God*, trans. M. Dods. *Basic Writings of Saint Augustine*, 2:17.
71. C. S. Peirce, "The Doctrine of Chances," *Popular Science Monthly* 12 (March 1878): 610.

72. Blaise Pascal, *Pensées* 194, trans. Thomas McCrie in *The Provincial Letters* (New York: Random House, 1941), p. 66.
73. Plato, *Symposium* 208 (trans. Benjamin Jowett).
74. Aristotle, *De Anima* 415 b 3–7 (trans. J. A. Smith).
75. Plato, *Symposium* 208 (trans. Benjamin Jowett).
76. Samuel Butler, *The Note-Books of Samuel Butler,* ed. Henry Festing Jones (New York: Dutton, 1927), p. 355.
77. *Chāndogya Upaniṣad* 7. 25. 1 (trans. Robert Ernest Hume).
78. Commentary on *Vedānta Sūtra* I. i. 1 (trans. George Thibaut), *A Source Book in Indian Philosophy,* p. 547.
79. J. B. Rhine, *New World of the Mind* (New York: Sloane, 1953), pp. 312–13.
80. Matthew 5:48 (RSV).
81. Betty Heinmann, *Facets of Indian Thought.* (New York: Schocken, 1964), p. 142.
82. Ibid., 142–43.
83. *The Complete Works of Swami Vivekananda,* Vol. 1. 11th ed. (Calcutta: Advaita Ashrama, 1962), p. 332.
84. Rabindranath Tagore, *Sādhanā* (New York: Macmillan, 1914), p. 153.
85. Mircea Eliade, *Patterns in Comparative Religion* (Cleveland and New York: World, 1963), p. 14.
86. Alfred North Whitehead, *Adventures of Ideas* (New York: Macmillan, 1933), pp. 353–54.
87. Aristotle, *Nicomachean Ethics* 1094 a 1. All selections from the *Nicomachean Ethics* are from the translation of W. D. Ross.
88. Ibid., 1094 a 3.
89. Ibid., 1094 a 18–22.
90. Ibid., 1094 a 22, 28.
91. Ibid., 1095 a 16.,
92. Ibid., 1095 a 19.
93. Ibid.
94. F. E. Peters, *Greek Philosophical Terms* (New York: New York University Press, 1967), p. 33.
95. Aristotle, *Nicomachean Ethics,* 1177 b 31–1178 a 1.
96. The word is *makários*, i.e., supremely happy.
97. Aristotle, *Nicomachean Ethics* 1178 b 8, 21–23.
98. Ibid., 1095 a 22.
99. Ibid., 1095 b 14.
100. Ibid., 1095 b 20. Happiness as pleasure has been viciously attacked in the West. William Makepeace Thackeray closed his novel *Vanity Fair* with these words: "Ah! *Vanitas Vanitatum!* Which of us is happy in this world? Which of us has his desire? or, having it, is satisfied?—come, children, let us shut up the box and the puppets, for our play is played out." Although John Stuart Mill was a hedonist, he did not believe that man had been strikingly successful in his quest for happiness: "If the motive of the Deity for creating sentient beings was the happiness of the beings he created, his purpose, in our corner of the universe at least, must be pronounced, taking past ages and all countries and races into account, to have been thus far an ignominious failure." (*(Three Essays on Religion* [London: Longman's, Green, Reader, and Dyer, 1874], p. 192.) Lewis Mumford has submitted, "If pleasure were in any sense the ultimate end of life, suicide by an inhalation of nitrous oxide, followed by a last sensible whiff of carbon monoxide, might be the last work in human bliss." (*The Condition of Man* [New York: Harcourt, Brace, 1944], p. 271.)
101. Aristotle, *Nicomachean Ethics,* 1096 b 14.
102. Ibid., 1096 a 6–7.
103. Ibid., 1099 b 1.

104. Ibid., 1178 a 29.
105. Ibid., 1095 b 22.
106. Ibid., 1095 b 23.
107. Ibid., 1095 b 24–26.
108. Ibid., 1099 b 1.
109. Ibid., 1163 b 4.
110. Ibid., 1178 a 33.
111. Ibid., 1178 a 34.
112. Ibid., 1177 b 5.
113. Aristotle, *De Anima* 434 b 23, 435 a 13 (trans. J. A. Smith).
114. Ibid., 434 b 24, 435 b 20.
115. Aristotle, *Nichomachean Ethics* 1152 b 5.
116. Ibid., 1175 a 36.
117. Ibid., 1156 a 8–12.
118. Ibid., 1178 b 8.
119. Ibid., 1178 a 7.
120. Ibid., 1177 a 20.
121. Ibid., 1177 a 16.
122. Ibid., 1179 a 23–32.
123. Epicurus, in *The Stoic and Epicurean Philosophers,* p. 50 (trans. C. Bailey).
124. Ibid., p. 51.
125. Ibid., p. 48.
126. Ibid., p. 43.
127. Ibid., p. 35.
128. Ibid., p. 41.
129. Ibid., p. 35.
130. Ibid., p. 14.
131. Ibid., p. 30.
132. Ibid., p. 91.
133. John Stuart Mill, *Utilitarianism,* chap. 2, in *Essential Works of John Stuart Mill,* ed. Max Lerner (New York: Bantam, 1961), p. 197.
134. Thomas Aquinas, *The Summa Contra Gentiles,* chap. 37 (trans. Laurence Shapcote), in *Basic Writings of Saint Thomas Aquinas,* 2:60.
135. Epictetus, *Encheiridion* 1 (trans. P. E. Matheson), in *The Stoic and Epicurean Philosophers,* p. 468.
136. Marcus Aurelius, *Meditations* 10, 6 (trans. G. Long), in *The Stoic and Epicurean Philosophers,* p. 563.
137. Ibid., 8, 59, in ibid., p. 552.
138. Ibid., 2, 1, in ibid., p. 497.
139. Ibid., 6, 2, in ibid., p. 526.
140. Ibid.
141. Ibid., 10, 8, in ibid., p. 564.
142. Ibid., 10, 15, in ibid., p. 566.
143. Ibid., 10, 3, in ibid., p. 562.
144. Immanuel Kant, *Foundations of the Metaphysics of Morals,* 1st sec., trans. Lewis White Beck (Chicago: University of Chicago Press, 1949), p. 55.
145. Ibid., p. 60.
146. Adapted from Confucius, *Analects* 11. 25 (trans. Arthur Waley).
147. Wang Chi, in Arthur Waley, trans., *Translations from the Chinese* (New York: Knopf, 1941), p. 114.
148. Po Chü-i, in Waley, trans., *Translations from the Chinese,* p. 137.
149. Edward Conze, *Buddhist Thought in India,* p. 71.

150. Bhikshu Sangharakshita, *A Survey of Buddhism*, p. 195.
151. Ibid., p. 188.
152. D. T. Suzuki, *Outlines of Mahāyāna Buddhism* (New York: Schocken, 1963), p. 341.
153. Conze, *Buddhist Thought in India*, p. 228.
154. *The Panchatantra*, trans. Arthur W. Ryder, p. 219. The publishers state that "an ounce of sense contained in the *Pañchatantra* is better than a ton of scholarship." (Ibid., p. x.)
155. Benjamin Walker, *Hindu World*, 1:275.
156. Troy Organ, *The Hindu Quest for the Perfection of Man*, p. 152. See pages 121–52 for a fuller treatment of *artha, kāma, dharma,* and *moksa*. The short quotation within is from the *Chāndogya Upanisad* 8. 4. 3.
157. Everett Shostrom, *Freedom to Be* (New York: Bantam, 1972), p. xvi.
158. *Gospel of Philip* 2. 53. 15–24 (trans. Wesley W. Isenberg), in *The Nag Hammadi Library* (New York: Harper and Row, 1977), p. 132.
159. Aurobindo, *The Life Divine*, p. 901.
160. Sarvepalli Radhakrishnan, *The Brahma Sūtra: The Philosophy of the Spiritual Life* (London: George Allen & Unwin, 1960), p. 153.
161. Sarvepalli Radhakrishnan, *The Philosophy of Sarvepalli Radhakrishnan*, ed. Paul Schilpp (New York: Tudor Publishing Co., 1952), p. 47. Alvin Toffler has said, "We tend to categorize individuals not according to the changes they happen to be undergoing at the moment, but according to their status or position between changes. We consider a union man as someone who has joined a union and not yet quit. Our designation refers not to joining or quitting, but to the 'non-change' that happens in between. For example, 'one who is moving to a new residence,' . . . 'one who is changing his job,' . . . 'one who is joining a church,' or 'one who is getting a divorce'.... This sudden shift of focus, from thinking about what people 'are' to thinking about what they are 'becoming' suggests a whole array of new approaches to adaptation." (*Future Shock* [New York: Random, 1970], p. 340.)

Recommended Readings

Chapter 1

Burtt, E. A. "A Basic Problem in the Quest for Understanding Between East and West." In *Philosophy and Culture—East and West,* edited by Charles A. Moore. Honolulu: University of Hawaii Press, 1962. Pp. 673–91.

Cassirer, Ernst. *An Essay on Man.* New Haven: Yale University Press, 1944. chap. 8.

Chan, Wing-tsit. "Philosophies of China." In *Twentieth Century Philosophy,* edited by Dagobert D. Runes. New York: Philosophical Library, 1943. Pp. 541–71.

———. *The Way of Lao Tzu.* New York: Bobbs-Merrill, 1963. Pp. 3–34.

———. "The Spirit of Oriental Philosophy." In *Philosophy—East and West,* edited by Charles A. Moore. Princeton: Princeton University Press, 1946. Pp. 137–67.

———. "The Story of Chinese Philosophy." In *Philosophy—East and West,* edited by Charles A. Moore. Pp. 24–68, also in *The Chinese Mind,* edited by Charles A. Moore. Honolulu: East-West Center Press, 1967. Pp. 31–76.

Chatterjee, S. C. "The Basis of World Philosophy." *Proceedings of the 28th Philosophical Congress* (India), 1933. Pp. 3–21.

Chatterjee, Tara. "The Concept of Sākṣin." *Journal of Indian Philosophy* 10, no. 4 (December 1982): 339–56.

Christian, James L. *Philosophy: An Introduction to the Art of Wondering.* New York: Holt, Rinehart and Winston, 1977.

Conger, George P. "An Outline of Indian Philosophy." In *Philosophy—East and West,* edited by Charles A. Moore. Pp. 12–23.

Datta, D. M. "On Philosophical Synthesis." *Philosophy East and West* 13, no. 3 (October 1963): 195–200.

Dewey, John. *Reconstruction in Philosophy.* New York: Holt, 1920.

Gutmann, James, ed. *Philosophy—A to Z.* New York: Grosset and Dunlap, 1963. Articles on "Chinese and Japanese Philosophy," "Esthetics," "Ethics," "Indian Philosophy," "Theory of Knowledge," "Metaphysics," and "Ontology."

Hahn, Lewis. "Philosophy as Comprehensive Vision." *Philosophy and Phenomenological Research* (September 1961), pp. 16–25.

Hocking, William Ernest. "Value of the Comparative Study of Philosophy." In *Philosophy—East and West,* edited by Charles A. Moore. Pp. 1–11.

Kantor, J. R. *Interbehavioral Philosophy*. Chicago: Principia, 1981. Chap. 1.

Knox, T. M. "Two Concepts of Philosophy." *Philosophy* 36 (1961): 289–308.

Moore, Charles A. "Comparative Philosophies of Life." In *Philosophy—East and West*, edited by Charles A. Moore. Pp. 248–320.

———. "The Comprehensive Indian Mind." In *The Indian Mind*, edited by Charles A. Moore. Honolulu: East-West Center Press, 1967, pp. 1–18.

———. "The Enigmatic Japanese Mind." In *The Japanese Mind*, edited by Charles A. Moore. Honolulu: East-West Center Press, 1967. Pp. 288–313.

———. "The Humanistic Chinese Mind." In *The Chinese Mind*, edited by Charles A. Moore. Pp. 1–10.

Munz, Peter. "India and the West: A Synthesis." *Philosophy East and West* 5, no. 4 (January 1956): 321–38.

Murty, K. Satchidananda. "Philosophical Thought in India." *Diogenes*, no. 24 (1958), pp. 17–31.

Nagel, Ernest. "The Mission of Philosophy." In *An Outline of Man's Knowledge of the Modern World*, edited by Lyman Bryson. New York: McGraw-Hill, 1960. Pp. 646–66.

Nikam, N. A. *Some Concepts of Indian Culture*. Simla, India: Indian Institute of Advanced Study, 1967.

Organ, Troy. *Western Approaches to Eastern Philosophy*. Athens, Ohio: Ohio University Press, 1975. Pp. 3–29.

Prasad, Rajendra. "Tradition, Progress, and Contemporary Indian Philosophy." *Philosophy East and West* 15, nos. 3 and 4 (July–October 1965): 251–58.

Radhakrishnan, S. *East and West*. New York: Harper, 1956.

———. "History of Indian Thought." In *A Source Book in Indian Philosophy*, edited by S. Radhakrishnan and Charles A. Moore. Princeton: Princeton University Press, 1957. Pp. xv–xxix.

Shastri, Prabhu Durr. *The Essentials of Eastern Philosophy*. New York: Macmillan Co., 1928.

Sheldon, W. H. "Main Contrasts Between Eastern and Western Philosophy." In *Essays in East-West Philosophy*, edited by Charles A. Moore. Honolulu: University of Hawaii Press, 1951. Pp. 288–97.

Smith, Huston. "Accents of the World's Philosophers." *Philosophy East and West* 2, nos. 1 and 2 (April–July 1957): 7–19.

———. "Western and Comparative Perspectives on Truth." *Philosophy East and West* 30, no. 4 (October 1980): 425–37.

Smith, John E. "The Need for a Recovery of Philosophy." *Proceedings and Addresses of the American Philosophical Association* 56, no. 1 (Spring 1982): 5–18.

Suzuki, D. T. *A Brief History of Chinese Philosophy*. London: Probsthain, 1914.

———. *Buddhist Philosophy and Its Effect on the Life and Thought of the Japanese People*. Tokyo: Kokusai Bunka Shinkokai, 1936.

Wadia, A. R. "On Philosophical Synthesis." *Philosophy East and West* 13, no. 4 (January 1964): 291–93.

Wang, Kung-hsing. *The Chinese Mind*. New York: John Day, 1946.

Watts, Alan W. *The Legacy of Asia and Western Man*. London: John Murray, 1937.

Chapter 2

Alston, W. P. *Philosophy of Language*. Englewood Cliffs, N.J.: Prentice-Hall, 1964.

Anscombe, G. E. M. *Intention*. Oxford: Blackwell, 1957.

Austin, J. L. *How to Do Things with Words*. Oxford: Clarendon, 1962.

Baird, A. C. *Rhetoric: A Philosophical Inquiry*. New York: Ronald, 1965.

Berkeley, George. *A Treatise Concerning the Principles of Human Knowledge*. Preface.

Bindeman, Steven L. *Heidegger and Wittgenstein: The Poetics of Silence*. Landham, Md.: University Press of America, 1980.

Black, Max, ed. *The Importance of Language*. Englewood Cliffs, N.J.: Prentice-Hall, 1962.

——. "The Labyrinth of Language." *Britannica Perspectives*. Chicago: Encyclopedia Britannica, 1968. 3: 1–171.

Bolinger, Dwight. *Aspects of Language*. New York: Harcourt, Brace, 1968.

Britton, Karl. *Communication. A Philosophical Study of Language*. College Park, Md.: McGrath, 1970. Chap. 1.

Carroll, John B. *The Study of Language*. Cambridge, Mass.: Harvard University Press, 1953.

Cassirer, Ernst. *An Essay on Man*. New Haven: Yale University Press, 1944. Chap. 8.

——. *Language and Myth*. New York: Harper, 1946.

Chase, Stuart, and Chase, Marian T. *Power of Words*. New York: Harcourt-Brace, 1954.

Chomsky, Noam. *Syntactic Structures*. The Hague: Mouton, 1957.

Condon, John C., Jr. *Semantics and Communication*. New York: Macmillan Co., 1966.

Dauenhauer, Bernard P. *Silence: The Phenomenon and its Ontological Significance*. Bloomington: Indiana University Press, 1980.

Flew, A., *Logic and Language*. Garden City, N.Y.: Doubleday, 1965.

Fromkin, Victoria, and Rodman, Robert. *An Introduction to Language*. New York: Holt, Rinehart and Winston, 1974.

Fromm, Erich. *The Forgotten Language*. New York: Rinehart, 1951.

Gardiner, A. *The Theory of Speech and Language*. Oxford: Clarendon, 1951.

Garey, Doris. *Putting Words in Their Places*. Chicago: Scott, Foresman, 1957.

Gellner, Ernest. *Words and Things*. Boston: Beacon, 1959.

Hayakawa, S. I. *Language in Thought and Action*. 3d ed. New York: Harcourt Brace Jovanovich, 1972.

Heidegger, Martin. *On the Way to Language*. Translated by Peter D. Hentz. New York: Harper and Row, 1971.

Heil, John. "Speechless Brutes." *Philosophy and Phenomenological Research* 42, no. 3 (March 1982): 400–406.

Heisenberg, Werner. *Physics and Philosophy*. New York: Harper, 1958. Chap. 10.

Hogben, Lancelot. *The Signs of Civilization*. London: Rathbone, 1959.

Hook, Sidney, ed. *Language and Philosophy*. New York: New York University Press, 1969.

Hopson, Janet L. *Scent Signals. The Silent Language of Sex.* New York: William Morrow, 1979.

Huxley, Aldous. "Education at the Nonverbal Level." *Daedalus* (Spring 1962): 279–93.

Katz, Jerrold J. *The Philosophy of Language.* New York: Harper and Row, 1966.

Kehl, D. G. "The Doublespeak of Academia." *National Forum* (Summer 1980). Pp. 36–37.

Korzybski, Alfred. *Science and Sanity.* 2d ed. Lakeville, Conn.: International Non-Aristotelian Library, 1947.

Landesman, C. *Discourse and Its Presupposition.* New Haven: Yale University Press, 1972.

Langer, Susanne K. *Philosophy in a New Key.* Cambridge, Mass.: Harvard University Press, 1942. Chaps. 1–5.

Locke, John. *An Essay Concerning Human Understanding.* Bk. 3.

Lyons, J. *Introduction to Theoretical Linguistics.* Cambridge: Cambridge University Press, 1969.

Matilal, Bimal Krishna. *Logical and Ethical Issues of Religious Belief.* Calcutta: University of Calcutta, 1982. Pp. 67–127.

Minnis, N., ed. *Linguistics at Large.* London: Victor Gollancz, 1971.

Minteer, Catherine. *Words and What They Do to You.* Evanston, Ill.: Row, Peterson, 1953.

Morris, Charles. *Signs, Language and Behavior.* New York: Prentice-Hall, 1946.

Mukerji, Dhan Gopal. *The Face of Silence.* New York: Dutton, 1926.

Mukhopadhyay, Kamal. *Austin's Philosophy of Language.* Ph.D. diss., University of Calcutta, 1983.

Nakamura, Hajime. *Ways of Thinking of Eastern Peoples: India-China-Tibet-Japan.* Honolulu: East-West Center Press, 1964. Pp. 2–43.

Ogden, C. K., and Richards, I. A. *The Meaning of Meaning.* 3d ed. rev. New York: Harcourt, Brace and World, 1930.

Olshewoky, T. M., ed. *Problems in the Philosophy of Language.* New York: Holt, Rinehart and Winston, 1969.

Ong, Walter. *Why Talk?* San Francisco: Chandler and Sharp, 1973.

Organ, Troy. "The Language of Mysticism." *Western Approaches to Eastern Philosophy.* Athens, Ohio: Ohio University Press, 1975. Pp. 160–80.

———. "The Silence of the Buddha." *Western Approaches to Eastern Philosophy.* Athens, Ohio: Ohio University Press, 1975. Pp. 181–98.

Partridge, Eric. *The World of Words.* London: Hamish Hamilton, 1938.

Pei, Mario. *Language for Everybody.* New York: Devin-Adair, 1957.

Piaget, Jean. *The Language and Thought of the Child.* New York: Harcourt, Brace and World, 1926.

Quine, W. V. *Word and Object.* New York: Massachusetts Institute of Technology, 1960.

Russell, Bertrand. *An Outline of Philosophy.* Cleveland and New York: World, 1960. Chap. 4.

Sapir, Edward. *Language. An Introduction to the Study of Speech.* New York: Harcourt, Brace, 1921.

———. *Culture, Language and Personality.* Berkeley and Los Angeles: University of California Press, 1956.

Searle, J. *Speech-Acts: An Essay in the Philosophy of Language.* Cambridge: Cambridge University Press, 1969.

Skinner, B. F. *Verbal Behavior.* New York: Appleton-Century-Crofts, 1957.

Sondel, Bess Selzer. *The Humanity of Words: A Primer of Semantics.* New York: World, 1958.

Trippett, Frank. "Why So Much Is Beyond Words." *Time,* July 13, 1981. Pp. 71–72.

Ullmann, Stephen. *Semantics: An Introduction to the Science of Meaning.* New York: Barnes and Noble, 1962.

Upadyaya, K. N. "The Significance of the Buddha's Silence." *The Philosophical Quarterly* 39, no. 1 (April 1966): 65–80.

Vendler, Z. *Linguistics in Philosophy.* Ithaca, N.Y.: Cornell University Press, 1963.

Wagner, Geoffrey. "The Language of Politics." In *Language in America,* edited by Neil Postman, Charles Weingartner, and Terence P. Moran. New York: Pegasus, 1969. Pp. 22–39.

Whatmough, Joshua. *Language. A Modern Synthesis.* New York: St. Martin's, 1954.

Whorf, Benjamin Lee. *Language, Thought and Reality: Select Writings of B. L. Whorf.* Edited by John B. Carroll. New York: Wiley, 1956.

Wittgenstein, Ludwig. *Philosophical Investigations.* Oxford: Blackwell, 1945. Secs. 65–77.

Ziff, P. *Semantic Analysis.* Ithaca, N.Y.: Cornell University Press, 1960.

Chapter 3

Ayer, A. J. *The Problem of Knowledge.* Baltimore: Penguin, 1956.

Blackwood, R. T., and Herman, A. L., eds. *Problems in Philosophy: East and West.* Englewood Cliffs, N.J.: Prentice-Hall, 1975. Pp. 107–265.

Chethimattam, John B. *Patterns of Indian Thought.* London: Geoffrey Chapman, 1971.

Church, Cornelia D. "Śaṅkara's Epistemology: A New direction for the West?" *Explanation: New Directions in Philosophy.* The Hague: Nijhoff, 1973. Pp. 22–40.

Conze, Edward. *Buddhist Thought in India.* Ann Arbor: University of Michigan Press, 1967. Pt. 3, sec. 4.

Datta, D. M. "Epistemological Methods in Indian Philosophy." In *Essays in East-West Philosophy,* edited by Charles A. Moore. Pp. 73–88. Also in *The Indian Mind,* edited by Charles A. Moore. Pp. 118–35.

Dennis, William Ray. "Empirico-Naturalism and World Understanding." *Essays in East-West Philosophy,* pp. 124–50.

Eddington, A. S. *The Nature of Physical Science.* Cambridge: Cambridge University Press, 1939. Chaps. 12, 13.

Haas, William S. *The Destiny of the Mind: East and West.* New York: Macmillan Co., 1956. Pp. 96–120, 159–84.

Hamblin, C. L. *Fallacies.* London: Methuen, 1970. Chap. 5.

Heimann, Betty. *Facets of Indian Thought.* New York: Schocken, 1964. Chaps. 4, 7, 8, 10, 11.

Hughes, E. R. "Epistemological Methods in Chinese Philosophy." *Essays in East-West Philosophy,* edited by Charles A. Moore. Pp. 49–72. Also in *The Chinese Mind,* edited by Charles A. Moore. Pp. 77–103.

Hu Shih. "The Scientific Spirit and Method in Chinese Philosophy." In *Philosophy and Culture—East and West,* edited by Charles A. Moore. Pp. 199–222. Also in *The Chinese Mind,* edited by Charles A. Moore. Pp. 104–131.

Jayatilleka, K. N. *Early Buddhist Theory of Knowledge.* London: George Allen and Unwin, 1963.

Locke, John. *An Essay Concerning Human Understanding.* Pt. 4.

Manno, Bruno V. "Creative Imagination as a Basis for Relating the Sciences and the Humanities: The Epistemological Perspective of Michael Polanyi." *Philosophy Today* 24, no. 2/4 (Summer 1980): 171–84.

Matilal, Bimal Krishna. "Error and Truth—Classical Indian Theories." *Philosophy East and West* 31, no. 2 (April 1981): 215–24.

———. *Logical and Ethical Issues of Religious Belief.* Pp. 128–151.

Mill, J. S. *A System of Logic.* Bk. 3, chap. 8.

Mitchell, Basil. *The Justification of Religious Belief.* New York: Oxford University Press, 1981.

Mohanty, J. N. "Indian Theories of Truth: Thoughts on their Common Framework." *Philosophy East and West* 30, no. 4 (October 1980): 439–51.

Montague, W. P. *The Ways of Knowing.* New York: Macmillan, 1925.

Moore, Charles A. "East-West Philosophy and the Search for Truth." In *Asia and the Humanities,* edited by Horst Frenz. Bloomington: Indiana University Press, 1959. Pp. 95–112.

Nakamura, Hajime. "Consciousness of the Individual and the Universal among the Japanese." In *The Status of the Individual in East and West,* edited by Charles A. Moore. Honolulu: University of Hawaii Press, 1968, pp. 141–60.

———. *Ways of Thinking of Eastern Peoples: India-China-Tibet-Japan.* Pp. 2–38, 41–172, 175–294, 297–342, 234–587.

Nikhilananda. "Concentration and Meditation as Methods in Indian Philosophy." In *Essays in East-West Philosophy,* edited by Charles A. Moore. Pp. 89–102. Also in *The Indian Mind,* edited by Charles A. Moore. Pp. 136–51.

Nisbett, R., and Ross, L. *Human Inference.* New York: Prentice-Hall, 1980.

Northrop, F. S. C. "The Complementary Emphases of Eastern Intuitive and Western Scientific Philosophy." In *Philosophy—East and West,* edited by Charles A. Moore. Pp. 168–234.

———. "Methodology and Epistemology Oriental and Occidental." In *Essays in East-West Philosophy,* edited by Charles A. Moore. Pp. 151–60.

Organ, Troy. "The Burden of Tradition." *Western Approaches to Eastern Philosophy.* Athens, Ohio: Ohio University Press, 1975. Pp. 104–7.

———. "Three into Four in Hinduism." *Western Approaches to Eastern Philosophy.* Athens, Ohio: Ohio University Press, 1975. Pp. 233–41.

Pears, David. *What is Knowledge?* New York: Harper and Row, 1971.

Peirce, Charles S. *Chance, Love, and Logic.* New York: Harcourt, Brace, 1923. Pp. 14–31. Originally published as "The Fixation of Belief" in *Popular Science Monthly*, November 1877.

Polanyi, Michael. *Personal Knowledge.* New York: Harper and Row, 1958.

Popper, K. *The Logic of Scientific Discovery.* London: Hutchison, 1959.

Quine, W. V., and Ullian, J. S. *The Web of Belief.* New York: Random House, 1970.

Raju, P. T. "Indian Epistemology and the World and the Individual." *The Status of the Individual in East and West,* edited by Charles A. Moore. Pp. 121–140.

———. "The Principle of Four-Cornered Negation in Indian Philosophy." *The Review of Metaphysics* 7, no. 4 (June 1954): 694–713.

Roth, Michael D., and Galis, Leon, eds. *Knowing: Essays in the Analysis of Knowledge.* New York: Random House, 1970.

Russell, Bertrand. "The Art of Drawing Inferences." *The Art of Philosophizing and Other Essays.* New York: Philosophical Library, 1968. Pp. 37–76.

———. *Human Knowledge.* Chicago: Scott-Foresman, 1965.

———. *Mysticism and Logic.* London: George Allen and Unwin, 1917. Chap. 10.

Scheffler, Israel. *Conditions of Knowledge.* Chicago: Scott-Foresman, 1965.

Stcherbatsky, F. Th. *Buddhist Logic.* New York: Dover, 1962. Vol. 1, pts. 3, 4.

Streng, Frederick J. *Emptiness: A Study in Religious Meaning.* New York: Abingdon, 1967. Chap. 9.

Suzuki, D. T. "An Interpretation of Zen-experience." In *Philosophy—East and West,* edited by Charles A. Moore. Pp. 109–29. Also in *The Japanese Mind,* edited by Charles A. Moore. Pp. 122–42.

T'ang Chün-i. "The Individual and the World in Chinese Methodology." *The Status of the Individual in East and West,* edited by Charles A. Moore. Pp. 101–19. Also in *The Chinese Mind,* edited by Charles A. Moore. Pp. 264–85.

Warren, Henry Clarke, trans. "Questions Which Tend Not to Edification." (*Majjhima-Nikya Suttas* 63, 72.) *Buddhism in Translations.* New York: Atheneum, 1963. Pp. 117–28.

Chapter 4

Alexander, S. "Self as Subject and as Person." *Proceedings of the Aristotelian Society* 11 (1911): 1–28.

Cassirer, Ernst. *An Essay on Man.* Chap. 1.

Charon, Jean. *Man's Search for Himself.* Translated by J. E. Anderson. London: George Allen and Unwin, 1967.

Copleston, F. C. "Know Thyself: But How?" *The Hibbert Journal* 41 (1942–43): 12–17.

Descartes, René. "Of the Nature of the Human Mind, and That It is More Easily Known Than the Body." *The Meditations Concerning First Philosophy.* Meditation 2.

Devaraja, N. K. *Philosophy, Religion and Culture*. Delhi: Motilal Banarsidass, 1944. Chap. 4.

Jung, Carl G. *Modern Man in Search of a Soul*. New York: Harcourt, Brace, 1933.

May, Rollo. *Man's Search for Himself*. New York: Norton, 1953.

Mellone, S. H. "The Nature of Self-knowledge." *Mind* 10 (1901): 318–55.

Nikhilananda, trans. *Self-knowledge. An English Translation of Śaṅkarāchārya's Ātmabodha*. Mylapore, Madras: Sri Ramakrishna Math, 1947.

North, Helen. *Sophrosyne. Self-Knowledge and Self-Restraint in Greek Literature*. Ithaca, N.Y.: Cornell University Press, 1966.

Nozick, Robert. *Philosophical Explanations*. Cambridge: Harvard University Press, 1981. Pp. 27–114.

Organ, Troy, "The Quest for Self-knowledge in the West and in India." *Darshana* 2, no. 1 (January 1962): 80–87.

———. "The Self as Discovery and Creation in Western and Indian Philosophy." *Western Approaches to Eastern Philosophy*, pp. 39–53.

Rhinelander, Philip H. *Is Man Incomprehensible to Man?* San Francisco: Freeman, 1973.

Ryle, Gilbert. *The Concept of Mind*. London: Hutchinson's University Library, 1949. Chap. 6.

Schuon, Frithjof. *Language of the Self*. Translated by Marco Pallis Macleol Matheson. Madras: Ganesh, 1959. Chap. 3.

Shoemaker, Sydney. *Self-knowledge and Self-identity*. Ithaca, New York: Cornell University Press, 1963.

Smith, Huston. *Forgotten Truth*. New York: Harper and Row, 1976. Chap. 4.

Watts, Alan W. *The Book on the Taboo Against Knowing Who You Are*. New York: Pantheon, 1966.

Chapter 5

Aristotle. *De Anima* 402 a 1–416 b 32. *Nicomachean Ethics* 1168 a 28–1169 b 2.

Bhattacharyya, Kalidas. "The Status of the Individual in Indian Metaphysics." In *The Status of the Individual in East and West*, edited by Charles A. Moore. Pp. 27–63. Also in *the Indian Mind*, edited by Charles A. Moore. Pp. 290–319.

Bradley, F. H. *Essays on Truth and Reality*. London: Oxford University Press, 1914. Pp. 409–27.

Bronowski, Jacob. *the Identity of Man*. Garden City, N.Y.: Natural History Press, 1971.

Campbell, C. A. *On Selfhood and Godhead*. London: George Allen and Unwin, 1957.

Castell, Alburey. *The Self in Philosophy*. New York: Macmillan Co., 1965.

Chan, Wing-tsit. "The Chinese Concept of Man in Chinese Thought." In *The Concept of Man in Comparative Philosophy*, Edited by S. Radhakrishnan and P. T. Raju. London: George Allen and Unwin, 1960. Pp. 158–205.

Chisholm, R. M. *Person and Object: A Metaphysical Study*. London: George Allen and Unwin, 1976.

Collins, Steven. *Selfless Persons. Imagery and Thought in Theravada Buddhism.* New York: Cambridge University Press, 1982.

Copleston, Frederick C. "The Psychophysical Constitution of the Human Person: Different Approaches." *Philosophies and Cultures.* Oxford: Oxford University Press, 1980. Chap. 5.

Descartes, René. "Of the Existence of Corporeal Things and of the Real Distinction Between the Mind and Body." *The Meditations Concerning First Philosophy.* Meditation 6.

Deussen, Paul. *The Philosophy of the Upanishads.* Translated by A. S. Geden. New York: Dover, 1966. Pp. 256–312.

Eastcott, Michael Joan. *The Story of the Self.* London: Rider, 1979.

Ewing, A. C. *The Fundamental Questions of Philosophy.* New York: Macmillan Co., 1951. P. 5.

Fair, Charles M. *The Dying Self.* New York: Columbia University Press, 1969.

Fang, Thome H. "The World and the Individual in Chinese Metaphysics." In *The Status of the Individual in East and West,* edited by Charles A. Moore. Pp. 23–46. Also in *The Chinese Mind,* edited by Charles A. Moore. Pp. 238–63.

Fung, Yu-lan. *A History of Chinese Philosophy.* London: George Allen and Unwin, 1937. Pp. 75, 119–31, 145, 286–89, 327–30.

Garnett, A. Campbell. *Reality and Value.* New Haven: Yale University Press, 1937. Chap. 3.

Glicksberg, Charles I. *The Self in Modern Literature.* University Park: Pennsylvania State University Press, 1963.

Groethuysen, Bernard. "Towards an Anthropological Philosophy." In *Philosophy and History. Essays Presented to Ernst Cassirer,* edited by Raymond Klibansky and H. J. Paton. New York: Harper and Row, 1963. Pp. 77–89.

Hampden-Turner, Charles. *Maps of the Mind.* New York: Macmillan Co., 1982.

Hocking, William Ernest. *The Self: Its Body and Freedom.* New Haven: Yale University Press, 1928.

Hoffmann, Yoel. *The Idea of Self East and West: A Comparison between Buddhist Philosophy and the Philosophy of David Hume.* Calcutta: Firma KLM, 1980.

Hofstadter, Douglas R., and Deanett, Daniel C. *The Mind's I.* New York: Basic Books, 1981.

Hume, David. *A Treatise of Human Nature.* Bk. 1, pt. 4; bk. 2, appendix.

Jackson, Edith. *The Self and the Object World.* New York: International Universities Press, 1977.

Johnstone, Henry W. *Problem of the Self.* University Park: Pennsylvania State University Press, 1970.

Korzybski, Alfred. *Manhood of Humanity.* New York: Dutton, 1921.

LaBarre, Weston. *The Human Animal.* Chicago: University of Chicago Press, 1954.

Lacan, Jacques. *The Language of the Self.* New York: Dell, 1975.

Lasing, R. D. *The Divided Self.* Middlesex: Penguin, 1967.

Laird, John. *Problems of the Self.* New York: Macmillan Co., 1917.

Lewis, C. I. *Mind and the World-Order.* New York: Scribners, 1929. Pp. 412–427.

Locke, John. *An Essay Concerning Human Understanding*. Bk. 2, chap. 27.

McMurrin, Sterling M. "The Individual in American Philosophy." In *The Status of the Individual in East and West*, edited by Charles A. Moore. Pp. 487–502.

Malalasekera, G. P. "The Status of the Individual in Theravāda Buddhist Philosophy." In *The Status of the Individual in East and West*, edited by Charles A. Moore. Pp. 65–76.

Mead, George Herbert. "Self." In *George Herbert Mead on Social Psychology*, edited by Anselm Strauss. Chicago: University of Chicago Press, 1964. Pp. 199–246.

Moore, Jared S. "The Problem of the Self." *The Philosophical Review* 42 (1933): 487–99.

Morris, Charles. *The Open Self*. New York: Prentice-Hall, 1948.

Morris, Desmond. *The Naked Ape*. New York: McGraw-Hill, 1967.

Myers, Gerald E. *Self: An Introduction to Philosophical Psychology*. New York: Pegasus, 1969.

O'Daly, Gerard. *Plotinus' Philosophy of the Self*. New York: Harper and Row, 1973.

Organ, Troy. "The Individual in East-West Discussions." *Western Approaches to Eastern Philosophy*, pp. 54–61.

———. *The Self in Indian Philosophy*. The Hague: Mouton, 1964.

Ortega Y Gasset. *The Dehumanization of Art and Other Writings on Art and Culture*. Garden City, N.Y.: Doubleday, 1948. Pp. 163–78.

Pannenberg, Wolfhart. *What Is Man?* Philadelphia: Fortress, 1970.

Parker, DeWitt H. *The Self and Nature*. Cambridge, Mass.: Harvard University Press, 1917.

Parsons, Howard. "Man East and West." In *S. Radharishnan Souvenir Volume*, edited by J. P. Atreya. Moradabad, India: Darshana, 1964. Pp. 337–52.

Penelhum, Terence. "Personal Identity." *The Encyclopedia of Philosophy*. Vols. 5 and 6. Edited by Paul E. Edwards. New York: Macmillan, 1967. Pp. 95–107.

Phenix, Philip H. *Man and His Becoming*. New Brunswick, N.J.: Rutgers University Press, 1964.

Raju, P. T., and Castell, Alburey, eds. *East-West Studies on The Problem of the Self*. The Hague: Martinus Nijhoff, 1968.

Regamey, Constantin. "The Individual and the Universal in East and West." In *The Status of the Individual in East and West*, edited by Charles A Moore. Pp. 503–18.

Reid, Thomas. *Essays on the Intellectual Powers of Man*. Essay 3.

Ricoeur, Paul, *Fallible Man*. Chicago: Regnery, 1965.

Royal Institute of Philosophy Lectures. Vol. 4: *The Proper Study*. London: Macmillan, 1971.

Royce, James E. *Man and His Nature*. New York: McGraw-Hill, 1961.

———. *Man and Meaning*. New York: McGraw-Hill, 1969.

Russell, Bertrand. *An Outline of Philosophy*. Cleveland and New York: World, 1960, Pt. 3.

Shukla, Pratap Chandra. *Concepts of the Soul in Indian Philosophy*. New Delhi: Newman, 1976.

Smith, Huston. *Forgotten Truth*. New York: Harper and Row, 1976. Chap. 5.

Spaulding, E. G. *What Am I?* New York: Scribners, 1928.

Śrinivasan, G. *The Self and Its Ideals in East-West Philosophy.* Trivandrum: College Book House, 1974.

Strunk, Orlo, Jr., *The Secret Self.* Nashville, Tenn.: Abingdon, 1976.

Suzuki, D. T. "The Individual Person in Zen." In *The Status of the Individual in East and West,* edited by Charles A. Moore. Pp. 519–33.

Symonds, Percival. *The Ego and the Self.* New York: Appleton-Century-Crofts, 1951.

Teilhard de Chardin, Pierre. *The Phenomenon of Man.* New York: Harper and Row, 1965.

Tournier, Paul. *The Meaning of Persons.* Translated by Edwin Hudson. London: SCM Press, 1957.

Warren, Henry Clarke, trans. *Buddhism in Translations.* Pp. 129–50.

Weiss, Paul. *Nature and Man.* New York: Holt, 1947. Chap. 12.

Wikse, John. *About Possession: The Self as Private Property.* University Park: Pennsylvania State University Press, 1977.

Williams, B. A. *Problems of the Self.* Cambridge: Cambridge University Press, 1973.

Wylie, Ruth C. *The Self-Concept.* Lincoln: University of Nebraska Press, 1979.

Yoshifumi, Ueda. "The Status of the Individual in Mahāyāna Buddhist Philosophy." In *The Status of the Individual in East and West,* edited by Charles A. Moore. Pp. 77–89.

Chapter 6

Anantharangachar, N. S. *The Philosophy of Sādhanā in Viśiṣṭādvaita.* Mysore: University of Mysore, 1967.

Chan, Wing-tsit. *A Source Book in Chinese Philosophy,* Princeton: Princeton University Press, 1963. Pp. 18–48, 788–89.

Childe, V. Gordon. *Man Makes Himself.* London: Watts, 1956.

Coe, George Albert. "A Realistic View of Death." In *Religious Realism,* edited by D. C. Macintosh. New York: Macmillan Co., 1931. Pp. 179–91.

Devaraja, N. K. "The Meaning of Life." *Philosophy, Religion and Culture.* Pp. 124–136.

Dubos, René, *A God Within.* New York: Scribners, 1972.

———. *So Human an Animal.* New York: Scribners, 1968.

Eisenberg, Leon. "The *Human* Nature of Human Nature." *Science,* April 14, 1972, Pp. 123–28.

Fang, Thome H. *The Chinese View of Life.* Taipei: Linking, 1980.

Ferkiss, Victor C. *Technological Man: The Myth and the Reality.* New York: Brazilier, 1969.

Frankl, Viktor E. *Man's Search for Meaning: An Introduction to Logotherapy.* New York: Washington Square, 1963.

Ghose, Aurobindo. *The Life Divine.* New York: Greystone, 1949. Pp. 900–47.

Ghose, Sisirkumar. "Lewis Mumford as Man Thinking." *Indian Journal of American Studies* 2, no. 2 (July 1981): 3–16.

Huxley, Thomas Henry. *Man's Place in Nature*. London: Watts, 1908.
Klemke, E. D., ed. *The Meaning of Life*. New York: Oxford University Press, 1981.
Larsch, Christopher. *A Culture of Narcissism*. New York: Norton, 1978.
Libby, Willard. "Man's Place in the Physical Universe." *New Views of the Nature of Man,* edited by John R. Platt. Chicago: University of Chicago Press, 1965. Pp. 1–15.
Llamazon, Benjamin S. *The Self Beyond: Toward Life's Meaning*. Chicago: Loyola University Press, 1973.
Mahoney, James. *Journey into Fullness*. Nashville, Tenn.: Broadman, n.d.
Medawar, P. B. *The Future of Man*. New York: Mentor, 1961.
Morris, Charles. "Comparative Strength of Life-Ideals in Eastern and Western Cultures." In *Essays in East-West Philosophy,* edited by Charles A. Moore. Pp. 353–70.
———. *Paths of Life*. New York: Harper, 1942.
———. *Varieties of Human Values*. Chicago: University of Chicago Press, 1956.
Morris, Desmond. *The Human Zoo*. New York: Dell, 1971.
Nikhilananda. *Hinduism: Its Meaning for the Liberation of the Spirit*. New York: Harper, 1958.
Nozick, Robert. *Philosophical Explanations*. Chap. 6.
Organ, Troy. "The Age of Hominization." *Western Approaches to Eastern Philosophy,* pp. 62–72.
———. "The Hindu Man." *Western Approaches to Eastern Philosophy,* pp. 73–92.
———. *The Hindu Quest for the Perfection of Man*. Athens, Ohio: Ohio University Press, 1970.
Orlans, Harold. "Some Attitudes Toward Death." *Diogenes,* no. 19 (Fall 1957), pp. 73–91.
Passmore, John. *The Perfectability of Man*. London: Duckworth, 1970.
Pico Della Mirandola, Giovanni. *Oration on the Dignity of Man*. (1487) South Bend, Indiana: Regnery/Gateway, 1956. Translated by A. Robert Caponigri.
Platt, John. *The Step to Man*. New York: Wiley, 1966.
Polanyi, Michael. *The Study of Man*. Chicago: University of Chicago Press, 1969.
Prasad, Rajendra. "The Theory of Puruṣārthas: Revaluation and Reconstruction." *Journal of Indian Philosophy* 9 (1981): 49–76.
———. "The Concept of *Mokṣa*." *Philosophy and Phenomenological Research* 31, no. 3 (March 1971): 381–93.
Radhakrishnan, S. *The Hindu View of Life*. New York: Macmillan Co., 1969.
Raju, P. T. "Religion and Spiritual Values in Indian Thought." In *Philosophy and Culture—East and West,* edited by Charles A. Moore. Pp. 263–92. Also in *The Indian Mind,* edited by Charles A. Moore. Pp. 183–215.
Rao, P. Nagaraja. *The Four Values in Indian Philosophy and Culture*. Prasaranga: University of Mysore, 1970.
Richards, Fred, and Richards, Anne Cohen. *Homonovus. The New Man*. Boulder, Colo.: Shields, 1973.

Rogers, Carl. *On Becoming a Person*. Boston: Houghton-Mifflin, 1961.

Russell, Bertrand. "A Free Man's Worship." *Mysticism and Logic*. Chap. 3.

Savery, Louis M., et al. *Shaping of a Self*. Winona, Minn.: St. Mary's College Press, 1970.

Sayama, Mike. *Samadhi: Self Development in Zen, Swordsmanship and Psychotherapy*. Albany: State University of New York Press, 1985.

Shepherd, Paul. *Man in the Landscape*. New York: Knopf, 1967.

Shostrom, Everett. *Freedom to Be*. New York: Bantam, 1971, Introduction, chs. 1–5.

Slater, Philip. *The Pursuit of Loneliness*. Boston: Beacon, 1970.

Te Taa, Henry. *In Pursuit of Fulfillment*. Roslyn Heights, N.Y.: Libra, 1980.

Teilhard de Chardin, Pierre. *The Future of Man*. Translated by Norman Denny. New York: Harper and Row, 1964, chs. 7, 10, 13, 20, 22.

Troxell, Eugene A., and Snyder, William S. *Making Sense of Things: An Invitation to Philosophy*. New York: St. Martins, 1976, ch. 11.

Tu Wie-ming. "The 'Moral Universal' from the Perspective of East Asian Thought." *Philosophy East and West* 31, no. 3 (July 1981): 259–77.

Vaught, Carl G. *The Quest for Wholeness*. Albany: State University of New York Press, 1982.

Watts, Alan W. *Psychotherapy East and West*. New York: Pantheon, 1961.

Weinberg, George. *Self Creation*. London: Raven, 1978.

Whyte, Lancelot Law. *The Next Development in Man*. London: Cresset, 1944.

Yankelovich, Daniel. *New Rules: Searching for Self-Fulfillment in a World Turned Upside Down*. New York: Random House, 1981.

Index

Adams, Henry, 111
Aiken, Jane Renkin, 52
Albright, W. F., 134
Alexander, Samuel, 143–45, 155
Alston, William P., 57
Anaximander, 106
Anaximenes, 106
Angell, J. R., 165
Anselm, 74
Aquinas, 21, 60, 84, 192
Aristotle, 20, 58, 60, 72, 74, 87, 88, 94, 103, 108, 112, 124, 129, 151, 165–68, 173, 186, 190, 191, 194, 200
Arnold, Matthew, 111
Āśmarathya, 103
Augustine, 39, 79, 108, 111, 112, 122, 184
Aurobindo, 123, 124, 146–50
Authority, 71–73
Axiology, 21, 33
Ayer, A. J., 83, 84

Bacon, Francis, 20, 21, 89, 90
Bādarāyana, 140
Barnes, Henry A., 57
Basho, 104
Bergson, Henri, 60
Berkeley, George, 22, 54, 77
Bharati, Agehananda, 23, 29
Bhattacharyya, Vidhushekhara, 161
Bias, 11
Black, Max, 82
Boas, George, 72
Bodhidharma, 64, 101
Bryant, William Cullen, 185
Buddha, 13, 63, 81, 95, 97, 101, 160, 161, 163, 186, 196

Bunyan, John, 183
Burgon, Dean, 81
Burtt, E. A., 96, 98
Butler, Samuel, 186

Calvin, John, 42, 123
Camus, Albert, 24
Carlyle, Thomas, 116
Carrel, Alexis, 112, 113, 122
Cassirer, Ernst, 109, 113
Chang Chen-Chi, 101
Chaucer, 173
Chaudhuri, Nirad C., 7, 31, 32
Chilon, 11
Chuang Tzu, 68, 183
Cicero, 14, 42
Clement of Alexandria, 133
Cleonbulus, 11
Clifford, W. K., 71
Cole, Luella, 176
Confucianism, 26, 35
Confucius, 13, 34, 48, 108, 135, 178, 186
Conrad, Joseph, 122
Conze, Edward, 97, 161, 165, 196
Copernicus, 26
Copleston, Frederick, 13, 29, 38, 143, 150, 156
Costill, David L., 71
Cratylus, 60

Dalgarno, George, 52
da Panicale, Masolino, 129
Darwin, Charles, 44, 45, 142
Das, N. C., 108
Death, 178–85
Deduction, 86–90
Democritus, 128, 129, 151

Dempf, Alois, 38
Descartes, René, 68, 85, 92, 108, 109, 110, 111, 112
Deussen, Paul, 125
Dewey, John, 20, 165, 168–69, 170
Diogenes, 129
Diogenes Laertius, 106, 182
Dionysius the Younger, 60
Dogen, 37, 101
Donatus, 188
Dostoevski, F. M., 24

Eckhart, 61, 64, 123
Eddington, A. S., 112
Eddy, Mary Baker, 181
Einstein, Albert, 79
Eisai, 101
Eisenberg, Leon, 127
Eliade, Mercea, 13, 29, 189
Eliot, Charles, 41
Eliot, T. S., 122
Empedocles, 129
Empiricism, 76–80, 83–84, 85
Epictetus, 193
Epicureanism, 20
Epicurus, 173, 182, 191, 192
Epistemology, 21, 33, 36
Essentialism, 23, 24
Euripides, 59, 107
Existentialism, 21, 23, 24, 29

Fichte, J. G., 154–56
France, Anatole, 72
Francis of Assisi, 129
Frankl, Victor E., 59
Fung Yu-Lan, 36
Fu Ta-shih, 104

Galileo, 85
Gandhi, Mahatma, 8
Gautama. *See* Buddha
Gelli, Giovanni Battista, 174
Glicksburg, Charles I., 122
Gueonon, René, 41
Güttinger, Fritz, 57

Haas, William S., 23, 28
Hall, Edward T., 43
Hall, G. S., 165
Haneda, Nobuo, 37
Hartt, Frederick, 129
Hegel, G. W. F., 60, 155

Heidegger, Martin, 24, 78, 113
Heinmann, Betty, 189
Heraclitus, 106, 107, 129
Hinduism, 7, 31, 32, 37, 81
Hippo, 129
Hippolytus, 133
Hitler, Adolf, 71
Hocking, W. E., 21, 29
Holmes, Oliver Wendell, Jr., 71
Hopson, Janet L., 44
Hsiuan-tsang, 87
Hsün Tzu, 135, 136
Hughes, E. R., 35
Hume, David, 39, 83, 119, 120, 121, 130, 137, 156, 159–60, 165, 182
Humphreys, Christmas, 161
Hurst, William Randolph, 181
Huxley, Aldous, 43, 57, 71
Huxley, Julian, 126, 145, 148
Huxley, Thomas, 142, 143

Immortality, 185–88
Induction, 86, 90–91
Inge, W. R., 41, 151
Intuition, 74–76
Ionesco, 122
Irenaeus, 132, 133
Iyer, Raghavan, 41

James, William, 14, 80, 82, 86, 115, 116, 117, 118, 121, 137, 165, 168
Jan Ch'iu, 195
Jaspers, Karl, 24, 78
Jastrow, Robert, 75
Jespersen, Otto, 44, 45
Johnson, Samuel, 77
Jorgensen, George, 117

Kafka, Franz, 24
Kant, Immanuel, 22, 25, 79, 104, 108, 109, 114, 115, 120, 121, 154, 155, 168, 194
Kao Tzu, 135
Katz, Jerrold J., 57
Keith, Arthur, 175
Keller, Helen, 43
Kierkegaard, Sören, 24, 43, 78, 125, 170, 171
Kipling, Rudyard, 113
Knowledge, ways of attaining, 69–81
Kokushi, Daitō, 118
Korzybski, A. H. S., 72
Kubler-Ross, Elisabeth, 180
Kung-hsi Hua, 195

Ladd, G. T., 165
Langer, Susanne K., 45, 46, 50
Language: origin of, 44–46; and thought, 56–59; uses of, 54–56
Lannoy, Richard, 33
Lao Tzu, 13, 108
Leibniz, 93
Leucippus, 151
Lewes, G. H., 143, 144
Liang, K'ai, 62
Lin Yutang, 87
Lippmann, Walter, 176
Livingstone, Richard, 31
Locke, John, 54, 159, 160
Loeser, Lewis, 179
Logic, 86–91
Logical positivism, 22, 29, 84, 111
Lovejoy, Arthur O., 7, 60
Lucretius, 182

Mahavira, 81
Mann, Thomas, 184
March, Robert H., 60
Marcus Aurelius, 179, 193, 194
Marx, Karl, 71
Maturity, 175–78
May, Rollo, 111, 121
Mead, George, 116
Meaning, 81–84
Mencius, 135, 136
Merton, Thomas, 42
Metaphysics, 21
Mill, John Stuart, 90, 91
Miller, Arthur, 122
Milton, John, 42
Monoimus, 133
Montaigne, 14
Moore, Charles A., 21
More, Thomas, 181
Morgan, Lloyd, 143, 144
Mukerji, A. C., 39, 108
Müller, F. Max, 37, 44, 45, 108
Murti, T. R. V., 161

Nāgārjuna, 63
Nakamura, Hajime, 57, 164
Nehru, Jawaharlal, 33
Neo-Confucianism, 35
Newman, J. H., 73
Nietzsche, F. W., 12, 24, 123
Nimbārka, 103

Noire, Ludwig, 44
Northrop, F. S. C., 21

Ogata, Sonaku, 64
Ogden, C. K., 52
Ontology, 21, 35
Oppenheimer, Robert, 60
Ortega y Gasset, José, 112
Orwell, George, 57
Overstreet, Harry A., 178

Paget, Richard, 45
Palmer, H. E., 52
Pandeya, R. C., 81
Parmenides, 151
Pascal, 185
Paul, Saint, 42, 81, 132, 134
Peirce, C. S., 185
Pepper, Stephen, 77
Periander, 11
Philosophy: Buddhist, 30, 37, 40, 61–65, 96–105; Chinese, 34–37, 108; comparison of Eastern and Western, 23–28, 37–40, 67; definitions of, 14–20; divisions of, 21–22; Eastern, 28–30; future of, 40–42; Indian, 32, 34, 35, 91–96, 108; professional and everyone, 12–13, 31, 35
Pieper, Josef, 60
Pittacus, 11
Plato, 7, 12, 20, 21, 28, 35, 58, 60, 79, 108, 115, 129, 130, 131, 132, 137, 150, 151, 175, 186, 187
Plotinus, 150–54
Po Chü-i, 195
Polanyi, Michael, 79
Pragmatism, 22, 29, 80, 83, 84, 86
Prigogine, Ilya, 146
Pythagoras, 11, 106

Radhakrishnan, S., 41, 189
Ramakrishna, 187
Rāmānuja, 157–58, 187
Rank, Otto, 121
Rationalism, 73–74, 85
Religion and philosophy, 13–14, 29–30
Renou, Louis, 7
Revelation, 80–81
Rhine, J. B., 188
Roosevelt, F. D., 71
Rossow, Robert, 38
Roy, Rammohun, 37

Russell, Bertrand, 23, 58, 83
Ryle, Gilbert, 121, 141–42

Sangharakshita, 99
Śaṅkara, 63, 68, 94, 103, 108, 123, 140, 141, 146, 149, 157, 161, 162, 186, 187
Sartre, Jean-Paul, 24, 78, 111, 168–72
Schafer, Thomas A., 134
Scheler, Max, 113
Schelling, F. W. J., 60, 155
Schlick, Morris, 111
Schopenhauer, Arthur, 32, 155, 177–78
Schrödinger, Erwin, 111
Schweitzer, Albert, 111, 134
Schwidetzky, George, 44
Science and philosophy, 13–14, 111
Self: Alexander's theory of, 143–45; Aristotle's theory of, 165–68; Aurobindo's theory of, 146–50; Buddhist theories of, 160–65; Chinese theories of, 134–36; Dewey's theory of, 168–69; Fichte's theory of, 154–56; Gnostic theories of, 131–34; Hume's theory of, 159–60; Indian theories of, 136–41; Plato's theory of, 130–31; Plotinus's theory of, 150–54; Sartre's theory of, 169–72; Teilhard's theory of, 145–46; Viśiṣṭàdvaita Vedānta theory of, 157–58
Self-evidence, 74
Self-knowledge: difficulty of, 112–22; importance of, 122–27; philosophy as, 39, 106–12
Self-realization, 173–75, 188–200
Sen, K. M., 31
Sen, Keshub Chunder, 37
Sextus Empiricus, 107
Shakespeare, 116, 122
Silence, 59–65
Sinari, Ramakant A., 96
Smith, Huston, 77
Socrates, 7, 13, 20, 107, 108, 111, 112, 130, 175, 181, 183, 186
Solon, 11
Sorokin, Pitirim, 111
Speech signs, 46–54
Spencer, Herbert, 20
Spengler, Oswald, 111
Spinoza, B., 178
Ssū-hsin Wu-hsin, 62

Stcherbatsky, T. I., 161
Steffens, Lincoln, 71
Stoicism, 20
Sunday, Billy, 73
Suzuki, D. T., 34, 62, 64, 98, 101, 102, 103, 104, 117, 118, 162, 164

Tagore, Rabindranath, 189
Takakusu, Junjiro, 30
Taoism, 26, 61, 118
Teilhard de Chardin, Pierre, 75, 126, 145–46, 148, 171
Tenacity, 70–71
Thales, 11, 13, 106
Thorndike, Edward L., 178
Tillich, Paul, 49, 50, 134
Toynbee, Arnold, 41, 111, 134
Truth, 84–86
Tseng Hsi, 195
Tseng Ts'an, 108
Tung Chung-shu, 136
Tu Wei-ming, 24
Tyller, Jorge, 75
Tzu-lu, 194

Vatsyāyana, 198
Vivekānanda, 189

Waismann, Friedrich, 14
Wang Chi, 195
Werkmeister, W. H., 37
Westermark, E. A., 175
Whitehead, A. N., 57, 58, 131, 190
Whittaker, Thomas, 24
Wilkie, Wendell, 27
Wilson, G. A., 125
Wing-tsit Chan, 27, 30, 37, 49, 88
Wittgenstein, Ludwig, 58, 63
Wong Ch'ung, 136
Wordsworth, William, 82

Xenophanes, 151

Yang Hsuing, 136
Yin-i' o-lo, 62
Yu-K'o, 75

Zen, 64, 101–5